marathon and half marathon

From Start to Finish

Published by A & C Black Publishers Ltd
36 Soho Square, London W1D 3QY
www.acblack.com

Second edition 2009
First edition 2004

ISBN 978 14081 1282 3

A CIP catalogue record for this book is available from the British Library.

Acknowledgements
Cover photograph © iStockphoto.com
Inside photographs p i, 3, 9, 10, 27, 28, 32, 44 top, 45, 46, 48, 69, 70, 72, 74, 77, 82, 83, 96, 98, 108, 120, 133, 135, 136, 140, 142, 144, 146, 148, 150, 152, 158, 168 © Mike King; p iii, 20, 25, 30, 33, 35, 36, 37, 42, 44 bottom, 51, 54, 55, 56, 57, 58, 59, 61, 62, 63, 64, 67, 80, 130, 190, 192 © Grant Pritchard; p viii, 40, 43, 86, 87, 126, 134 © istockphoto.com; p 78 © Richard Smith/Corbis; p 124 © Randy Faris/Corbis; p 154, 156, 159, 160, 208, 209 © PA Photos
Illustrations by Louise Parker
Designed by Lilla Nwenu-Msimang
Cover designed by James Watson
Commissioned by Charlotte Croft
Edited by Kate Turvey
Running kit kindly supplied by Asics and adidas

This book is produced using paper that is made from wood grown in managed, sustainable forests. It is natural, renewable and recyclable. The logging and manufacturing processes conform to the environmental regulations of the country of origin.

Typeset in 14 on 10pt DIN-Regular by Palimpsest Book Production Ltd, Grangemouth, Stirlingshire

Printed and bound in China by C&C Offset Printing Co.

acknowledgements

A big thank you to all those people who contributed their time, expertise and insights to this marathon project! My gratitude goes to John Brewer, now director of sport science at Lucozade, who was instrumental in the development of the first edition of this book. Pauline Beare and Peg Jordan from the Women's Running Network gave feedback on various chapters; Dr Sharon Dixon, biomechanist at Exeter University, read my sections on running technique and shoes with a critical eye, for which I am very grateful. Alastair Bryan-Jones furnished me with lots of useful information on ultra running and mountain marathons.

My thanks also go to Charlotte Croft and Kate Burkhalter for putting the book together so well, and to the photographers Mike King and Grant Pritchard. Finally, a huge thank you to all the marathoners who took the time and effort to offer their feedback, tips and experiences of the ultimate endurance sport. I hope you all continue to smash your PBs.

sam murphy

contents

introduction

I'll be honest with you – I thought I knew pretty much everything I needed to know about running marathons when I wrote the first edition of this book, back in 2003. But, six years on, I have to admit I've learned a whole lot more since! Enough to have the publishers groaning at the many pages of extra material I produced for this revised version. In part, the new information comes as a result of personal experience. I've run more, raced more – achieving some new personal bests along the way – and, perhaps more importantly, have succeeded in staying injury-free. But the changing face of sport science is another important reason to update the book. Researchers are constantly looking for ways to help us run further and run faster, recover more easily and avoid injuries, whether that is in terms of how we train, what we eat and drink, what we wear, or even how we think. My aim is to translate the science into user-friendly marathon training strategies, to help you achieve your potential whatever your fitness level or experience.

Another big change in the UK running scene over the past five years has been the burgeoning popularity of the half marathon. The Great North Run, for example, is now the biggest mass-participation running event in the world, while two brand new events – the Royal Parks Foundation and Run to the Beat half marathons – both notched up more than 10,000 participants on their first outings. While much

of the advice in this book is just as apt for a half marathon as for a full one, there are some specific considerations for running a 'swift half', which I've addressed in a special new section that begins on page 191. You will also find three half marathon training programmes, each offered at a 'first timer' and 'experienced' level, in this new chapter – ideal for anyone who is training for a half marathon as the main event, or as a stepping stone to the full distance.

Sam Murphy, 2009

Introduction to the first edition

The population is divided into those who have completed a marathon and those who have not. Not long from now, you'll be joining the ranks of those who have. Welcome, and congratulations! The marathon is unique among sports events. It's doubtful that you'll ever get to play against Andy Murray at Wimbledon – your local football team isn't likely to get the chance to compete against a Premiership club, and yet you can limber up on the same start line as the marathon greats, run the same course and distance, and cross the same finish line (if a little later), that they do. That's what makes embarking on the marathon journey so magical. Like, say, climbing Mount Everest, it is many people's idea of the ultimate challenge – daunting and exciting in equal measures. Unlike conquering Everest, however, running a marathon is surprisingly achievable for the majority of people. But it takes preparation, knowledge, inspiration and dedication. Imagine if you were to climb Everest – the preparation would start months in advance, you'd have expert assistance in planning your route, determining how far you are going to cover each day, what you are going to eat and drink, what you're going to wear, what you'll do if you encounter an injury or adverse weather. You'd study the mountain, listen to the advice and stories of others who have gone before, and become familiar with the challenges, risks and pitfalls involved in your task.

Yet many of the thousands of people who embark on the ultimate running challenge each year have no idea where to begin, how much running they need to do, what they should wear, eat and drink, how and why they should warm up, stretch, cool down, take rest days . . .

The end result is that many ditch the idea long before the big day, others drop out before they cross the finish line, and still others don't achieve the result they hoped and believed they would. This book is designed to guide you through the whole process, so that won't happen to you! While I can't get up and train for you on those dark wintry mornings, I can certainly help you prepare in the best possible way in order to reach your goals, I can inspire and inform you, and ensure that you are as ready as you possibly can be, by the time you reach the start line. If your goal is to complete rather than compete – then you are in the right place. And the good news is that it is perfectly possible to train for a marathon without giving up your job, your friends, your hobbies, your sex life, your Friday night out or your favourite food treats. Nor does it have to take over every waking minute. The key to success is to train, not strain. And *Marathon – from Start to Finish* is here to show you how – every step of the way. Whether this is your first ever marathon, or one of many, it can help make your race a success.

See you on the start line . . .

1

starting out

❖ 0–26.2 miles

THE CHALLENGE OF RISING FROM THE SOFA TO COMPLETE THE MARATHON

Whichever way you put it – 26.2 miles, 42 km – the marathon is a long way, and an immense physical and mental challenge for all those who tackle it, whether they finish in 2½ or 5½ hours. The physiological demands involved are a far cry from those of normal daily life.

Take a typical day at the office – heart rate seldom rises above 70–80 beats per minute, you only break into a sweat if the computer system crashes, and you may cover a total distance on your feet of 2–3 kilometres. Drinking is limited to a few cups of tea or coffee and the odd glass of water, and the closest you get to a physical challenge is having to climb the stairs if the lift isn't working. Things don't change much at home – feet up in front of the TV, remote control nearby and, at the end of the day, a total energy expenditure of around 2500 calories if you're a man, a tad under 2000 if you're a woman. That is the same number – give or take – that you'll be burning in the course of running the marathon in a few months' time.

In the process of running 26.2 miles, you'll take in the region of 40,000 strides, 20,000 with each leg – two to three times your body weight being exerted on each landing. If you weigh 70 kg, that's a force equal to 5.6 million kg going through your joints (it's no wonder we shrink by as much as 2 cm during the race). Your heart rate will rise to approximately 150 beats per minute, assuming you are running at around 70 per cent of your maximum aerobic capacity (the pace most non-elite marathoners instinctively choose, according to research from Loughborough University).

In a 4-hour marathon, that equals a total of 36,000 beats – twice as many as normal – enabling you to pump 25–35 litres of blood around your body each minute. Compare this to a cardiac output of only 4–5 litres a minute at rest and you can see that the heart needs to adapt in the same way as any other muscle to the extra demands placed upon it. Your breathing rate will also go through the roof – increasing to approximately 40 breaths a minute compared to a resting rate of between 12 and 18 breaths a minute.

It's enough to make you exhausted just thinking about it! So what changes need to take place, in order to facilitate the transformation from couch potato to accomplished endurance athlete? Broadly speaking, they can be divided into four areas, as discussed below.

Improved cardiovascular and respiratory fitness

A stronger heart, lungs and circulatory system will get more oxygen and nutrients into and around the body, and dispel carbon dioxide and waste products more efficiently – enabling you to run further and faster without tiring. Beneficial changes take place at many levels. For starters, the lungs become more efficient at taking in air, so you are able to bring a greater volume of oxygen into the body. The actual volume of blood circulating in your body increases, as does the number and size of red blood cells – and this determines how much oxygen can be carried to the heart, from where it is transported around the body. Then, once the oxygen-rich blood reaches the muscles, increased capillarisation – a greater number and density of capillaries – enables you to extract more of this much needed oxygen from the blood. A trained runner might have five to seven capillaries per muscle fibre, compared to the three to four a sedentary person might have.

Improved fuel utilisation

The body can use carbohydrate, fat or, to a lesser extent, protein as fuel for energy production, but its preferred – and most efficient – source is carbohydrate, which it stores in the muscles and liver as a substance called glycogen. The problem is that it can store only a limited amount – enough for perhaps 90 minutes to 2 hours of exercise. Regular training teaches the body to expand its glycogen stores – studies show increases of up to 40 per cent in trained runners. In addition, aerobic training enhances the body's capacity to use fat as a fuel by as much as 30 per cent, thereby 'sparing' precious glycogen (not to mention improving health and trimming away excess pounds).

Improved muscular strength and endurance

Strong, fatigue-resistant muscles are able to contract for prolonged periods without tiring, are less susceptible to injury and quicker to recover from physical activity. A few months of marathon training will make day-to-day exertions feel like a breeze. What's more, regular running increases the number and size of 'mitochondria' in the muscle cells, the powerhouses in which glycogen is broken down to produce energy – think of it as employing more workers to get a job done.

Stronger tendons, ligaments and bones

Stronger connective tissues and bone will be better able to withstand the rigours of repetitive impact, and reduce the risk of stress fractures and injuries to joints. In fact, contrary to popular belief, running improves joint health and reduces the risk of osteoarthritis. Stanford University researchers monitored 539 runners and 423 non-runners over a 20-year period and found that the non-runners suffered worse 'wear and tear' on their joints than the runners.

This, then, is your Everest to climb. Provided you train wisely, consistently and regularly, rest assured that the adaptations outlined above *will* happen, and you will make it to the start line – and finish line – without succumbing to injury, boredom or burnout. Read on to find out how . . .

⁘ Are you ready to run?

DETERMINING YOUR STARTING POINT AND COMMITMENT

Whether you are already a regular runner or haven't even been out to buy a pair of trainers yet, it's a good idea to see just how fit (or unfit!) you are before embarking on a running programme. This will enable you to begin at a safe and effective level, rather than plunging in with both feet and ending up injured or totally disillusioned.

If you have any doubts about your ability to start running, if you have been completely sedentary for more than a year, or if you are a woman over 55 or a man over 45, it is advisable to get a check-up from your GP before you start. In addition, visit your GP if you answer 'Yes' to any of the following questions:

⁘ Has your doctor ever said that you have a heart condition?

⁘ Do you feel pain in your chest when you do physical activity?

> In the past month, have you had chest pain when you were not doing physical activity?

> Do you lose your balance because of dizziness, or do you ever lose consciousness?

> Do you have a bone or joint problem (such as osteoarthritis or osteoporosis), or an injury that could be made worse by physical activity?

> Are you currently taking medication for high blood pressure or a heart condition, *or* is your blood pressure higher than 140/90?

> Are you pregnant or have you recently had a baby?

> Is your body mass index (BMI) greater than 30 (*see* box)?

> Do you have a parent, brother or sister who has or has had premature heart disease (in men under 55 or women under 65)?

> Do you have any other medical condition (such as diabetes), which may affect your ability to run, or do you know of any other health factor that may affect your readiness for physical activity?

If you answered 'No' to all the questions above, you get the go-ahead to start training, but do read the following advice first.

Running just 10 miles a week burns 1000 calories and cuts your risk of heart disease. Research published in the *British Medical Journal* found that men who ran for an hour or more each week at 10-minute mile pace had a 42 per cent reduced risk of coronary heart disease compared with men who did not run. So get those trainers on . . .

> If you are suffering from an injury, pain, infection or illness of any kind, delay starting training until it has passed or been addressed.

> If you have suffered overuse injuries in the past or have any kind of postural or biomechanical abnormalities (such as a scoliosis or leg length discrepancy), it is advisable to visit a physiotherapist or podiatrist for an assessment before you begin running.

Body mass index (BMI)

BMI is a measure of body weight in relation to height and is used to determine whether someone is overweight. It's not ideal, however, as it does not distinguish between weight from fat and weight from muscle (so a highly muscled person may appear to be overweight when they are not).

The figure is arrived at by simply taking your weight (in kilograms) divided by your height (in metres), squared. So, for example, if your height is 1.70 m, and your weight is 70 kg, your BMI would be:

$$70/(1.7 \times 1.7) = 24.22$$

The ideal range is 18.5–24.9. If your BMI is over 30, you should consider starting with something less impactful than running, to avoid putting undue stress on your system, or aim to lose some weight before you begin a running programme. Don't worry too much if your BMI is below 18.5, as long as you are in good health (and, in the case of women, are menstruating normally).

>	Below 18.5	underweight
>	18.5–24.9	optimal range
>	25–29.9	overweight
>	30+	very overweight

The 1½ mile (2.4 km) run test

Good cardiovascular fitness is the lynchpin of distance running, and the 1½ mile run test will give you a snapshot of your current aerobic condition, helping you determine when, and at what level, to begin training, as well as offering a way of monitoring your improvement.

Walk or jog for 5 minutes (or two laps of an athletics track) to warm up. Then time yourself running 1½ miles (2.4 km). If you can't run the whole way, walk where necessary. You can use an athletics track (1½ miles is six laps) or use the odometer in your car to measure the route. Don't worry if it's not exact – as long as you use the same route next time so that you can make comparisons. To see how you fare relative to your age and gender, use the table below to benchmark your current performance, set targets and monitor your progress.

Levels	Under 30		30–34		35–39		40–44		45–49		50–54		55–60		Levels
	M	F	M	F	M	F	M	F	M	F	M	F	M	F	
Excellent	08:15	10:00	08:30	10:30	09:00	11:00	09:15	11:30	09:30	12:00	09:45	12:45	10:00	13:00	Excellent
Very good	08:16	10:01	08:31	10:31	09:01	11:01	09:16	11:31	09:31	12:01	09:46	12:46	10:01	13:01	Very good
	09:45	12:00	10:10	12:30	10:40	13:00	11:05	13:30	11:30	14:00	12:20	14:55	13:10	15:40	
Good	09:46	12:01	10:11	12:31	10:41	13:01	11:06	13:31	11:31	14:01	12:21	14:56	13:11	15:41	Good
	10:30	13:00	11:00	13:30	11:30	14:00	12:00	14:30	12:30	15:00	13:30	16:00	14:30	17:00	
Average	10:31	13:01	11:01	13:31	11:31	14:01	12:01	14:31	12:31	15:01	13:31	16:01	14:31	17:01	Average
	11:15	14:00	11:50	14:30	12:20	15:00	12:55	15:30	13:30	16:00	14:40	17:05	15:20	18:10	
Below average	11:16	14:01	11:51	14:31	12:21	15:01	12:56	15:31	13:31	16:01	14:41	17:06	15:21	18:11	Below average

How committed are you?

What you are capable of achieving on race day isn't just down to your fitness level. It's also determined by how much time, effort and commitment you are able and willing to put in. It may be that you simply want to get round in one piece, and intend to put in only the bare minimum of effort – or you may be planning to go all-out and do everything you can to ensure you cross the finish line in a time you are proud of. Whatever your feelings about your marathon goal, the training programmes in this book have been designed to accommodate you, so don't worry if you weren't planning to devote six days a week to your training. But if you can't realistically fit in even three days a week, the chances are you won't achieve the fitness level that a full marathon demands. Here's something worth bearing in mind before you sign the entry form: there will always be only 24 hours in each day. So, even if you intend to train only three times per week, that still means something else in your life will have to make way for your training. It's remarkable how many people fail to acknowledge this. You'll find some helpful advice on fitting in your training on pages 29–31, but don't make life hard for yourself by trying to pile on too much pressure during your marathon build-up.

The questions below will help you think about your commitment level.

:· How many days a week can I train?

:· Is there a major commitment in my life between now and my race that may conflict (such as a wedding, house move, career challenge or visiting relative)?

:· Is my finish time important to me, or do I just want to 'get round'?

:· Is my lifestyle stable enough to enable me to schedule in runs?

:· What do(es) my partner/family feel about me running the marathon? (It will help if you have some support pledged for tasks that are normally your responsibility.)

why we are here

Your brain will benefit as much as your body from regular exercise. A study undertaken by the University of Illinois found that a 30-minute bout of treadmill running improved decision making, reaction time and the number of correct answers given in a computer-based test.

How long do I need?

If you've yet to take your first running steps, learn how to get started safely and successfully by reading the next chapter. The beginner's running programme it contains will help you reach the point at which you can run continuously for 30 minutes. Then you can gradually build up your mileage and pace, using the advice and information presented in the rest of the book.

I advise making your race debut at a shorter-distance event, such as a 10 km or half marathon, before you take on the marathon challenge. Starting from scratch, you will need a minimum of six months to get marathon fit (ideally longer). I also recommend devoting some of your training time to improving your strength and core stability, to minimise the risk of injury (see the 'Runner's strength' workout on pages 61–64.)

If you already run a couple of times a week and can comfortably sustain 30–45 minutes, the challenge is to make running a more regular fixture in your life – you'll probably find that the deadline presented by entering a marathon will help you achieve this! Make sure you give yourself enough time to build up your mileage and running frequency before embarking on one of the training programmes on pages 169–189.

For experienced runners who already train regularly, the aim is to gear your sessions more specifically towards completing a marathon, to ensure you achieve the best time you are capable of. You'll learn how to do this over the next few chapters, or you can follow one of the training programmes on pages 169–189.

⠶ First steps
GETTING UP AND RUNNING – A GUIDE FOR NEW RUNNERS

If this is your first foray into running, or if you haven't run in a long time, you need to proceed sensibly. My motto is 'make haste slowly'. Even if you already participate in another sport or activity, such as cycling or swimming, and have a good level of aerobic fitness, you will need to give your musculoskeletal system time to adapt to the specific demands of running – so be patient.

Getting off on the right foot

The number one beginner's mistake is to push too hard, too soon. That might mean trying to run too fast, too far or too often – or all three! While it's great to be enthusiastic, overdoing it will leave you feeling sore, exhausted and disillusioned. The softly-softly approach gives your body (and brain) time to adapt to the new challenge, and makes the whole experience of becoming a runner more enjoyable and less likely to result in injury.

So what is an appropriate level to start at? Well, as you'll see from the 'Absolute beginner' programme, over the page, the first few weeks of training should entail mixing walking and running. Far from being a cop-out, walking is an important component of a start-up running programme and, indeed, can have a place in more experienced runners' schedules, too. As you progress, it's simply a matter of gradually reducing the length of walking breaks, so that your running bouts get progressively longer. Stick with it and within eight weeks you should find yourself able to run continuously for 30 minutes.

What about pace?

Although, not too long from now, there will be runs during which I encourage you to run beyond your comfort zone, now is not that time. You should be running at a pace at which you can hold a conversation and breathe without gasping. It doesn't matter if that pace is barely above walking speed – you'll benefit far more from working at 'conversation pace' than attempting to go faster than is comfortable. Working at this level of effort helps to build the foundations of fitness on which you will later build.

Only when you can run comfortably at a steady pace for 30–45 minutes, and have been doing so for 6–12 weeks should you begin to introduce other elements into your training, such as speed work or interval sessions. Attempting to progress too quickly, and without having built a solid foundation, could cause the whole thing to come tumbling down.

Absolute beginner's programme

The eight-week programme over the page aims to get you to a position where you can run continuously for 30 minutes. You don't have to follow the schedule to the letter, but it's a good template to ease you into regular running, and for aspiring marathoners (and half marathoners), is the first step of your journey.

How it works

Each week there are three runs – but if you wish to repeat the first session to make four in total, then do so (you will progress to the 30-minute goal faster). The last run of the week is the 'challenge', which will eventually become your 'long run' (*see* page xx) when you are ready to begin training for your event in earnest.

Try to run on non-consecutive days, to allow recovery time, and don't attempt to run every day. Don't worry if you don't feel ready to cut down the walking intervals on the exact weeks stated or, indeed, if you feel more than ready to cut them down early – everyone progresses at different rates. Remember, make haste slowly.

You could perform an alternative activity to running as a fourth session, or follow the 'Runner's strength workout' on page 61, which will make your running muscles perform better, fatigue less and be more resistant to injury.

Start every session with a warm-up (page 49), and finish with a cool-down and stretch (page 51). Start as you mean to go on!

Don't give up

Becoming a runner isn't easy – there will be times when your old sedentary lifestyle beckons, when the weather is foul and you can hardly bear to drag yourself out the door, and when the aches and pains hardly seem worth it. But keep going! You'll find tips on staying motivated on pages 75–78. Rest assured, a few weeks from now you will begin to reap the benefits of a healthier lifestyle, a fitter body and a more focused mind. I promise, you'll never look back!

Week 1	Week 2	Week 3	Week 4
Walk for 3 minutes, run for 2 minutes and repeat 4 times (20 min)	Walk for 2 minutes, run for 2 minutes and repeat 6 times (24 min)	Walk for 1 minute, run for 3 minutes and repeat 6 times (24 min)	Walk for 1 minute, run for 4 minutes and repeat 5 times (25 min)
Walk for 3 minutes, run for 2 minutes and repeat 4 times (20 min)	Walk for 2 minutes, run for 2 minutes and repeat 6 times (24 min)	Walk for 1 minute, run for 3 minutes and repeat 6 times (24 min)	Walk for 1 minute, run for 4 minutes and repeat 5 times (25 min)
Challenge: Walk for 3 minutes, run for 2 minutes and repeat 5 times (25 min)	Challenge: Walk for 2 minutes, run for 3 minutes and repeat 5 times (25 min)	Challenge: Walk for 1 minute, run for 4 minutes and repeat 5 times (25 min)	Challenge: Jog for 10 minutes (walk as and when you need to), rest for 2 minutes and repeat (22 min)

Week 5	Week 6	Week 7	Week 8
Walk for 1 minute, run for 4 minutes and repeat 6 times (30 min)	Run for 8 minutes, walk for 1 minute and repeat 3 times (27 min)	Run for 10 minutes, walk for 30 seconds and repeat 3 times (31.5 min)	Run for 15 minutes, walk for 1 minute and repeat (31 min)
Walk for 1 minute, run for 4 minutes and repeat 6 times (30 min)	Run for 9 minutes, walk for 1 minute and repeat 3 times (30 min)	Run for 10 minutes, walk for 30 seconds and repeat 3 times (31.5 min)	Run for 15 minutes, walk for 30 seconds and repeat (30.5 min)
Challenge: Jog for 8 minutes, walk or rest for 1 minute and repeat two more times (26 min)	Challenge: Jog for 10 minutes, rest or walk for 30 seconds and repeat 3 times (31.5 min)	Challenge: Run for 15 minutes, walk or rest for 1 minute and repeat (31 min)	Challenge: Run for 30 minutes non-stop

2 smart training

⁖ The truth about training

WHY RUNNING THE SAME PACE, SAME DISTANCE, SAME ROUTE DAY AFTER DAY WON'T GET YOU ROUND THE MARATHON

Ask anyone who has run a marathon, and they'll probably tell you that the hardest part isn't the 26.2-mile run itself – it's the training. Think of it this way – the race lasts a few hours, the training goes on for months! There's no denying that there's some hard graft to be done between now and race day, but knowing what to do, how and when to do it, and why you're doing it goes some way towards making the task easier. It gives every training session a point, rather than simply being more miles to note in your training log.

Just running for the sake of it – mile after mile at the same speed, covering the same distance around the same route – is pretty boring for even the most committed runner, and it certainly won't help you reach your marathon or half marathon potential. To understand why, let's have a look at the principles of training, and how they relate to going the distance.

Progressive overload

When you take your first faltering steps on the road to running fitness, you will find that you progress in leaps and bounds. The run that felt like a near-death experience in week one will barely have you breaking a sweat in a couple of months' time. Sadly, though, this doesn't mean that training gets easier and easier as you go along. What it means is that as you reach each new level of fitness you need to increase the challenge to your body – effectively moving the goalposts further away. Why? Because your body will continue to adapt and get fitter only when the challenge placed upon it is greater than that which it can already handle. This is a principle known as 'progressive overload', and it holds true whether you are a running newbie or an aspiring Olympian. The 'overload' refers to the amount of work, or 'stress', you place on your body, while 'progressive' hammers home the point that piling on the workload all at once simply won't work. Training has to be increased little by little in order to avoid injury, illness or burnout. It is widely believed that increasing your training volume by approximately 10 per cent per week (but not *every* week) enables you to progress safely and effectively. For example, you might increase a 60-minute steady run to 65–70 minutes – not to 90 minutes!

But (to make things a little more complicated) just as attempting to progress too much, too quickly won't work, nor will failing to apply *enough* overload. If you get stuck in a 'comfort zone', and fail to increase the speed, distance or frequency of your runs as you get fitter, further adaptation will cease and you could end up falling short of the physiological changes your body needs to become a better runner.

Specificity

The adaptations your body makes as a result of progressive overload are determined by the type of training you do. What does that mean? It means to get better at something, you need to gear your training towards the specific demands of that sport or activity. That's why swimmers swim, climbers climb, dancers dance and runners run. While your heart neither knows nor cares whether you're dancing the tango or running 5 km (it's all cardiovascular exercise, after all), being specific about the type of exercise you do is the best way of developing the muscles, tendons and ligaments – as well as the neuromuscular pathways – that are going to be needed for your event. However, this doesn't mean that there isn't scope for runners to include some different types of training in their programmes – in fact, there are some very good reasons to do so, which we'll explore on pages 66–68. But it does mean that the core part of a training programme for a marathon has to be running.

Rest and recovery

If you think marathon training has to mean seven days a week, maximum effort every time, you are mistaken. Such a regime will leave you stale, fatigued, ill or injured, and you'll never achieve the performance you are capable of. Why? Because your training regime is missing one essential, but often overlooked, element: recovery! It is during recovery that the body undergoes the physiological adaptations triggered by the training. Take it away and you are not giving your body a chance to develop, nor giving any minor injuries or ailments a chance to heal. When it comes to marathon training, 'no pain, no gain' and 'if some is good, more must be better' are definitely not appropriate mantras to be chanting. But how do you know when to rest and when to train? Or how much rest is enough?

It's important to schedule rest into your programme, rather than just having a day off when you're too tired to run. Coaches talk about the 'hard/easy rule' – the notion that hard training sessions should be followed by easy ones, or by no training at all. Research from Ball State University found that most runners need 48–72 hours to recover fully from a hard training session, so you won't be doing yourself any favours by pushing hard too often. Structuring your training using the hard/easy rule enables you to train consistently without overstretching yourself. And, remember, those terms 'hard' and 'easy' are relative and individual to you (one person's 'comfortable' may be another person's 'tough').

I mentioned the '10 per cent' increase guideline above – the notion that increasing your mileage/time on your feet by 10 per cent per week is an appropriate rate of progress. But you cannot continue to build indefinitely. Many athletes use a 'three weeks hard, one week easy' system to allow time to consolidate the benefits their training has brought on, and to recharge for the next training period. I have used a similar system in the training programmes on pages 169–189.

A final consideration as far as rest is concerned is to listen to what your body is telling you. If you wake up exhausted, and are suffering from stiffness, and aches and pains, then you should give running a miss regardless of what your training schedule says. It's essential to pay heed to your body's messages. As running coach Malcolm Balk likes to say, 'listen to the whispers and you won't have to hear the screams'.

Reversibility

In the same way that the body adapts to the stimulus of training, it also adapts to an absence of training! The sad fact is, you can't store fitness, so if you stop training, all your hard-earned gains can be lost. Research from Odense University in Denmark found that a month of inactivity resulted in a 20 per cent drop in that all-important glycogen storage, for example, while a study review in the journal *Sports Medicine* concluded that running performance is likely to decrease by 3–5 per cent after three to four weeks of sitting on the sofa. Of course, as we've seen, that doesn't mean to say that you should never take a day off (in fact, performance often improves after a few days' rest). The key is ensuring that you get the right balance of training and recovery.

Applying the principles of training

OK, so you know you need to run, that you need to progressively increase the challenge of your runs, and that you need to schedule in some rest days, but not too many. So far, so good. But what does this actually boil down to, in terms of structuring your programme?

The three key variables you have to play with are encompassed within the acronym FIT: frequency, intensity and time. In other words, how often, how hard and how long are you going to run?

The factors to bear in mind when you are figuring out your answers to these questions are your age and level of experience, your health status and fitness, your personal goals and the amount of time you have to dedicate to training.

Frequency

As far as frequency is concerned, you need to be able to run at least three times per week in order to train for a marathon. Four to six sessions per week would enable you to cover greater mileage – but you need to consider whether an increased volume of training may leave you fatigued or susceptible to injury.

Intensity and time

Intensity and time (or distance) are like two ends of a seesaw. As one goes up, the other must come down. For example, you might try to run faster in a particular session, so you shouldn't try to go further, too. Why? Because that doesn't represent *progressive* overload – it's simply 'overload', and is likely to see you ending up in the sports injury clinic.

If you are a novice runner, there are more benefits to be gained from focusing on time, rather than intensity. Running longer, rather than harder, will help you maximise your aerobic fitness, on which you can later build strength and speed. But for more experienced runners, and those seeking to compete rather than complete, as far as the marathon is concerned, it is important to vary both intensity and distance in your training, in order to work on different elements of fitness. For example, Swedish researchers found that the best way to increase the volume of the heart is through steady-paced running, while the best way to increase cardiac output (the amount of blood pumped out by the heart per minute) is to run at high intensity – the perfect example of why you need a variety of different sessions in your weekly schedule.

Many new marathoners make the mistake of

focusing too heavily on mileage or 'time on feet', without paying enough attention to higher-quality sessions. It's an easy mistake to make – after all, on the big day itself you'll be running at a fairly constant, less-than-maximal pace for a prolonged period. But training only in that way will not enable you to reach your full potential.

Monitoring intensity

It's easy enough to keep tabs on how often you are running, and for how long, but what about intensity? There are a number of different methods you can use to monitor your effort – let's look at three of the most common.

Heart rate

The more effort you put into a run, the greater the number of times your heart has to beat per minute, in order to pump sufficient blood to the working muscles. So your heart rate (the number of times your heart beats per minute, measured as bpm) is a good measure of how hard you are working. A heart rate monitor (*see* page 46) enables you to keep tabs on your heart rate during exercise and is a worthwhile investment. But heart rate has to be viewed in context in order to be useful. For example, simply knowing that your heart is beating at 140 bpm doesn't give you much information. But if you know that your maximum heart rate is 180 bpm, then you know that 140 bpm represents 77 per cent of your maximum, which is far more meaningful. Why? Because it enables you to modify your pace where necessary, in order to achieve lower or higher heart rates – and because it provides a useful measure of progress: as you get fitter, you'll be able to run the same pace at a lower percentage of your maximum heart rate.

Using heart rate effectively

There are two important figures you need in order to use heart rate effectively. Your maximum heart rate (MHR) – the highest number of times your heart is capable of beating in 1 minute – and your resting heart rate (RHR) – the number of times it beats when you are completely at rest.

The only way to get a true measure of the first is to have a maximal exercise test at a sports medicine clinic or laboratory, which can be expensive and isn't recommended for everyone. That's why the formula 220 – age = MHR is often used, to give a ballpark figure. This formula can be wildly inaccurate – as much as 20 beats out – which is why I don't recommend using it in isolation.

But when RHR is subtracted from estimated MHR, you get something known as 'heart rate reserve', and this can be used to give a more accurate working heart rate range. This is called the Karvonen method (*see* the example in the box).

It's worth noting that we tend to talk about heart rate ranges, rather than specific figures. In the example below, the runner wanting to work at 70 per cent of his maximum might try to stick within a range of 140–146 bpm.

The Karvonen method

Example: You are 40 years old. Using the 220 – age formula, your maximal heart rate would be 220 – 40 = 180 bpm. Your resting heart rate (ideally recorded before rising from bed or taking any food or caffeine) is 60 bpm.

Let's say we want to work out what your heart rate would be at 70 per cent effort:

> 70 per cent = (MHR – RHR) x 70 per cent + RHR

> 70 per cent = (180 – 60) x 70 per cent + 60

> 70 per cent = 120 x 0.7 + 60

> 70 per cent = 144 bpm

RPE

A simpler way of determining the intensity you are working at is to use your 'rate of perceived exertion' (RPE). Put simply, how hard do you feel you are working? This is measured on a scale (the scale I use in this book is from 1–10). The benefit of RPE is that it is truly individual: one person's conversation pace may be another's near-maximal speed, for example. Also, as you get fitter, your pace at any given RPE will quicken, so you'll be able to run at, say, 6–7 RPE, a little bit faster. Given that RPE isn't related to a physiological reading, or a specific pace, it also takes into account that you might be feeling a bit low on energy, or extra zippy, on a particular day. So you may still feel that you are working at 7 out of 10, but you are actually moving at a slightly slower or faster pace. While RPE sounds a little unscientific, research from the University of Exeter found that our built-in ability to assess how hard we are working is surprisingly accurate. When volunteers were asked to 'rate' how hard they were working on a scale of 6–20 (with 6 being completely inactive and 20 being on the verge of exhaustion), their estimates correlated closely with how hard they were *actually* working, as measured by their heart rate and oxygen uptake.

Pace

How fast you are going is another obvious way of monitoring your effort, and now that GPS systems and other speed–distance devices, such as Nike+ (*see* page 46), are widely available, this is easy to do.

Pace tends to be more useful to runners who have the experience to know what their 'race pace' is for various distances. For example, if you ran your last marathon in 4 hours 10 minutes, your pace was approximately 9½ minutes per mile. This time, you want to run it in under 4 hours, so you know you need to run 30 seconds per mile faster and can therefore ensure you incorporate training runs at this pace in your marathon build-up.

Coaches who advocate using pace point out that it is the only truly objective measure. No matter what your heart rate or RPE says, if you need to be running 9-minute miles to achieve your goal, then that's all there is to it. Other coaches believe that always running on pace is too stressful, and doesn't take into account fluctuations in energy level, health, nutrition and hydration status. My experience of training for a marathon entirely on pace reflected this, although I do think it's useful to gauge your pace at least some of the time, to give you a clearer idea of what you are capable of in training and racing.

To summarise, perhaps the best approach to monitoring your efforts is to use a combination of methods rather than getting too hung up on a single one. That's the value of top-of-the-range GPS systems, which combine heart rate monitoring with real-time pace and distance feedback. The sessions described in the next chapter and included in the marathon training programmes offer a heart rate range and effort level. It is, of course, impossible to suggest a specific pace, but I have included some guidelines to help you ascertain your own personal pace for different sessions.

Finally, remember that many factors – including the terrain, the weather, your own energy levels and health – will affect your running, so you must keep your monitoring in perspective.

Now you know about the principles of training and the demands of the marathon, we can take a look at some specific sessions and what place they might hold in your marathon training programme.

⁘ Way to go

THE LOWDOWN ON DIFFERENT TYPES OF RUN AND THEIR BENEFITS FOR MARATHON TRAINING

There are many ways to run: long and slow, short and fast, repetitive bursts of hard effort, up hills, down hills and on all manner of different surfaces. None is bad, all of them work (in terms of improving fitness), but some are more effective for marathon training than others. Which ones?

Before trying to answer that question, it is important to acknowledge that running is not an 'exact' science. There is no completely right or totally wrong way of training, which is why no two elite athletes train in exactly the same way. That said, certain methods of training will optimise the time you have available, and lead to the best returns from your training miles.

The long run

Why do it? The long run is, without doubt, the most important training session for budding marathoners. A study by scientists from Hong Kong looked at factors predicting the successful completion of a marathon and found that the number and length of competitors' long runs was a more important factor than total weekly mileage. As well as proffering great physiological benefits, such as increased blood volume, improved oxygen extraction from the blood (due to more capillaries), enhanced fat utilisation and calorie expenditure, stronger connective tissue and greater muscular endurance, the long run will develop the mindset and willpower that you'll need to keep going, and give you confidence that you can beat the marathon distance.

How do I do it? The traditional approach is to set aside one weekly session for a long run. 'Long' is a relative term. If you are a beginner, then long may mean only 40 minutes to start with, but the crucial thing is to gradually extend the long run, taking into account the principle of progressive overload. Increasing your long run by 10 per cent, or 1–2 miles, at a time is a reasonable rate of progress. But don't extend your long run week in, week out. It's important to have a break from long runs every few weeks, either to take a rest or to put your training to the test at a race.

A question that I often get asked is 'How long should my longest long run be?' I'm afraid the answer is very much dependent on the person asking. If you pressed me, I'd say at least a couple of 20-mile training runs is advisable, but I hadn't run beyond 16 miles when I made my marathon debut and I got round fairly comfortably. When you are deciding how far to run, remember to factor in recovery – it takes time for the body to recover from 3 hours pounding the pavements!

What about pace? For the first few weeks of marathon training, your long runs should be at a pace that feels easy – you are building your foundation of aerobic and muscular endurance (*see* the panel 'Pace yourself', page 171, for guidance on how different levels of effort should feel). However, if you only ever run your long runs at a slow plod, you can't expect your body to suddenly produce the goods on the big day and not only run further than ever before, but also at a faster pace than you've achieved in training. That's why I recommend that, as the weeks go on, you introduce some long runs – or sections of your long runs – at a slightly faster pace. It's especially good to introduce these faster bouts in the second half of a long run, when the body is getting fatigued, as that is how you will feel when you're reaching the second half of the race itself.

Try this If you are daunted by the long run, adopt a walk/run strategy to help give you the confidence you need to be on your feet for prolonged periods. An ideal walk/run ratio for marathon training is 8 minutes running, 2 minutes walking (it's also easy to keep track of on your sports watch). You can gradually reduce the walking breaks as you get more accustomed to being on your feet for long periods of time – or you can opt to run the race using a walk/run plan (*see* page 134).

Steady runs

Why do it? Steady running is exactly what it says on the tin. It is an essential part of your marathon or half marathon training, because, unlike speed work and hills, it doesn't require much recovery but still enables you to put the miles in and reap fitness benefits. Steady runs are what I think of as my 'sanity runs'. They aren't long or fast enough to be daunting – they are simply enjoyable training miles, run at a pace that will improve heart health, oxygen delivery to the muscles, fat utilisation and muscular endurance. (This is likely to be the pace at which you run on race day, too, so it's great 'race pace' practice.)

How do I do it? Steady runs should be performed at a comfortable pace. You are able to maintain a conversation, but it's not effortless – your chatting should be slightly breathless!

Try this A 30–50-minute steady run. Try to maintain an even pace rather than starting out fast and slowing down.

Recovery runs

Why do it? Recovery running – provided it is done at the right pace – facilitates better recovery than doing nothing, helping to clear waste products from the muscles. It also enhances fat burning (due to the low intensity) and adds to your weekly mileage and 'time on your feet'. Your challenging runs should be balanced by plenty of recovery runs or rest days to keep you fresh.

How do I do it? The crucial thing is to ensure that the pace really is easy – so easy that you feel guilty! Keep these runs fairly short: 20–40 minutes is ideal.

Try this The day after a tough session, instead of resting, try a really easy-paced recovery run for 20 minutes. See how you feel on your next run, compared to when you took a full rest day.

Threshold running

Threshold running has you teetering on the brink of what's called your lactate or anaerobic threshold (*see* box on page 18). This isn't a pace at which you'll feel comfortable chatting, which is why the session is kept short and sharp, or even divided into segments with a short recovery in between each one. Working at an intensity that equates to the lactate threshold will gradually push it upwards, so that you can produce energy aerobically at a higher intensity. It also gets your body accustomed to exercising with lactic acid in the muscles (improving lactate tolerance) and to clearing lactate acid from the muscles more efficiently. A group of French scientists who monitored high-standard runners during a six-week training programme that included threshold runs found that the runners experienced significant physiological improvements in aerobic capacity, resulting in shaving up to 2 minutes off their 10 km time. The other essential pay-off from threshold running is an improvement in leg turnover (cadence) and running economy.

How do I do it? Most people reach their lactate threshold at around 85 per cent of their maximum heart rate, although this can vary – fitter runners may not reach their threshold until they are closer to 90 per cent, while those new to running may hit it sooner. Determining your threshold pace isn't easy unless you have access to a high-tech physiology laboratory, but a good estimate is that you should just about be able to force out a few words, rather than hold a proper conversation.

Don't overdo threshold running. One session per week is enough to have an impact. Only consider incorporating two weekly threshold runs if you are running five days per week or more. Even then, you'd probably still be better off selecting a different type of speed session, rather than repeating the same type of training twice.

What's all this about lactate threshold?

When sufficient oxygen is flowing through the bloodstream to meet energy needs, such as at an easy running pace, the mitochondria, or 'engine rooms', in the muscle cells can use it to produce energy with minimal fuss and effort. But when there isn't enough oxygen coming through to meet demand, such as when you are exercising heavily, the muscle cells have to produce energy without oxygen, or anaerobically. This is far less efficient, since it results in the accumulation of heat and a substance called lactic acid, which makes the muscle very acidic and hampers muscular contraction. The lactic acid is continually being removed, but if it is produced at a faster rate than it can be taken away, then it builds up in the muscle and, before you know it, you've crossed the 'lactate threshold' (also sometimes called the anaerobic threshold). Physiologically, the lactate threshold is the last point at which lactate is being removed as fast as it is being produced. Running at a pace that is equal to this point effectively pushes the threshold upwards, so you can run faster without crossing it.

Try this To dip your toes into threshold running, try splitting the session into long intervals with a short recovery. For example, run 2–4 x 8 minutes with a 2-minute recovery between each effort.

Interval training

Interval training involves interspersing fast efforts of running with periods of recovery. The intensity (speed at which the effort is run), length of the effort (either distance or time), length of the recovery interval and volume (number of efforts) can all be changed to suit the needs of the runner and the event they are training for.

Why do it? As well as boosting endurance, interval training will improve leg turnover and strength, and get you accustomed to working at a higher heart rate and effort level. It will also improve your running technique and your 'economy' (your ability to run faster at any given heart rate), one of the key factors in successful marathon running according to a report in the journal *Sports Medicine*. The great thing about interval training is that it enables you to put in a good deal of quality work without completely exhausting you or being psychologically daunting, thanks to those recovery periods.

How do I do it? Traditionally, intervals are done on an athletics track but there is no need to confine yourself to one – anywhere with fairly even, flat terrain will do fine, or you may even use hills as part of your interval training. The number of intervals that can be completed will depend on your level of fitness, and the intensity and length of the effort. A session focusing on building speed endurance should allow less time to recover than a session focusing on pure speed, relatively speaking. For example, if you ran 1 km intervals, you might take 1½ to 2 minutes to recover before setting off again. If, however, you ran 400 m, you might take 2–3 minutes to recover. This is for two reasons: first, you'll be completing the 400 m reps a lot faster than you will the 1 km reps; second, if you are looking to boost speed, as in the shorter session, you need to allow the body to recover completely each time, while in the former session the onus is on improving endurance, so a full recovery isn't necessary. If you feel tired halfway through an interval session, slow down the pace of the run rather than increasing the length of the recovery period.

How often should I do it? One session per week of interval training is sufficient for marathon and half marathon training. If your time is limited, opt for a threshold session instead of intervals – it is more specific to the event you are training for.

Try this Four to six 3-minute efforts with a 2-minute recovery jog or walk between each one. French research suggests that this is the optimal way to develop aerobic capacity (VO_2max). The mark of a successful interval session is when all your reps are roughly the same length of time/distance. If you go faster or further on your first one and then deteriorate, then you started out too fast. A good lesson to learn on pace judgement!

Fartlek

'Fartlek' running has its origins in Scandinavia, and is really just a less structured version of interval running. Translated, the term means 'speed play', and it simply involves runners putting in faster or harder bursts when they feel ready, during a steady run (often on mixed terrain and inclines).

Fartlek training is often portrayed as a great introduction to intervals and speed work without being too intimidating. However, the lack of structure may not work for beginners who don't know how much effort – and how many reps – to put in to make the session count. I find it is best used on days when you don't feel up to a full interval session but still want to get some faster-paced work in.

VO_2 max for beginners

The maximum rate at which oxygen can be extracted from the air and used by the muscle is called your maximal oxygen uptake, or VO_2 max. It is largely determined by your genetics (as well as sex, age and body size) but that doesn't mean you can't improve it through regular training (most of us are far from our genetic potential). VO_2 max on its own is not a good predictor of performance in distance running – although research shows that there is a strong relationship between marathon performance and the percentage of VO_2 max that can be sustained for the duration of the race. Highly trained runners in one study were able to maintain 82 per cent of their VO_2 max for an entire marathon. Studies suggest we can increase VO_2 max by 5–25 per cent through exercise (that's where those above-threshold interval sessions come in). As a general example, a sedentary man may have a VO_2 max of 30 ml/kg/min, while a highly trained man may be closer to 70 ml/kg/min. Legendary marathoner Grete Waitz had a VO_2 max of 73.3 ml/kg/min.

why we are here

Being a runner makes you sexier! Not just because you've got a lithe, toned body, but because you are more sexually responsive. An American study of 8000 women aged 18–49 found that of those who exercised three times a week, 40 per cent reported greater arousal, 31 per cent had sex more often and 25 per cent found orgasm easier to achieve.

A word about 'race pace'

You will almost certainly come across the term 'race pace' during your marathon training. Unsurprisingly, it refers to the pace at which you intend to run your race. But don't make the mistake of thinking that race pace should be a given intensity, like a threshold run or recovery run. It is very individual and will differ according to the length of the race (ie. your 5km 'race pace' won't be the same as your half marathon 'race pace'). One study found that most recreational runners work at around 70 per cent of their maximum heart rate during a marathon – elite runners may be closer to 85 per cent.

As far as your long run (*see* page 16) is concerned (the session that is most specific to marathon running), if you are a slower runner, race pace is likely to be the same, or slower than, the pace at which you perform your long runs. Faster runners, on the other hand, will run the race considerably faster than the pace at which they'll perform their long runs in training. The pace is simply too challenging for them to be able to perform long runs week in, week out, compromising recovery and risking injury and illness. However slow or fast you are, it is great to have an idea of the sort of pace you might be able to sustain on marathon day to enable you to get the intensity right in training. Read more about figuring out your marathon pace on page 125.

Hill training

A hill session is one that uses gravity to add to the overload on your body. While any run that takes in undulating territory could be considered 'hill training', a hill session is usually more structured, doing 'repeats' on one particular hill.

Why do it? Even if your marathon is flat, it is worth including some hill work because you'll have to work harder to overcome the extra resistance that gravity causes, developing the muscles, ligaments and tendons and enhancing cardiovascular fitness. In a study from the University of Georgia in Greece, scientists monitored a group of athletes during both

level and uphill running, and found that there was over 20 per cent more activation of the muscle fibres on hills.

How do I do it? Choose a hill that has a gentle gradient if you are new to this kind of training, and a moderate gradient if you're a more experienced runner, but not more than 10 per cent. Forget about Everest-style inclines, your technique will suffer too much for it to be beneficial. Run up the hill at a swift pace, jogging back down to recover, before running straight back up. It's important to run off the top of the hill rather than allowing yourself to slow down when the peak is in sight.

How often should I do it? One weekly hill session is plenty during your marathon training, and, like threshold training and intervals, it needs to be balanced with steady and recovery runs. If you live in a hilly area, make sure you aren't overdoing it and ending up with three or four hilly runs per week.

Try this Find a road with a longish gradual hill (say, up to a 2-minute climb) and lamp posts or rubbish bins for markers. Start at the bottom and run at a swift pace to the first marker, then recover by jogging back to the bottom. Next run to the second lamp post, and so on, until you reach the top, then work your way back down again in the same manner. You can also use the incline on a treadmill for your hill sessions.

Kenyan hills

Former Commonwealth Games marathoner and running coach with Full Potential, Keith Anderson coined the phrase 'Kenyan hills' to describe a session that he learned while training with Kenyan runners in Africa in the lead-up to the Kuala Lumpur games. In this kind of hill session, you don't race up the hill and jog back down, but run up at a steady to swift pace and back down at the same pace, allowing less recovery. You also get to work on your leg turnover on the downhills (*see* opposite). Anderson reports that the Kenyans would practise this kind of hill work for an hour at a time – but start with shorter blocks of 5–10 minutes. You could use Kenyan hills in place of a threshold training session, as the effort level is similar.

Downhill running

While not a bona fide running session in its own right, there is a place for downhill running in your training, even if you are not going to be making descents on race day. A slight decline enables you to work on your leg turnover with less resistance, and is a good training aid that strengthens the legs and improves speed. If you are going to be running lots of descents on race day you must practise in training, since downhill running puts a lot of stress on the muscle fibres, due to the high proportion of eccentric muscle contraction involved. This type of muscle contraction is known to lead to a greater strengthening of the muscles, but at the same time can cause significant muscle soreness up to 48 hours later, so make sure you avoid doing too much too close to an important training session or race.

∴ Perfect motion

THE IMPORTANCE OF GOOD TECHNIQUE – AND HOW TO ACHIEVE IT

Observe a good distance runner and you'll see poetry in motion. Their movement is strong and purposeful, yet fluid and relaxed. It's also economical, both in the sense that they don't squander energy on unnecessary side-to-side or vertical movements, and in terms of how much oxygen they need to fuel their efforts. Studies show that elite distance runners use 5–10 per cent less oxygen to maintain a given pace than either elite middle-distance runners or recreational distance runners, and part of the reason for this is their efficient running form.

There is undoubtedly a genetic component to good form (so you can blame your parents for that shuffling gait), but the good news is that running form tends to improve, over time, as a result of training. And, even better, many aspects of less-than-perfect technique are simply bad habits, which can be changed quite easily. You will find plenty of tips on how to improve your running technique throughout this chapter, but first let's look at the biomechanics of running, and the hotly debated area of foot strike.

The biomechanics of running

Just take a look at any group of runners and it soon becomes clear that, as with dancing, everyone has their own individual style. Some lollop, others bounce from foot to foot, others have a short, snappy stride . . . but in spite of our weird and wonderful individual variations, the general movement pattern that propels us forward in running is the same. You land on one foot, the knee bending simultaneously and the muscles of that leg working eccentrically (while lengthening) to decelerate the body and absorb shock. While one foot is in the 'stance' phase (in contact with the ground) the opposite leg is pulling through, its weight providing the momentum to move the body forward, assisted by the muscular effort (and stored elastic energy) of the calves and hamstrings, as well as the pumping action of the arms.

The 'stance' phase of the foot lasts approximately 0.2 seconds, but an awful lot happens during this time. In a rearfoot strike (the most common gait pattern among runners), the foot lands on the outside edge of the heel, and then rolls slightly in and forward. The arch flattens to help dissipate the impact (this is the pronation phase we hear so much about). As the opposite leg pulls through and the stance foot gets ready to push off into the next stride, it moves into a 'supinated' position (the arch stiffens) to give leverage. This leverage, along with the extension of the hip, knee and ankle, propels the body off the ground, typically allowing you to be airborne (the 'float' phase) for approximately 0.5 seconds.

But what if you don't land on your heels? Increasingly, many running coaches are now actively encouraging a forefoot or midfoot strike, rather than a heel strike. There are running techniques (such as the 'Pose method') and even shoes (like the Newton range, *see* 'Further information', page 212) to help facilitate this.

A large part of the argument focuses on the fact that, if we run barefoot, we don't land on the heels. In other words, a forefoot/midfoot strike is a more natural way to run, allowing the structures of the foot, ankle and lower leg to work as they were designed to. What's more, proponents of a forefoot/midfoot strike say that landing on the heel on an outstretched leg acts as a 'brake', halting forward momentum,

What happens in a forefoot strike pattern?

Forefoot strike patterns are less well documented than rearfoot ones but, according to sports biomechanist Dr Sharon Dixon, the forefoot tends to strike the ground in a supinated position (with a stiffened arch) before pronating (rolling in), forcing the rearfoot into a degree of pronation. 'An inward rotation of the foot will generally occur for all strike patterns,' she explains. Does this mean that forefoot strikers need the same support and stability from their shoes as heel strikers? Not entirely. 'Most overpronation issues relating to footwear are for heel strikers, so the stability features of running shoes would not be so relevant for forefoot strikers,' she says. However, while some forefoot strikers don't make any heel contact at all, others allow the heel to touch down after making initial contact with the forefoot. 'These runners may make some use of the overpronation-related features of a traditional running shoe,' says Dr Dixon. Find out more about footwear on page xx.

sending strong impact forces up the body and requiring additional energy to overcome.

In other words, it's not just about what part of the foot strikes the ground first but about *where* the foot strikes the ground. The two are closely related. To see how, try running on the spot. You'll find that it's difficult to land on your heels – you pretty much have

to land on the front half of the foot. Now progress to jogging forward, and you'll see that your foot is landing beneath your knee, rather than out in front of it. If you now make a concerted effort to make the foot land out in front of the knee, you'll find you need to switch to a heel strike, and, according to the forefoot strike camp, will be running less efficiently.

Let me offer a few thoughts on this. First, it's generally accepted that most recreational runners are heel strikers, while a greater proportion of elite distance runners are forefoot strikers. Second, if asked to sprint, most of us run more on our toes than our heels. This might suggest that forefoot/midfoot running is faster, or more efficient, than heel striking (or it may simply be that many elite runners started off on the track as youngsters, where they learned to run on their toes). An interesting study published in the *Journal of Strength and Conditioning Research* looked at foot strike among 415 elite runners at the 15 km mark of a half marathon and found that 74.9 per cent of them were rearfoot strikers, and the remainder were midfoot and forefoot strikers. So much for elite runners all being mid/forefoot strikers, eh? However, it also found, when looking at the finish times of the race participants, that a greater proportion of midfoot strikers came further up the pack than rearfoot strikers, lending further support to the idea that forefoot striking is a more efficient way to run fast.

But what about injury risk? Research from the University of Delaware has shown that a rearfoot strike induces loads that are more associated with tibial stress fractures (shin splints), while a forefoot strike is associated with mechanics that place a runner at greater risk of Achilles tendinitis. What's more, if the foot lands beneath the knee, rather than extended out in front, the stride length is shorter and you will therefore need to take more strides to cover a given distance. This, it could be argued, might increase your injury risk by increasing the number of impacts (*see* 'Stride and tested' on page 26). Overall, the message is that, rather than being associated with a higher or lower injury risk, different foot strike patterns are simply associated with *different* injury risks.

Which brings us to the question, should you try to change the way you run? Some coaches firmly believe that there is one 'correct' way to run, which all runners should strive to achieve, while others are of the opinion that everyone has a unique gait pattern, and as long as we are running comfortably and injury-free, there really is no need to make alterations.

It's interesting to note that practically everyone who falls into the 'one way to run' camp recommends landing on the forefoot or midfoot. There are no coaches that I know of imploring us all to land on our heels. But the 'if it ain't broke, don't fix it' camp point out that the body makes compensations and adaptations in respect of its biomechanical imperfections and inadequacies, so forcing change may create problems rather than solve them.

So what's the bottom line? Both minor and major discrepancies in running gait can cause problems, but they don't always. There are runners who look like an injury waiting to happen but they never seem to get problems, and others who appear bio-mechanically efficient who are plagued with injury. It's also worth remembering that some of the world's top runners don't have what could be described as perfect technique and still pull off amazing athletic achievements. What's more, research reported in *Sports Injury Bulletin* suggests that sudden changes in volume or intensity of running are a greater cause of injury than faulty mechanics. If you do decide to change your technique you need to bear in mind that it takes time. If you are midway through a marathon training programme, now is not the time to start making major alterations to your gait pattern.

I decided to work on changing my gait pattern just after the London Marathon in 2008 and it took me the remainder of the year to get to a stage where I was comfortable running for reasonable periods of time in a new way. (I managed to reduce my PBs in the 10 k, 10 mile and half marathon as a result, though.) But I did get some calf soreness and minor Achilles problems along the way, and I think it's important to be aware that you may end up creating problems that weren't there before, even if you also succeed in eliminating others.

Ask yourself the following questions to help you decide whether you need to make changes:

- Do I suffer from lots of injury problems?
- Have specific faults in my technique been identified?
- Am I willing to put in the time and effort to experiment with a new running technique?
- Is it that important to me to perfect my running style?

High Q

Another issue regarding foot placement concerns where the foot lands in relation to the body's 'midline'. Ideally, the foot should be in alignment with the hip and knee, but, in some cases, the leg 'rolls in' so that the foot lands closer to the midline than the knee or hip. This is believed to be more common in people who have a high 'Q angle' – the angle between where the quadriceps muscle attaches to the kneecap and where it attaches to the pelvis. A greater angle, often linked to wider hips, has been associated with a greater incidence of running-related leg injuries such as runner's knee and ITBF syndrome. Simply trying to make your feet land straighter won't work, but improving your strength and flexibility by doing some of the exercises on pages 61–64 can help you develop a more efficient stride.

Ten tips for better form

1. Relax – it's impossible to run well if you aren't relaxed. Be aware of common tension sites, including the hands (unclench those fists and relax your thumbs), the jaw and forehead, and the shoulders. Research shows that when we clench the jaw, neural signals are sent along the spinal cord, causing us to 'brace' our posture and tense up.

2. The foot should strike the ground beneath the body, in line with your centre of gravity. Think of the foot strike as a 'glancing blow'. Don't deliberately 'push off' the toes as your foot leaves the ground or clench them inside your shoes.

3. Don't grip with the front of your ankles, particularly on hills. Many of us have a tendency to run with rigid ankles, which doesn't help with shock dissipation or a smooth stride. (Swimming – kicking the legs as in front crawl or back stroke – can help mobilise inflexible ankles.) Think of your legs moving in a 'cycling' action from the hip joint. So the knee comes up in front while the heel travels up towards the bottom (the range of movement will be greater when you are running fast, smaller when you are jogging).

4. Run tall, with an upright posture, or a slight forward lean from head to toe. Try not to bend forward from the waist or 'sit' on the hips. Visualise yourself growing taller with every step. Running tall requires a certain amount of muscle strength and stability as well as know-how (*see* the 'Runner's strength' workout on page 61 for more details).

5. Don't try too hard. Running isn't a battle against the ground or the air. Imagine it as a controlled 'topple' forwards – all you need do is put your legs and arms out and you're on your way!

6. You only need try running with your hands in your pockets to realise how much your arms count in running. Imagine they are pistons, propelling you forward, with elbows bent to around 90 degrees. Don't allow the arms to swing across the torso (it's fine if they roll in a little), and put some effort in on the back swing – the arm will spring forward on its own.

7. As mentioned above, clenched fists are not conducive to relaxed running, but that doesn't mean you should let your wrists and hands flop around like a ragdoll, either. Runners are often advised to imagine they are holding a crisp between each thumb and forefinger, tight enough to hold it without crushing it. I prefer to let my thumbs curl in to my palms, but in a 'relaxed clench' position.

8. Your head weighs approximately 7–10 lb (depending on how clever you are!), so be smart and look ahead, not down, otherwise the weight of it will throw your upper spine forward and make your lower back arch, putting a lot of stress on the skeleton. Focus on the ground 10–20 metres ahead.

9. Run light – think of running over the ground rather than into it – spending as little time on the ground as possible. Don't bounce from foot to foot. Vertical movement is one of the biggest wastes of energy.

10. Monitor yourself as you run. Practise running through a 'body scan' from top to toe. Are you gritting your teeth, or are your arms coming across your body? After taking stock, address any tension, tightness or pain, then regroup and carry on.

Running techniques

Malcolm Balk, a Canadian running coach and Alexander Technique teacher, has developed a method of running that has helped many runners (including me) stay injury-free, improve performance and get more enjoyment from their sport. Balk's 'Art of Running' uses Alexander Technique principles to help runners increase their kinaesthetic awareness, and stop forcing and controlling their movement.

Another technique that promises to reduce injuries and enhance performance by minimising wasted effort is the 'Pose method', developed by Dr Nicholas Romanov, a Russian running coach now based in the United States. Danny Dreyer, creator of Chi Running, also promises to reduce injury rates and enhance technique with his running method (see 'Further information', page 212, for more details).

Stride and tested

How fast you run is a product of how big your stride is and how many steps you take, both of which increase as you speed up. But which is most important? Well, one study found that elite distance runners (competing in 800 m to 26.2 mile races) had a cadence of 185–200 steps per minute (spm) – 92–100 per leg). The majority of recreational runners take significantly fewer steps than this, suggesting that increasing cadence is a sensible way of upping speed.

You can easily work out your own cadence by counting the number of times one foot strikes the ground in 60 seconds and multiplying this figure by two. If your cadence is below 180 spm, you may want to consider speeding it up a little. (I found using a metronome very helpful in doing this. I set the metronome to 4–6 beats per minute quicker than my existing cadence, and then jogged on the spot in time to its beat as part of my warm-up, to get my neuromuscular pathways accustomed to the faster rhythm. I would then try to maintain this on the run, periodically counting my steps to see how I was faring. Over a period of weeks I comfortably increased my cadence by 10 spm.) If your cadence is already above 180, you may want to consider addressing stride length. However, in experiments in which runners instinctively pick their most economical stride length, and are then asked to increase it, their perception of effort increases and they use more oxygen, suggesting it may be counter-productive to consciously aim to extend your stride. Perhaps the best way ahead is to ensure that your stride length is optimal by working on your flexibility and running technique rather than actively trying to take bigger steps.

Uphill technique

The most common mistake runners make when taking to the hills is to look down, taking the hefty weight of the head forward and throwing the spine out of alignment. Leaning forward also reduces the involvement of the hamstrings, giving you less propulsion. Instead, look ahead, shorten your stride a little, use your full range of hip extension (which will reward you with steely glutes!) and use your arms to help propel you upwards. Don't try to maintain the same pace you had on flat ground. The golden rule is 'even effort, not even pace'.

Downhill technique

Running downhill might sound a lot easier than running uphill, but the knees and quads can take a real pounding, not just because of the increased impact but because the thigh muscles are contracting eccentrically (to decelerate you), which causes more microtrauma (microscopic damage) in the muscle. To descend less painfully, relax, particularly in the thighs and at the front of the ankles, and don't 'brake' or lean backwards. Take your arms wider for balance, but ensure you don't inadvertently take your legs wider, too. Don't look down at your feet – it's tempting to do so if you are running on a rough trail, but try to pick your route a few metres ahead and trust your feet to follow it.

Breathe easy

There are lots of theories on the best way to breathe during running. For the record, research suggests that most elite marathon runners use a 2–2 breathing pattern (that is, they breathe in for two footstrikes and out for two footstrikes). However, I believe the best way to breathe is the way that comes most naturally to you. As for the common advice that runners should breathe in through the nose and out through the mouth – or, indeed, inhale and exhale through the nose – a study from Liverpool John Moores University showed that once exercise is moderately hard, the most efficient way of breathing in and out is through the mouth, not the nose. Besides, for much of the summer, my nose is way too blocked up to breathe through anyway, and the only true advantage I can see is that I don't swallow quite so many flies . . .

3

making tracks

❖ Fitting in your running
MARATHON TRAINING IN THE REAL WORLD

For many of us, life is a constant race against time – we juggle work, family commitments, chores and social activities, and there never seem to be enough hours in the day. So how, exactly, are you going to cram in all those hours of marathon training? You'll be glad to know that this book takes a practical approach to marathon training – the programmes are geared not only towards varying levels of experience and fitness but also to how much time you have available. You'll find full details on pages 169–189, but in the meantime let's look at some of the strategies people have used to fit their training into a busy life with success.

Planning counts for a lot. A study published in the *British Journal of Social Psychology* tracked a group of runners training for a marathon over a one-year period. They found that working out how, when and where you're going to do your training makes it more likely to happen. And be specific in your planning. Recent research from Germany found that people who outlined their goals in a detailed way (for example, 'I will run before work every Monday, Wednesday and Friday') were more likely to still be

exercising after two weeks than people who set more vague goals, like 'I will exercise in my free time.'

Talking of time, is there an ideal time to run? Yes – the ideal time to run is the time that suits you best. It may be that you love to get up and run first thing, or that you find running helps you to unwind in the evening. Fine. While research shows that between 4 and 7 pm the body is at its most receptive to training (body temperature, muscle strength and flexibility peak between these hours), this doesn't always fit in with our lifestyles. One study found that early-morning workouts could leave your immune system compromised and make you more susceptible to infections. It's to do with hormone levels rising and falling throughout the day, and the fact that saliva, which protects the membranes against airborne germs, is less abundant in the morning. But don't be too quick to generalise with regard to these findings – the study was on swimmers, and their training volume was massive. Other research has shown that people who exercise first thing in the morning are more likely to stick with an exercise programme than are those who leave it until

later in the day (and are more likely to put it off altogether).

Real-life training solutions

Be an early bird

Run before anyone else is up. That way, your running is over and done with before the day has properly started. To resist pressing snooze on the alarm clock, have your kit ready (on the radiator, if it's winter), your watch handy and your bottle filled – then you won't have to think too much.

Advantages

It leaves your evenings free. It doesn't affect your partner or family.

Disadvantages

It may still be dark. The lack of people around could make early runs unsafe. You may feel tired later in the day.

Run to (or from) work

You get Mondays off from running because this is the day that you carry in all your work and training clothes for the week – and shower gear. The rest of the week, you run to the office and get showered and changed and take public transport home.

Advantages

It saves money and releases you from the stress of commuting. It means you use your time productively. It also doesn't impinge on family or partner time. (You may not want to run home from work if it means navigating busy streets, but if you take running gear in the car and park at the station, you can run a circular route from there.)

Disadvantages

Pollution and traffic; unpleasant surroundings (possibly); need to leave earlier to allow time to stretch, shower and change.

Lunch hour runs

These are best used for shorter, faster runs to allow you to warm up, cool down and stretch without going over the allotted hour. Treadmills can be handy, because there'll be showers and changing facilities on tap.

Advantages

It gives you an energy boost for the afternoon. It leaves your evenings free for other things. It gives you a mental break from work.

Disadvantages

Time is always of the essence, so even if you're feeling great you can't just keep running. Not all offices have showering facilities. You need to make time to eat. You don't get to socialise with work colleagues.

One-way ticket

Rather than doing an 'out and back' route, run from home to a local pub or café and get a friend or partner to meet you there with the car, or take a train or bus somewhere and run back.

Jog a dog

Walking the dog is something you have to do anyway, so why not take him running with you? If your route is too long for Rover to come the whole way, circle back to the car or your house, deposit him there with a bowl of water and continue on.

Advantages

You get an important job done without wasting time. You get more fun from your run with a canine companion. You get a fitter dog! See pages 81–82 for tips on running with a four-legged friend.

Disadvantages

You can't leave the dog in the car on a hot day. Some dogs don't like to run, or aren't able to. Your run may be interrupted by the dog's antics. There's also the risk of tripping or colliding with your companion.

Getting others involved

:• Get the kids to help with your fundraising activities if you are running for charity.

:• Get someone to set up a 'drinks station' for you to practise drinking on the run.

:• Enter local races as part of your training. Many events have fun runs on offer for children to get involved in, or bouncy castles, fêtes and face painting to keep them entertained.

:• Don't allow running to clash with regular family or partner activities, such as Sunday lunch or Friday-night cinema visits – it's the fastest way to get people to resent your running!

:• Encourage friends, kids or partners to come for a day in the country, where they can walk or bike at a leisurely pace while you run – you can then all meet up afterwards for tea and cakes!

:• Book a weekend away somewhere nice to run and take the family – even if you do two runs, that's only 2–3 hours out of the weekend 'family time'.

:• Consider taking the whole family to your marathon venue so it becomes something for them to look forward to as well as you.

:• Get some support from work. If they aren't initially very enthusiastic, tell them about the research from New York which found that people who train for a marathon become more goal-focused, disciplined and mentally tough in other areas of their lives, too.

Wherever and whenever you choose to run, make a pledge right now to keep your training in perspective. There will always be times when you simply can't stick to what you had planned, and times when your body will be screaming for rest. It is vital that you listen and pay heed to the call if you are to make it not just to the finish line, but to the start line, with a smile on your face.

why we are here

Research published in the *New England Journal of Medicine* found that running three days a week for four weeks significantly improved concentrations of good HDL cholesterol and lowered risk factors for heart disease. The results were superior to those seen in women who walked for exercise.

Running and the menstrual cycle

Does where you are in your menstrual cycle affect your running? The research is inconclusive. One study, from the University of Adelaide, found that women felt more sluggish early in their cycles and burned less fat when they exercised earlier in the month. Other research suggests that the hike in progesterone at the end of the luteal phase (towards the end of the cycle, leading up to the next period) boosts metabolic rate, but also stimulates fluid retention. That said, Olympic records have been set by women in all stages of their menstrual cycles.

If you suffer from pre-menstrual syndrome (PMS), you'll be glad to hear that a study published in the *Journal of Psychosomatic Research* found that three months of regular exercise successfully reduced premenstrual symptoms. Active women generally report less menstrual cramping, bloating and breast tenderness than their less active peers, but they are not entirely symptom free. If it's period pain that is cramping your style, the best painkillers are ibuprofen and naproxen sodium, both part of the non-steroidal anti-inflammatory drug (NSAID) family. And, hard as it may be to believe, researchers think that intense training eases period pain more effectively than more prolonged, gentler exercise. Try doing your hill training or intervals when you have period pain, to see whether this works for you. It may be that the endorphins released in response to exercise help mask the pain. Conversely, if your symptoms are more mood-related, gentle aerobic exercise is more effective, say researchers from Duke University.

❖ Where to run

THE PROS AND CONS OF DIFFERENT SURFACES

There's no end of places that you can run: parks, playing fields, nature trails, country lanes, urban streets, orienteering routes, towpaths, cycle paths, athletics tracks, beaches, public footpaths . . . Marathon training is the perfect way to discover your local area, and explore a little further afield. Buy a local map or check out internet mapping sites to get an idea of where the footpaths and greener areas are. Of course, you'll be road running, too, but it's important to vary your surfaces and avoid doing all your running on hard surfaces, which increases the overall amount of impact on your joints. Then again, a report in the journal *Sports Medicine* found that running cross-country puts you more at risk of injuries resulting from slipping or losing your footing, such as falls or sprained ankles! Let's look at some of the options . . .

Going off-road

Much of the pleasure from running comes from its potential to provide an escape from the humdrum of daily life – and running in the fresh air, in wide open spaces and among pleasant scenery is undoubtedly more motivating than a busy cityscape. In fact, research from the University of Essex suggests that exercising in natural surroundings is psychologically more beneficial. And it's good for your body, too. One study found that running at the same pace on rough terrain compared to a flat road burned 26 per cent more calories – so regular off-road training will make that road run feel all the easier.

Running on softer terrain will also save your joints from the constant, relentless impact of pavement or road. Not only that, but running on varied surfaces and rolling terrain places an extra demand on the

ligaments, tendons and muscles, according to research from the University of Western Australia. Paula Radcliffe is one of many elite endurance athletes who do much of their training off-road, to reap the benefits of the more forgiving surface and varied terrain.

Trail and grass are the ideal compromise as far as the advantages and disadvantages of off-road running are concerned. Challenging, but not so much that they'll slow you down too much. Unstable, but not so much that they'll pose biomechanical problems.

If you choose to run on the beach, try to avoid highly cambered beaches, which will throw your spine and pelvis out of alignment. You'll also need to go easy on soft sand, as the 'give' of the surface enables your feet to sink and puts extra stress on your calf muscles and Achilles tendon.

Whatever the surface, don't expect to run at the same pace off-road as you do on-road. Instead, aim to run at the same effort level or heart rate.

Don't fear to tread

Many new runners first experience running on the treadmill. It's only when they get up to 20–30 minutes that they start wondering about running outdoors. While you may have 'graduated' to outdoor running by now, there is still a place for the treadmill in a marathon training programme, especially when it comes to timed efforts. There are also the 'safety and softy' factors to consider: it may be too dark or icy to run outdoors, or you simply may prefer to stay inside when it's wet and cold.

However, it would be foolish to do all your marathon training on the treadmill, since although the general movement pattern is the same, the biomechanics are subtly different. For a start, you aren't moving forward but running on the spot; second, your stride length is generally shortened; third, many people have a tendency to look down rather than ahead, misaligning the head and spine as they do so. Research suggests that it takes 6 minutes to get accustomed to running on a treadmill. And, of course, you don't have wind resistance to contend with, or any uneven surfaces.

So how can you use the treadmill to your advantage?

Do a time trial
Your ability to precisely control the environment makes the treadmill a good location for monthly time trials. Warm up first, then select your time (12 minutes is a good test) or distance and go for it. Keep a record of your results to monitor progress.

Make use of the incline button
Researchers at Brighton University found that setting the treadmill gradient to 2 per cent more closely mimicked outdoor conditions.

Don't shy away from hills even if your intended marathon is as flat as a pancake. Hills build leg strength and boost endurance. Try some hill repeats on the treadmill with a jog recovery on the flat.

Go for speed
Whether it's a sustained 20–30-minute effort, or an interval session, you can more precisely control your speed and sustain your effort on a treadmill than out in the real world, where you may slack off without really noticing.

Getting on track

If you live close to an athletics track, make use of it. Don't see it as an exclusive club for the elite runner, but as a convenient, flat training option, offering a responsive surface and measurable distances. Nowadays, you are just as likely to see someone walking round the outside lane of the track as you are to see middle-distance runners hurtling round the bends. It's also very handy in that you can leave a drink by the side of the track, throw off a layer of clothing once you've warmed up, or nip to the loo – all within a few metres of the clubhouse or changing rooms. Most tracks charge a small usage fee, although if you join a running club that trains at the track, this will probably be included. One word of warning, though: if you are susceptible to Achilles tendon or calf problems, approach the track with caution. The super-bouncy surface has lots of give, but it can put additional stress on the lower leg.

The long and winding road

If you are training for a road-based race, it makes sense to do some of your training on hard surfaces, to enable your musculoskeletal system to adapt. Some 95 per cent of British roads are made from asphalt – but often, when we say 'road running', we actually mean pavement running, and concrete pavements are actually ten times harder than asphalt roads. I'm not suggesting you should put your life at risk by battling traffic on the road instead of running on the pavement, but you may be able to swap pavements for, say, a traffic-free cycle trail or a quiet country lane. And for those of you who live in rural areas where road running is a necessity rather than a choice, take comfort in the fact that you are putting less stress on your joints than are pavement-hoggers . . . and wear high-visibility clothing.

⋮ Going shopping
THE SHOES, KIT AND GADGETS YOU NEED TO GET STARTED

This section is devoted to my favourite activity (other than running, of course): shopping. First we'll look at the basics – running shoes and kit – and then check out some useful extras.

Running shoes

First things first: running shoes. Given that a force equal to two to three times your body weight passes up through the body every time your foot hits the ground (and that's at a steady pace on the flat), footwear that helps protect and support the foot is vital. According to US health and fitness organisation IDEA, inadequate heel cushioning can cause heel spurs and insufficient shock absorption can increase the risk of lower leg stress fractures and lower back pain while poor fit can cause ankle and knee problems. To maximise comfort and performance, and minimise the risk of injury, you need the right shoe.

So where do you begin the search? There are shoes to suit all shapes, sizes, biomechanical differences and budgets. Even for the most experienced of runners, the choice can be mind-boggling. The best solution is to visit a specialist sports or running shop that stocks a wide range of brands and has knowledgeable staff. Many stores offer gait analysis on a treadmill, to provide more information about your footwear needs. But bear in mind that gait analysis equipment is useful only if the person testing you has the knowledge and experience to translate the findings into usable advice.

RUNNING SHOE ANATOMY

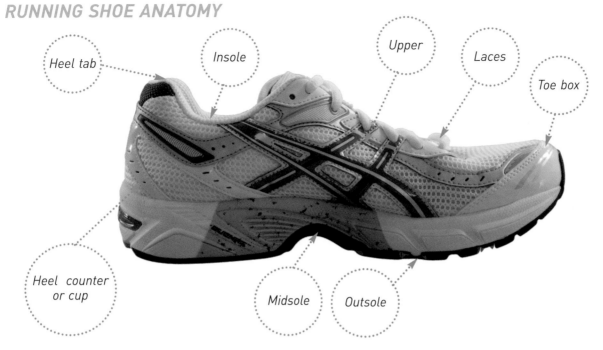

Heel tab

Insole

Upper

Laces

Toe box

Heel counter or cup

Midsole

Outsole

Questions asked at the running store:

- ⫶ Can I take a look at/measure your feet?
- ⫶ How many miles/hours do you/will you train?
- ⫶ Are you training for something specific?
- ⫶ How much do you weigh?
- ⫶ What trainers have you worn in the past?
- ⫶ Do you/have you had any injury problems?
- ⫶ What is your budget?
- ⫶ Where do you train (what sort of terrain)?
- ⫶ What are the shoes principally for (racing 5 km may necessitate different running shoes than training for a marathon)?

If they don't ask you any of these questions, or simply try to sell you the most expensive pair of running shoes they stock without good reason, take your custom elsewhere.

What to look for in a running shoe

You need to be prepared to spend at least £60 for a reputable brand and model. Think of it like this: good shoes might not last longer than cheaper shoes but, as with a good-quality paint, you'll get a better finish. Your first and foremost consideration when buying your first pair of running shoes, should be comfort. It doesn't matter if it's the latest, greatest most expensive model in the shop, if it doesn't feel comfy, don't buy it. And certainly don't expect to 'wear it in'. Trainers should feel good straight away – the acid test is if you can run in them for the first time and forget that they are new.

Comfort also means good fit. There should be the width of your index finger between your longest toe and the end of the shoe. Don't buy a size 8 just because all your shoes are a size 8. If size 8½, or even size 9, feels better, opt for that. Different brands vary widely, both in length and width.

The second most important consideration is shock absorption, or cushioning. A study published in the *International Journal of Sports Medicine* concluded that shoe cushioning could reduce the effect of impact forces on spinal structures – so it's not just your feet you are protecting. Shock-absorbing material may come in the form of an air capsule, foam or gel, and the key factors are the level of shock absorption the shoe offers, and whereabouts in the shoe it is positioned. The majority of running shoes are designed for heel strikers (those who make first impact with the ground on their heels), but with the recent interest in forefoot running (*see* page 22) some manufacturers are now producing shoes more suitable for forefoot strikers.

A third important factor is how stable the shoe is. A large percentage of runners overpronate (*see* page 22), and 'stability' or 'motion control' shoes are designed to attenuate the effects of this. Stability shoes usually have a 'dual-density' midsole. This means that the material on the medial side of the shoe is harder than that placed on the lateral side, to prevent the foot rolling inwards. Another common stability aid is a medial post (an insert of high-density foam or plastic), which aims to limit the rate and extent of pronation as the foot lands.

The flexibility of a shoe is also something you need to assess. A stiff, inflexible shoe will require more energy to flex than a bendier sole (making it less than ideal for lighter runners, who won't have the force to flex the sole). Good flexibility in the forefoot is particularly important if you are a forefoot striker (landing on the front half of the foot) because it will allow the tarsophalangeal joint (the 'knuckle' of the foot) to flex naturally, but make sure you don't entirely sacrifice cushioning for flexibility.

Shoes vary widely in weight – there could easily be a difference of 140 g between two different models. Generally speaking, there is a trade-off between weight and support – in other words, the lighter a shoe is, the less support and fewer stability features it is likely to offer. Many experienced marathoners have 'racing shoes' that are lighter but less supportive than their training shoes. They can get away with wearing them for the duration of a race (and benefit from their lighter weight) but they opt for more support during training.

A final consideration is where you will be doing your training. If a significant amount of your training is likely to take place off-road, it's worth investing in a pair of shoes designed specifically for off-road use. Since you'll be running on softer, more slippery and less stable surfaces, off-road shoes will give you more grip (traction), thanks to lots of knobbly bits (lugs) on the outsole of the shoe that grip without slipping. The upper part of the shoe will usually be more robust to protect your toes from rocks and tree roots – many now incorporate a water-resistant Gore-tex layer, too.

Bearing all the above in mind, you may find that you need (or want) more than one pair of running shoes – for example, a solid, stable pair for long runs and a lighter more responsive pair for faster training and races. Or perhaps a pair for running trails and a pair for the roads. There are two good reasons for investing in more than a single pair. First, running in different shoes varies the stress placed on the muscles of the feet and lower legs, reducing your chances of developing an overuse injury. And, second, giving your trainers a break between uses allows time for the midsole to decompress – it can take up to 24 hours to return to normal.

Determining your foot type and shoe needs

Make a wet footprint

The imprint your foot leaves gives an idea of whether you have particularly high- or low-arched feet, which may affect your gait. I say 'may', because arch height and gait pattern are by no means inextricably linked, as demonstrated by many research papers. For example, I have high-arched feet but I still over-pronate. Dip your feet in water and then walk across a flat, even surface, such as concrete, hard sand or even a sheet of cardboard. Can you see the entire silhouette of your foot or is it more of an outline, with just heels and toes showing?

> Toes and forefoot plus heel show, joined by a broad band: indicates normal or 'neutral' foot-strike.

> Entire foot shows: indicates low or flat arches, associated with overpronation.

> Toe prints plus heel but little in between: indicates high arches, which are associated with excessive supination, or underpronation.

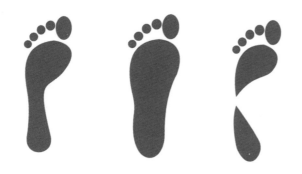

Jump on a pressure plate

Pressure plate analysis involves running over a pressure-sensitive mat, which records how much force is exerted when your foot lands and which areas of the foot display the highest force measurements during footstrike. A digital image of the foot is created, indicating the areas of peak pressure and giving some clues as to what type of shoe will best meet your needs. The adidas FootScan machine is installed in a number of specialist running shops across the UK and the service is provided free of charge.

Go for analysis

Many running shops now offer a gait analysis service. This is normally carried out by a staff member who has been trained by a shoe manufacturer, and it can be very useful, but bear in mind that it isn't the same as seeing a physiotherapist or podiatrist. You should consider having a full gait analysis (see box on page 40) at a sports injury clinic or the like, if you have recurring injuries as a result of running. Otherwise, a shop-floor service will probably suffice.

The ten commandments of shoe shopping

1. Never buy cross-trainers or shoes designed for anything other than running in place of desig-nated running shoes.
2. Shop for trainers in the afternoon, or, even better, after a run, when feet are slightly bigger.
3. Stand, don't sit, when assessing the amount of space in the front of the shoe. You need approxi-mately an index finger's width beyond your longest toe (which isn't always the big toe).
4. Try both shoes on together. Everyone has one foot slightly larger than the other.
5. Be particularly picky about fit around the heel. A study from the University of Illinois found that a poor-fitting heel cup could cause ankle and knee problems.
6. Expect instant comfort. If the shoe doesn't feel great as soon as you put it on, don't buy it.
7. Run at least a few steps in shoes that you try on, either around the shop or on a treadmill, if one is provided.
8. Don't be seduced by gimmicks. All the big shoe companies introduce 'revolutionary' technologies that have disappeared by the following season.

Gait analysis – step by step

Gait analysis should be conducted by a podiatrist, biomechanist or physiotherapist (a podiatrist/physiotherapist team is ideal). The consultation will start with some questions about your general health, any joint or muscular problems, past injuries and your current running regime. The consultant will then take a look at your posture in standing and assess the function of some important 'stabilising' muscles. Then you'll hop on to the treadmill (perhaps barefoot at first) and you'll be videoed walking and running. Make sure they film you running in trainers, too, unless you plan to train for the marathon barefoot! Afterwards, the practitioner will take you through the video, showing you, frame by frame, where any problems lie. You may be given stretches and exercises to do to improve the strength and function of particular muscles, or you may be prescribed orthotics. (An investigative feature in *Runner's World* magazine found that nearly all podiatrists recommended orthotics, even in the absence of injury problems.) These are special insoles that go inside the shoe to correct, or at least minimise, faulty movement patterns. Off-the-peg orthoses, which cost under £100, may help if you have a very minor biomechanical problem, but custom-made ones, designed to cope with more serious problems, can cost £300 or more. If you are in the market for gait analysis, ensure that the podiatrist or physio that you see has a specialism in running. See 'Further information' (page 213) for more on gait analysis and podiatry.

9. Try shoes on with your sports socks and, if you wear them, orthotics.
10. When you find the perfect pair, buy two! Shoe companies have an annoying habit of changing models each year, so you may never find the exact same pair again.

Maintenance and replacement

Running shoes don't last forever. In fact, if you count miles, 300 to 500 miles (depending on how heavy you are and the type of surface you run on) is considered the average life span. Even if there are no signs of wear, you should replace running shoes after 500 miles of use (Paula Radcliffe changes her shoes every three weeks!). To maximise the life of your trainers, keep them just for running, rather than wearing them for the gym and other activities, don't wear them without socks (especially if you want to keep some friends), and never put them in the washing machine. If they get wet, remove the insoles and allow them to dry naturally (stuffing them with dry newspaper, which you replace as it becomes soaked, helps speed up the drying process).

Knot a problem

You've got perfect fit in the forefoot, but your heel is slipping around. What to do? Adjust the laces. Do a normal 'criss-cross' lacing pattern up to the last-but-one hole. Then thread each end of the lace through the last hole on its own side, pulling a little bit of lace up to create a loop. Now take the end of each lace and thread it through the loop on the opposite side. When you pull the laces tight, you will notice the firmer heel fit.

Alternatively, get a pair of 'shoe driers' – thick insoles filled with beads that absorb moisture. Muddy running shoes are best cleaned with warm soapy water and a brush. Again, allow them to dry naturally – using a heat source can damage the midsole and melt the glue holding the shoe together.

Socks

Simple? Yes. Inexpensive? Yes. Potential for disaster, if wrong? Huge! If you are regularly active and still buy three pairs of cotton sports socks for a fiver, you're missing out on the technical fabrics and features of the true performers, such as an absence of seams, or flat-stitched seams that don't chafe and cause blisters, sweat-wicking fabrics with anti-fungal properties, two-layer construction, better shaping (socks marked 'left' and 'right', no less) and even extra cushioning at the points of impact.

A good pair of socks needs to be absorbent, since your feet will produce large quantities of sweat when running, but the sweat then needs to be wicked away from the feet in order to prevent blisters and chafing. Cotton socks, while absorbing moisture efficiently, aren't able to do anything with it, so they cause the fabric to swell, and create friction. Technical fabrics, such as Coolmax or Dri-fit, are a much better bet,

maintaining their shape and fit, and keeping runners' feet drier.

The style of sock you prefer is an individual choice. I like thick socks with good padding, but other runners like thin, lightweight ones. See what works best for you. Another sock style worth considering is compression socks, the below-the-knee tight-fitting type worn by many of the elite distance runners. Compression socks are designed to reduce muscle oscillation (wobbling), which helps minimise microtrauma, and to aid venous return (blood flow to the heart). I like to wear these for long runs and long races, as, even if they don't improve my performance, they definitely hasten recovery.

Running kit

Not so long ago, you had to choose between fashion and function when buying running kit but, happily, that's no longer the case and there are some great ranges out there that have all the sweat-wicking, non-chafing, wind- and waterproofing properties, as well as good looks. But what are the essentials? That depends on the time of year and climate in which you are going to be doing most of your training, so I have divided kit into winter and summer options. In general, you should opt for manmade technical fabrics rather than cotton. These are able to wick moisture away from the skin over 50 per cent faster than cotton. Layering thin garments is better than opting for one big, thick item, since sweat can move more easily between thin layers.

Kitting yourself out in the right gear will certainly make you feel the part, but there is also a comfort and convenience factor not to be sniffed at: ease of movement, better ventilation, protection from the elements, reflective strips for safety, and pockets for on-the-run items such as MP3 players, keys and coins.

Spring and summer running kit essentials

Bottom half

Shorts: Choose between traditional running shorts (a loose fit, with an inner pant) and 'cycling style' Lycra shorts. If you opt for the former, make sure they aren't too baggy, because excess fabric could cause inner-thigh chafing, not to mention reducing your aerodynamism! Also look for flat or protected seams, particularly around the waistband, to avoid chafing. An antibacterial gusset liner is useful in tighter-fitting shorts if you are prone to yeast infections. An internal pocket is handy if you don't like to carry stuff while you run.

OR

Lightweight, breathable long pants/tights: Not everyone likes to run in shorts, and provided they are made from a cool, lightweight fabric, long pants are fine. They are particularly good if you frequently include trail runs in your weekly regime and need protection from nettles, brambles and ticks.

Top half

Sports bra: No woman should set foot out the door without a proper sports bra. Read all about why, and how to find the right one, in the box below.

Vest: A running vest must fit perfectly – too loose and you will be continually hoisting the shoulder straps back on, too tight and you will not get a cool flow of air around the chest and may end up suffering from soreness under the armpits.

OR

T-shirt: Choose one that is loose-fitting enough to allow air flow but not overly baggy. Look for lightweight, breathable fabrics. Zipped tops enable you to increase ventilation if you want to. A short-sleeved T-shirt will be cooler than a long-sleeved one – it's useful to have one of each.

Hat/visor: On sunny days, a visor, or a very lightweight, breathable baseball cap, is a good option to protect your face.

Essential chick kit

Recent research from the University of Portsmouth found that breasts can move as much as 21 cm during impact exercise. This movement, in a figure-of-eight-type pattern, can cause severe discomfort and, over time, causes the supportive Cooper's ligaments to stretch. A sports bra helps to minimise movement and make exercise more comfortable. There are two main styles: 'encapsulated' bras separate and support each breast in its own cup and sometimes have underwiring for extra support, while 'compression' bras press the breasts against the rib cage to reduce movement. The former style is usually advised for larger-breasted women, the latter for flatter-chested women, but the University of Portsmouth study found that encapsulated styles worked better for women of all bra sizes. It also revealed that the extent of breast motion was just as great during jogging compared to sprinting. So ladies, no excuses!

Choosing the right bra

- Comfort and fit come first. The bra should be snug but not so tight that it restricts your breathing (you should only be able to hook one finger beneath the band). It should be level all the way round, not riding up at the back. Look for flat seams, to avoid chafing.

- The straps should be wide enough to give proper support and not dig into your skin, but soft enough not to chafe. They should also be adjustable, since the fabric will stretch over time and you'll need to shorten them.

- As with all sports kit, cotton isn't ideal. Technical fabrics like Coolmax or Supplex wick away sweat so that your body stays dry and comfortable, and you avoid chafing.

- If your breasts noticeably change size throughout your menstrual cycle, you may need to consider buying sports bras in different sizes to suit the time of the month.

- A crop top is not a sports bra. A study published in the *Journal of Science and Medicine in Sport* found that a crop top did not restrict breast movement as efficiently as a designated sports bra.

- Just like running shoes, sports bras have a limited life span. After frequent washing, the elastic will begin to slacken and the level of support will be reduced. Sports bra specialist LessBounce.com recommends changing a sports bra after 30–40 washes, although you may find you can extend its life a little by adjusting the straps and using a tighter hook on the back.

See 'Further information' (page 212) for details of sports bra manufacturers and suppliers.

Autumn and winter running kit

Layering is the secret to warm and comfortable winter running. Even when it's really cold outside, a bulky sweatshirt will feel heavy and stifling after a mile or two.

Bottom half

Tights: Most runners wear tights for cold-weather training – they are a much better option than heavy cotton jogging bottoms, which will soon be sweat-soaked and perhaps rain-drenched. The main difference between different tight options is the fabric – in general, 'shinier' high-Lycra content tights are less warm than thicker, softer pairs with a matt finish. If you don't like the feel of a 'second skin', trackster-style tights offer a looser fit. Try on lots of pairs to ensure they feel comfortable – be particularly picky about the fit around the crotch (a low-hanging crotch is extremely uncomfortable!) and check that the tights are long enough. Also make sure that seams along the legs don't rub or chafe. Reflectivity is important for running in the dark.

Shell trousers: Looser-fitting soft shell trousers have the advantage of being wind-proof, or even waterproof, but bear in mind that greater water resistance usually comes with less breathability. These can be a useful second layer in extreme weather conditions.

Top half

A base layer: Base layers are designed to be worn next to the skin, to wick away sweat and prevent you from getting damp and chilly. They are tight-fitting (in order to do their job properly) and made from technical fabrics. On colder days, opt for a thermal base layer.

Mid layer: A second, looser-fitting layer provides extra warmth by trapping body heat. This could simply be your summer running T-shirt, worn on top of the base layer, but technical fabrics, such as Windstopper soft shell, offer more protection from the elements, along with a degree of water-resistance. Reflectivity is useful if this is going to be your top layer of clothing (if you don't need a jacket).

Waterproof jacket or gilet: A lightweight water-proof that has been designed for running is essential. Why? Because it offers features such as back and underarm ventilation, shaped sleeves and two-way zips, which bog-standard waterproofs won't have. A jacket with zip-off sleeves, to turn it into a gilet, is perfect for different weather conditions, or pick one that packs away into itself, like a cagoule, in case you need to remove it mid-run.

Hat and gloves: It is important to keep your extremities warm when you are out running in cold temperatures. Even these are available in technical fabrics, although you can easily make do with a fleece or wool 'beanie' hat and a cheap pair of gloves. That said, high-tech fabrics can offer warmth without weight or bulk, and have useful extras, such as reflectivity and 'grippy' finger panels to enable you to operate your sports watch without removing them.

Top gear
Drinking vessel

It is worth investing in a designated running drinks bottle, which is easier to hold than a mineral water bottle. For longer training runs, especially those where you won't be passing any signs of civilisation, you might consider a 'hydration system' (a backpack with a water bladder inside and a drinking tube that reaches round to your mouth). Bumbag-style 'fuel belts' are another option. These hold a few small bottles, allowing you to distribute the weight of your fluid more evenly, and also enabling you to grab and drink easily without fumbling around.

   The smallest, lightest hydration solution of all is a £1 coin, with which you can buy a drink en route – and the change can be dispensed into a charity box.

Sunglasses

Sports sunglasses are a must if you are training in bright sunlight – prolonged exposure to UVA and UVB rays without eye protection can increase the risk of eye damage. Sport sunglasses are designed to stay on even when you are moving around a lot, and usually have a wraparound style and a sweat-resistant nosebridge to prevent slippage. There are two other advantages of sunglasses: first, they make a barrier between you and the rest of the world, helping to ease any feelings of self-consciousness; second, they prevent flies and dust getting in your eyes.

Monitoring tools

If I were to advise a runner to buy one gadget, it would be a heart rate monitor – which consists of a chest strap and a wrist watch to which the monitor constantly sends heart rate information. Cheaper than GPS, it still offers unbiased feedback on your workout, both during and afterwards. Most models enable you to set the upper and lower boundaries of your exercise intensity (based on your personal data), and record both peak and average heart rate during a session, along with calories and the percentage of fat burned. Higher-end options allow you to download data on to your computer, or track your distance and speed via a 'footpod' (a cheaper but less accurate alternative to GPS). Only pay out for functions you think you'll use, and make sure the watch face is clearly readable and the buttons easy to press on the run.

Another option is a speed/distance monitor. This consists of a foot-mounted device that transmits data to either a heart rate monitor or, in the case of the Nike+ Sports Kit, your iPod. Speed/distance monitors are not as accurate as GPS but they give you a reasonable estimate of your pace and how far you've run, and can be calibrated to increase accuracy.

Global positioning systems (GPS) are the most comprehensive monitoring tool, giving you real-time information on your pace and distance while you run. You can also download your route and session data on to your PC afterwards (some do this wirelessly), giving you the option of comparing and contrasting your performances. Some GPS devices now come with a chest strap for heart rate monitoring – enabling you to track every aspect of your performance, from heart rate to calorie expenditure, maximum speed to metres climbed. Great, if you want to get really geeky! If, on the other hand, you simply want to know how long you have been running for, a simple sports watch will do the job. Useful features include a countdown timer for interval training, a 'split time' function to record laps, a backlighter for running in the dark, and big, easy-to-press buttons so you don't accidentally fail to record that new PB!

Backpacks

Just any old backpack won't do if you are running with provisions. What you need is one that straps firmly to the body without chafing (straps that fasten across the chest and around the waist or hips give a snugger fit), and that has a vented, breathable padded back, so that you don't end up with a giant sweat patch on yours. Other useful features to look out for are side pockets for drinks bottles, and flat-zipped compartments for keys and other jangly things.

4

staying strong, flexible and injury-free

⋰ Routine procedures

HOW, WHEN AND WHY TO WARM UP, COOL DOWN AND STRETCH

In chapter two, we looked at the essential principles underpinning your training regime. This chapter deals with further aspects of the training itself. First, let's take a look at how to prepare for each run – warming up – and how to wind down afterwards – by cooling down and stretching.

The warm-up – why and how

A warm-up helps bridge the gap between stationary and 'in motion', allowing the body and mind time to respond and adapt to running. The warm-up has a number of functions; most importantly, it raises body temperature, increases heart rate, redirects blood flow away from the internal organs to the working muscles and mobilises the joints. Articular cartilage, which cushions the joint surfaces, does not have its own blood supply but relies on nutrients being delivered by synovial fluid, to reduce friction between the bone surfaces. Movement promotes the arrival of fresh fluid to soak the articular cartilage, as well as making it less 'sticky'.

Warming up will also enhance your performance. Research from the Institute of Sports and Preventive Medicine in Germany demonstrated that a warm-up improved range of motion, while a study from the University of Strathclyde in Glasgow found that it reduced the accumulation of lactic acid following an all-out sprint.

Here are a few of the other benefits of a warm-up:

- improved oxygen uptake by the muscles, since haemoglobin, the oxygen-carrying molecule, releases its oxygen more readily at higher temperatures

- increased speed and efficiency of muscle contraction

- greater economy of movement

- a reduced risk of muscle straining or tearing (a warmed-up muscle is less susceptible to injury than a cold one, says research in the *American Journal of Sports Medicine*)

- a warm-up also helps to put you in the right mental state for a run – giving you time to focus your thoughts on the forthcoming session, and temporarily put worries and daily stresses aside.

How to do it

Warming up is an active process – don't confuse warming up with stretching (*see* panel). While studies clearly show that a warm-up reduces injury risk and improves performance, there is no evidence that static stretching (in which you hold a position for a short period) does either of these things.

Start your warm-up with some gentle mobilisations of the major joints (this is particularly important if you've been sitting down all day or have just got out of bed). Even though running is predominantly a lower-body activity, you don't want to start running with stiffness or tension in other areas. Work from the head to the feet, mobilising the neck, shoulders, spine, waist, hips, knees and ankles. All your movements should be very gentle – not vigorous swinging but controlled circling, bending and extending. Next, take a walk, either on the spot or forwards, gradually increasing your speed and range of movement to break into a slow jog. Once you are feeling warm and slightly breathless, you can either

pick up the pace to begin your run or spend a few moments on some dynamic flexibility work (sometimes called dynamic stretching). This involves working through the specific movement patterns involved in running; the purpose of this is to 'switch on' the right neuromuscular pathways and optimise range of motion. Typical dynamic warm-up activities for running include hamstring swings, heel flicks and skipping shown on page 51.

A warm-up should take at least 5 minutes – if you are doing a short, fast session or race, the warm-up should be longer and more thorough than if you are embarking on a slower, more prolonged run. This is partly because you don't want to spend precious minutes getting up to speed in a shorter session, but also because faster running and racing puts you at greater risk of injury. Don't allow too much time to pass between completing the warm-up and beginning the activity – otherwise the benefits will be lost.

Should I stretch before I run?

Increasingly, opinion is shifting away from pre-run static stretching. A review in the journal *Physician and Sportsmedicine* in 2005 concluded that stretching immediately before exercise does not prevent injury, and that it reduces force and power output by 2–5 per cent (perhaps not enough to affect your long run, but potentially enough to make a difference if you were racing a 5 km event). Dynamic stretching is now the favoured form of flexibility training within a warm-up, with static stretching saved for *after* a run. However, there is a personal element to this. If you feel the need to stretch before you run, then you will probably perform better if you do so. But one thing's for sure: never stretch cold muscles – always warm up for a few minutes first.

Warm-up exercises

Hamstring Swings

Heel flicks

High knee skipping

The cool-down – why and how

Once you've accomplished your run, it's tempting to leave it at that and get on with your day, but cooling down – or warming down, as it's sometimes called – is every bit as important as warming up. All it really means is coming to a gradual, rather than a sudden, stop. This prevents you from suffering undesirable effects such as dizziness, blood pooling in the veins and a sudden drop in blood pressure. It also prepares your body to return to a resting state. A study in the journal *Physiology of Sport and Exercise* found that a gradual cool-down helped to remove lactic acid from the muscles more quickly than complete rest, which may reduce the likelihood of cramping or muscle spasm, and goes some way towards preventing muscle stiffness and hastening recovery.

How to do it

All you need to do is slow down your running speed to a gentle jog and then a walk. Maintain this until your breathing and heart rate have returned to normal. Then get ready to stretch. You can get showered and changed into something warm and comfortable before stretching – you don't need to do it the moment you walk in the door; 20 minutes or so won't allow the muscles to get too cold.

Stretching – the truth

Few subjects in running are as hotly debated as that of stretching. Does it improve performance, does it reduce injury risk – is it, indeed, worth doing at all? New research, published in the *Journal of Strength and Conditioning Research*, found that distance runners who performed the worst in a 'sit and reach' test (which measures hamstring and lower back flexibility) had the best running economy! But, on the other hand, a study review in the *Clinical Journal of Sports Medicine* found that flexibility training improved running speed. Meanwhile, Swedish researchers suggest that, while stretching improves range of motion, this had no bearing on running performance, either negatively or positively.

While the dispute rages on, we can do one of two things – wait for the science bods to make up their minds, or look at the current evidence and make our own decision.

Personally, I think flexibility work is hugely important – particularly for anyone who sits down most of the day and for those of us past the first flush of youth! Chris Norris, a physiotherapist and author of *The Complete Guide to Stretching*, points out that 'body tissues must be taken through their full range of motion to maintain their extensibility and elasticity. When this does not occur, the muscle can shorten permanently and alter the function of a joint.' While we can't categorically say that stretching will reduce injury risk or improve performance, it will help to restore muscles to their optimal length after the continual contraction involved in running, and it will help to maintain range of motion in the joints and prevent tightness and imbalances between muscle groups.

Using improved range of motion as their parameter of 'benefit', researchers reporting in *Physician and Sportsmedicine* concluded that a regime of regular static stretching, holding each stretch for 30 seconds, was advisable.

It's not known whether our physiological capacity for stretching improves over time, enabling us to stretch further, or whether regular practice simply increases our stretch 'tolerance' – in other words, our ability to hold a position without pain. Whichever is correct, these gains make it all the more likely that you'll continue to stretch – and, who knows, maybe even enjoy it!

How to do it

Many runners are a law unto themselves when it comes to stretching practices, so don't just copy someone else's routine – you may well be picking up inappropriate stretches and missing out on important ones. Always know what muscle or muscles you are stretching, and ensure you use good technique. The stretch routine on pages 54–57 is based on the static stretching protocol. This is the kind of stretching most of us are familiar with, in which you take the muscle to a point at which it feels tight and taut, and hold the position. There are, of course, other ways to stretch – for example, active stretching, in which you contract one muscle to its fullest capacity in order to stretch the opposite (antagonistic) muscle to its greatest outer range, and proprioceptive neuromuscular facilitation (PNF), which sets out to 'trick' the stretch receptors into allowing the muscle to extend further. Some research suggests that PNF techniques offer marginally greater increases in range of motion compared to static stretching, but they do take a bit more effort and may increase the risk of injury. Meanwhile, a study published in the *Journal of Orthopaedic Sports and Physical Therapy*, found that continuous static stretching was superior to active stretching. So, for the purposes of marathon training, we'll stick to static stretching. This is a very safe and simple method, and good to use post-workout, since it is relaxing and doesn't require you to do anything other than maintain the position.

How long?
The American College of Sports Medicine recommends holding stretches for 20–30 seconds, repeating each stretch two to four times. But research in the journal *Physician and Sportsmedicine* found that some muscle groups need to be stretched for longer than others, and that injured muscle tissue may need longer in order to increase the range of motion (for example, it took five stretches to 'release' the hamstrings, compared to just 15 seconds to improve range of motion in the hip abductor muscles). Flexibility varies from joint to

joint – you may find your calves and hamstrings have an impressive range of motion while your lower back is as stiff as a board, or that your right side is stiffer than your left. If this is the case, work harder on the tighter side – otherwise you'll simply maintain the imbalances.

How far?

Stretch until you feel tension and a slight 'irritation' in the muscle but not pain. As the muscle relaxes, you can move slightly deeper into the stretch and hold again. Do not bounce in and out of your 'end' position unless you want your muscles to snap like overstretched elastic bands!

How often?

You should stretch after every run – particularly your long run and tougher sessions. In fact, if you can stretch daily that's even better, suggests research in the *Clinical Journal of Sports Medicine*.

Full body stretch for marathon runners

The routine on the following pages addresses all the muscles a runner needs to stretch. Perform it after every run if you can. Hold each position for 20–30 seconds (per side, if appropriate) and, ideally, perform each stretch twice.

1 Hamstrings

Stand face on to a support between knee and hip height. Extend one leg and place it on the support, with the foot relaxed. Your supporting leg should be perpendicular to the floor. Now hinge forward from the hips (don't round your back), keeping the pelvis level and the knee of the extended leg straight. Feel the stretch along the back of the supported thigh. You don't need to pull your toes back towards you – the only reason this intensifies the stretch is because it adds the sciatic nerve into the equation. If your hamstrings are really tight, repeat this stretch with your leg slightly across the midline and then slightly outside the midline and then with the knee slightly bent.

2 Quads

Stand tall with feet parallel and then lift your right heel, taking your right hand behind you to grab the foot. Bring the pelvis in to a neutral position and gently draw the foot up towards your bottom, keeping knees close together. It doesn't matter if your stretching thigh is in front of the supporting one, as long as you experience a stretch.

3 Upper and lower calves

Stand facing a support, feet a stride length apart with back leg straight and front leg bent. Make sure your back foot is pointing directly forwards. Press the back heel into the floor so that you experience a stretch in the middle of the calf muscle (1). Hold. Now bring the back leg in a little, bend the knee and flex the hips, so that the stretch moves down to the lower part of the calf and Achilles tendon (2). Make sure you keep most of your weight on the non-stretching leg.

1   2

4 Inner thighs (adductors)

Sit on the floor with knees drawn in to chest and feet flat on the floor. Drop knees open to the sides and use your elbows to gently press the legs open (1). Don't round the back; sit up tall. Hold, then extend the legs out to the sides and hinge forward from the hips (2).

5 ITB/tensor fascia latae

Stand tall, and cross one leg behind the other, sliding it away from you until you feel a stretch in the back leg hip. Bend the supporting leg and lean the torso in the direction the back leg is stretching to increase the stretch.

6 Hip flexors

Assume a lunge position, allowing the back knee to go to the floor, and the toes to face down. Tighten the tummy muscles and extend forwards from the back hip, until your front knee is at 90 degrees. You should feel a stretch along the front of the rear leg's hip and thigh.

7 Shins (tibialis anterior)

Kneel on a mat, gently lowering your weight on to your haunches and placing hands on the floor for support. Now lift one knee off the floor, feeling a stretch along the front of the shin and ankle.

8 Glutes/outer thighs (abductors)

Sit against a wall with legs outstretched. Cross your right foot over your left thigh and put the foot flat on the floor. Now take your left arm around the right knee and gently pull it around towards the shoulder (rather than hugging directly to chest), sitting up tall. Feel a stretch in the bottom and hip of the bent leg.

9 Hip rotators (piriformis)

Lie face up on the floor and bring one knee into your chest, the other foot flat on the floor. Now grasp the ankle of the bent leg and, stabilising the knee with your other hand, gently pull it across the body until you feel a deep hip stretch in the lifted leg.

10 Lower back
Lie on your back with knees bent and feet flat on the floor. Take your arms out to the sides. Now drop your knees towards the left, keeping the shoulders on the floor. Hold, then bring the knees back to the centre and drop to the right. Finish by drawing your knees in to your chest and linking your arms around them.

Stretched for time?

In an ideal world, we would all spend 15 minutes stretching after every run, but unfortunately that isn't always a luxury we can afford. So, if you are short on time, what are the crucial muscles to stretch? Focus on those that you usually find most tight, rather than just going for the obvious ones.

Nerve stretches
Nerve stretching can help free up nerves that have become compressed or shortened as a result of bad posture or repeated poor movement patterns, and is particularly important after an injury, since it prevents swollen soft tissues sticking to the nerve and hampering neuromuscular pathways. But nerves should be treated carefully – never hold a nerve in a stretched position, like you would with a muscular stretch. Instead, you 'pulse' in and out of the stretched position. The sensation should be of tightness and tingling rather than pins and needles and outright pain. Turn the page for three key nerve stretches.

why *we are here*

Regular aerobic exercise helps you sleep better. A Stanford University study found that people who exercised for at least 40 minutes, four times a week, fell asleep twice as fast and woke up feeling more refreshed than non-exercisers.

1

The slump

This position stretches the sciatic nerve, focusing on the lower back, glutes and hamstrings. Sit on the edge of a table, link your arms behind your back and begin rolling forward through the spine, starting by taking the chin to the chest. Simultaneously straighten one leg, pulling the toes up towards you and locking the knee. Gently swing the leg 20 times. Perform on the other leg, and then repeat on both sides.

2

Point and flex

This exercise mobilises the sciatic nerve where it meets the calf and Achilles tendon, and is great for tightness in this area. Lie on your back, hooking a scarf or belt over one foot and extending that leg up overhead. Lock the knee out then flex and point the foot 20 times. Swap sides, and repeat on both sides.

3

The Thomas stretch

This mobilisation stretches the femoral nerve and helps loosen tight hip flexors and quads. Sit on the edge of a bench or table, and pull one knee in to your chest and roll backwards, allowing the other leg to hang over the table edge, completely relaxed, but in line with your torso (not dropping out to the side). Now lift your head to your chest and swing the 'hanging' leg back and forth 20 times, using as great a range of motion as you can. Swap sides. Repeat on each side.

⋰ Body maintenance

HOW TO STAY STRONG AND INJURY-FREE THROUGHOUT MARATHON TRAINING

Our bodies may be designed to move, but they aren't necessarily designed to withstand regular, repetitive motion in a single direction, which is what they get with distance running. Perhaps that's why, in a typical year, nearly two-thirds of runners suffer an injury bad enough to put them out of action. Despite being fantastic exercise, running isn't an 'all-round' form of activity – it uses predominantly the lower body muscles, for a start, and it uses them in a very specific, repetitive way. The upshot is that some muscles are likely to get short and tight, while others become weak and lengthened. If you want to reduce the risk of injury and maintain a strong, healthy, balanced body (not to mention maximise your running performance), it's important to supplement your running training with some complementary exercises.

The 'Runner's strength workout' on page 61 addresses the key running muscles – both those that actually power your movements as well as those that help to stabilise the joints while you run. If you can find the time, I recommend performing the whole workout one to three times per week. But, if not, you can still benefit by selecting the most relevant exercises from the workout to suit your own particular 'weak links' – for example, if you have had niggles or injuries in a specific area, or have suffered from back pain. The area worked in each exercise is indicated, to help you choose the right moves. Runners can have weaknesses or niggles anywhere, but there are some key problem areas that come up time and again. Read on to see if any of the following issues ring bells with you. The most relevant exercises from the Runner's strength workout are indicated for each problem.

Four common problems and how to address them

Poor core stability and lower back pain

The premise of core stability is that if the stabilising muscles of the abdominals and back (often described as the core) are functioning properly, they will protect the spine, enhance posture, minimise the risk of injury, and improve sports technique and performance. Think of the core stability muscles as an 'internal corset' that keeps the pelvic girdle and spine in perfect alignment, and provides a stable base from which the limbs can move. Without good core stability, the lower back tends to arch and the pelvis 'tips' forward, compromising the ability of the muscles that attach to it (such as the hip flexors and hamstrings) to work properly and increasing the risk of lower back pain. A recent study, published in the *Journal of Strength and Conditioning Research*, found that six weeks of core stability training resulted in a significant improvement in 5 km run time, so it's well worth considering.

So what's the key to gaining core stability? It's a case of learning how to engage the correct muscles and then improving their endurance, rather than hitting the gym to lift weights. Often, core stability is down to inefficient recruitment (the stabilising muscles have 'forgotten' what to do) rather than a lack of strength per se. Try exercises 1, 2, 3 and 5 in the Runner's strength workout (page 61) to improve core stability. The stretch on page 57 and nerve stretch on page 58 can also help alleviate lower back pain.

Pelvic instability and glute weakness

The muscles that stabilise the hip when the foot lands during running are the gluteals, particularly the gluteus medius and minimus, and the deep hip stabilisers: the piriformis and obturators. If these are weak (and they often are, since they spend so much time in a lengthened, unused position while we are seated), a muscle called the tensor fascia latae steps in to compensate. Since this attaches to the iliotibial band, it can cause the latter to become over-tight or inflamed. Weak glutes also affect your hip extension in running, reducing stride length. An indicator of poor pelvic stability is when you aren't able to keep your pelvis stable and level when you lean back against a wall and lift each knee alternately up in front of you. Try exercises 4–8 and 10.

Calf/shin imbalance

The calves work very hard during running, particularly in decelerating the foot on landing. If you progress your mileage and speed too quickly (or if you have particularly tight calves), the Achilles tendon, which attaches to the calf muscles, can become sore and inflamed. Meanwhile, the 'agonist' (opposite) muscles along the front of the shins, the tibialis anterior, can suffer if the calf muscles become overly strong in comparison. Exercise 9 will help work the calf muscles in a functional way, while the stretch on page 58 (point and flex) will help to mobilise the sciatic nerve in the calf area. Regular shin and calf stretches, such as those on pages 54 and 56, are also essential.

Knee maltracking

If you've ever suffered from a sensation of 'heat' behind the kneecap or been told you have 'runner's knee', it may be that your knee joint mechanics aren't up to scratch. The kneecap sits in a groove on the front of the thighbone, on which it slides up and down. If for some reason it is slightly off-kilter, it can cause irritation and inflammation under the kneecap. Often the reason for this is that the kneecap is being pulled out of line by tight lateral structures at the outside of the knee joint, such as an overtight iliotibial band, or it may be that the innermost quad muscle, the vastus medialis obliquus (VMO), is too weak. You can sometimes spot knee maltracking simply by standing in front of a mirror with your feet facing forwards, slightly apart. If the kneecap is tilted, or points left or right rather than straight ahead, it is indicative of maltracking. The knee rolling

inwards when you stand on one leg and bend your knee is another telltale sign. Try exercises 7 and 8.

The Runner's Strength workout

This workout is designed to do three things: improve your core stability, get your other stabilising muscles functioning properly, and strengthen your key running muscles. This will enhance your movement patterns, co-ordination and proprioception, reducing the likelihood of you being put out of action by an injury. You may choose to do all the exercises, or just select those that seem most appropriate to you.

The exercises

1 **Toe touchdowns**

Aim: to strengthen the core stabilisers in the abs and back. Good for lower back pain sufferers.

Lie on your back with knees bent and feet flat on the floor. Place

one or both hands under your lower back (palms facing down) and contract your abdominals and pelvic floor until you feel your back press against the hands. Maintaining this pressure, slowly lift one foot off the floor until your thigh is at a 90 degree angle (1). Pause, then lift the other foot off the floor to join it (2). Continuing to maintain the same pressure on your hands, lower the first foot to the floor, then the second foot. Repeat. Don't be afraid to stop, 'regroup' and try again with this exercise!

2–3 x 8 repetitions

2 **Side bridge**

Aim: to strengthen the lateral stabilisers in the trunk.

Lie on your side, supporting yourself on the elbow and forearm, with your legs stacked and body aligned. Keeping the navel pulled into your spine, raise up on to the elbow. Visualise trying to keep the lower side of your waist lifted away from the floor. Hold for 5–10 seconds, then release.

Do 2–3 reps on each side

3 *Plank*

Aim: to strengthen the core stabilisers and lower back with the body fully extended and working against gravity.

Lie face down on the floor, propped up on your elbows, with feet and knees together. Engage the core, and lift the hips and knees off the floor, forming a straight line from heels to crown. Hold for 10 seconds, but don't forget to breathe.

Do 3–5 repetitions

4 *Hip hitch*

Aim: to improve gluteal strength and pelvic stability. Stand sideways on a step, with your support leg bent at about 25 degrees and the other leg hanging over the edge (1). Now 'hitch' the hip, so that the pelvis becomes level (2). Hold for 2 seconds, then sink back down and repeat. Swap sides.

Do 2–3 x 8 on each side

1 2

5 *The bridge*

Aim: to strengthen gluteals, lower back and hamstrings, and improve pelvic stability. Lie on the floor with knees bent and feet flat. Raise the body up enough to allow the

1 2

pelvis to clear the floor, Hold for 10 seconds, then release (1). Once you can do this comfortably, do the same as above, but once your pelvis is raised, alternately extend one leg and then the other, without allowing the pelvis to rock from side to side (2).

Do 3–5 reps (for the alternating legs, do 3 x 10 leg lifts)

6 Hip opener

Aim: to activate and strengthen the glute medius and deep hip rotators.

Lie on your side, with pelvis square, and hips and knees bent (1). Leaving the heels

together, slowly lift the top knee by turning out at the hip but only go as far as you can without letting the pelvis or back twist (2). Hold for 5 seconds, then lower and repeat.

Do 3–5 on each side

7 Single-leg squat

Aim: to strengthen the glutes and the muscles supporting the knee joint, particularly the innermost quad, the vastus medialis obliquus (VMO).

Stand with feet hip-distance apart and arms out to the sides. Lift your right leg up in front and, keeping the pelvis level, bend the left knee. Ensure your knee is aligned over your middle toe and don't allow it to roll in as the leg bends. Straighten completely between each rep. Swap sides.

Do 2–3 x 10 on each side

8 Step-up

Aim: to strengthen the running muscles (the quads, hamstrings, glutes and calves) through a similar range of motion.

Stand in front of a step or stair, with your right foot placed upon it, knee bent to approximately 90 degrees (1). Now take your weight on to the right foot and straighten the leg, driving up with your left knee at the same time (2). Take the left foot back to the floor with control and immediately repeat. Swap sides between sets.

Do 2–3 x 10 on each side

9 *Calf raise*

Aim: to improve lower leg muscle balance and strengthen the calf through the lowering phase, when it works hardest during running.

Stand on a stair or step with your heels extending over the edge (1). Rise up on to the toes (2) and then drop slowly back down. Work through the full range. When this gets easy, perform with one leg at a time.

Do 3 x 10 repetitions

1   2

10 *Ball curl*

Aim: to strengthen the hamstrings eccentrically (while they lengthen), as they are used in running. Also strengthens the lower back.

Lie on your back with your

1   2

feet raised up on a Swiss ball. Lift your body off the ground, to form a straight line from shoulders to feet (1), and then roll the ball in towards your bottom by bending your knees (2). Draw it in as far as you can, pause, then roll it back out until your legs are straight, then repeat.

Do 2–3 x 10 repetitions

Seven ways to reduce the risk of injury

1. Rest up. It's crucial to incorporate rest into your schedule. You need at least one day a week of no vigorous exercise.
2. Don't neglect your flexibility work, warm-up or cool-down. These aren't just for professional athletes but an essential part of any runner's training.
3. Don't allow niggles to go neglected. If anything hurts when you come back from your run, take the weight off it and ice it for 8 minutes, either with an ice pack or using ice massage (*see* page 113). This can help reduce inflammation. If it still hurts the next day, don't run on it, but rest and, if necessary, see a sports medicine expert.
4. Don't overdo things. The number one reason for injuries, according to the journal *Sports Injury Bulletin*, is doing too much, too quickly.
5. Free up your knees. Chartered physiotherapist Alan Watson recommends 'patella mobilisations' for all marathon runners. These help to prevent tight structures causing the kneecap to get misaligned and you can do them in front of the TV or at work. With your leg straight out in front of you but relaxed, move the kneecap medially, laterally and diagonally in a firm, repetitive pulsing motion. (A tea towel can help you get a good grip.) Then bend the leg a little and push the kneecap directly down. You'll need to do 20–30 in each direction.
6. Get a rubdown. While numerous studies conclude there is no proof of the benefits of sports massage, the fact that nearly all elite athletes consider it to be an important part of their regime cannot be ignored. Sports massage involves specific techniques and is a very deep tissue massage, which encourages fresh supplies of oxygenated blood to reach the muscle tissues and flush out metabolic waste products and toxins. More importantly, perhaps, it frees up the collagen fibres around each muscle sheath, and prevents 'sticking'. In a recent study published in the *British Journal of Sports Medicine*, researchers found that a massage given 2 hours after exercise reduced the intensity of soreness 48 hours later, although it did not improve function in the muscles that had been working. It also feels good, which is an important factor in staying motivated.
7. Be 'body aware' all the time, not just when you are running. There's no use in hunching over your computer all day, or slumping in front of the TV in the evening, only to then try to perfect your posture when you are running. Good posture – including core stability – is something you should strive for 24 hours a day.

⁝ Cross-training

HOW TO BECOME A BETTER RUNNER WITHOUT RUNNING

Cross-training simply means mixing other activities into your training week. It might be for pleasure, for further performance benefits or, if you are injured, simply out of necessity.

But will cross-training make you a better runner? Going back to those principles of training, remember 'specificity'? The idea that, to get better at distance running, you have to run long distances. Well, in a way, cross-training flies in the face of specificity, because it implies that taking part in other activities will improve performance in your main activity (marathon running).

So what does the evidence say? Researchers at California State University looked at five weeks of mixed cycling and running (alternate days) compared to a running-only programme of equal intensity. After five weeks, both groups had maintained aerobic performance, suggesting that cross-training could be of benefit. Another study, published in the journal *Medicine and Science in Sport and Exercise*, looked at the effects of cross-training versus running for six weeks on 5 km run time and found similar improvements in both subject groups. These results support the use of cycling as a form of cross-training to maintain running fitness – but, remember, it didn't improve performance over and above running alone, which begs the question, why not stick to running?

The role and value of cross-training have a lot to do with what you expect to get out of it. Is it a way of getting cardiovascular exercise without the impact of running? Is it a way of balancing your programme by using muscles that running doesn't use? Is it a mental break as much as a physical one? Is it a strategy to keep training while injured? These questions deter-

mine whether cross-training is appropriate and, if so, what type. A long-term research project from Johns Hopkins University looked at professional female swimmers over a seven-year period and found that as many injuries were sustained in cross-training activities as were caused by swimming. This demonstrates that engaging in activities you aren't used to needs to be done with caution.

However, there are times when cross-training is useful, and even essential. Your heart and lungs may get a fantastic aerobic workout if you go out cycling and aren't accustomed to it. Even though you aren't pounding the streets they can't tell the difference. But you do need to make running your main activity in order to allow your musculoskeletal system to adapt to the demands of running.

Cross-training for aerobic fitness

For those new to running, mixing in non-impact activities may help protect you from injury while still giving you sufficient cardiovascular exercise to get round the marathon course. According to the journal *Peak Performance* (backed up by the studies cited above) the most effective aerobic cross-training activity for runners is cycling. It uses similar muscles to running and can be sustained for long periods. The cross-trainer (elliptical trainer) is another good option for runners. Research from Dublin found that fitness gains after 12 weeks training on the elliptical trainer were the same as those made using a treadmill. However, other research has found that while calorie burn was similar in both activities, the exercisers in the study felt they were working harder on the elliptical

trainer – possibly because they weren't used to it. If you choose to take the impact off your joints by cross-training on the elliptical, try to let go of the handles as soon as you are accustomed to the machine. Use your arms in a 'running' motion to more closely mimic your sport.

Other aerobic cross-training options

* Swimming is impact-free, improves ankle flexibility and upper body strength, and allows hip flexors to lengthen.

* The Stairclimber is a good substitute for hill work, honing in on the quads and glutes.

* Walking: you will gain many of the fitness benefits from the lower end of the intensity spectrum (such as improved fat utilisation, better muscular endurance and connective tissue strength) through walking. The impact is significantly lower.

* Sport – games such as tennis and football are still high-impact but are multi-directional (so use different muscles). They also tend to be more stop–start than running.

Cross-training for strength

Do endurance athletes need to lift weights to improve performance? Increasingly, I believe that strength training is an excellent form of cross-training for runners, and there's evidence to back me up. A recent study in the journal *Medicine and Science in Sports and Exercise* found that eight weeks of strength training exercise resulted in improved running economy and increased time to exhaustion at maximal running speed among well-trained endurance runners. There was no change in body weight, or in VO_2 max. In another study, conducted at the University of Connecticut, there was an average 4.6 per cent improvement in running economy as a result of resistance training for six weeks or more.

So how can pumping iron help you run faster? Scientists believe it is a combination of factors: stronger, more fatigue-resistant muscles and better neural (nerve) input for more efficient and economical movement. But to ensure that you do the right type of resistance training for your running muscles, you need to know a little about muscle fibre types.

There are two principal types of muscle fibre in the body – we all have some of both, but the type that predominates varies from person to person, and the intensity and duration of an activity determines what fibre type is preferentially recruited. Endurance athletes tend to have a lot of 'slow-twitch', or type 1, fibres (muscle biopsies on marathon runners have revealed as many as 80 per cent slow-twitch fibres). These fibres are highly resistant to fatigue, but tend to be recruited mainly at low intensities. Fast-twitch fibres (type 2), on the other hand, are associated with muscle power, strength and speed – and are recruited at very high intensities. (That's why speed training is so beneficial: it gets all your muscle fibres working.)

However, there are two types of type 2 fibres: type 2a and type 2b. While 2b are the hardcore high-intensity sort, the type 2a fibres are more middle-of-the-road, and, depending on the type of training you do, can be made to act more like type 1 or type 2b fibres. Endurance training will make them type 1 'wannabes', while the wrong type of resistance training – hard efforts of lifting weights over a short period of time – is likely to make your type 2a fibres more like 2b fibres. The way to go is to opt for a high number of repetitions with a low weight (many body weight exercises – such as squats, lunges, push-ups and dips – are ideal). This way, you'll gain what is known as 'muscular endurance', as well as benefiting from stronger connective tissues (ligaments and tendons), increased calorie expenditure (due to higher muscle mass) and use of the muscles that don't get used in running. Researchers from the University of Maryland got volunteer novice exercisers to cycle to exhaustion and recorded their times. They then put them on a thrice-weekly strength training programme for 12 weeks. At the end of the period, leg strength had increased significantly (as might be expected) but cycle time had also increased, by 33 per cent.

Cross-training as a necessity

Sometimes cross-training isn't just for fun or variety – it's a necessity. If you are injured, and unable to withstand the high forces of running, or are returning from an injury and need to proceed with caution, cross-training is a useful tool for maintaining – or at least minimising the loss of – fitness. The best activity to do is the one that causes no pain in your injured area – it could be cycling or elliptical training, so you will need to test out different activities to see what feels right. One of the most effective, and least impactful, options is aqua-running. It's perfect, since the mechanics are barely different from running on land, and research has shown that it can be as aerobically challenging, partly because water has 12 times the resistance of air. You can perform water running with or without a buoyancy belt (it's harder without). This device is secured around your hips so you don't have to work so hard not to sink. If you're giving water running a try, bear the following tips in mind.

- The water must be deep enough for you to move your legs without touching the bottom of the pool.

- Remember to use your arms in a running motion rather than paddling.

- Try to hit the pool off-peak – not only to avoid curious onlookers, but so that you get the space you need to train.

- Aim for a leg turnover of roughly half your land leg turnover speed.

- Don't lean forwards – stay upright.

- Don't be afraid to take breaks on your first few attempts – this is tough training, so go for 3–5-minute bouts with a 30-second recovery in between – 15–20 minutes total is sufficient to start with.

- Mimic your running sessions, rather than paddling monotonously for the same time and at the same speed every visit.

∴Running in later years

ADVICE ON HAPPY, HEALTHY RUNNING FOR RUNNERS OVER 50

Flexibility begins to decline in our twenties; bone density and muscle mass deteriorate by as much as 60 per cent between the ages of 30 and 80 years. Metabolic rate and VO_2 max also begin to slide down the slippery slope before we've hit 40. Bearing all this in mind, it's a miracle that any of us 'more mature' runners can function at all, let alone run a marathon! But, of course, it is running that delays and attenuates many of these changes, not to mention safeguarding general health. As we have seen throughout this book, there are many reasons 'Why we are here', and enhancing health and increasing longevity are among the best.

Studies show that running reduces your risk of suffering coronary heart disease, high blood pressure, diabetes and obesity. Research from Stanford University found that runners experience less muscular and joint pain in old age than non-runners. Running preserves bone and muscle, keeps connective tissues healthy, and aids blood circulation and digestion. It even helps you maintain hearing sensitivity, according to research from Miami University.

What about the cardiovascular system? One piece of research found that six months of regular endurance exercise increased VO_2 max by 30 per cent in 60–70 year olds; another found that the calf muscles of athletes still competing over the age of 60 years had an equal number and size of mitochondria as those of a group of twenty-somethings in the same race. So age, per se, doesn't necessarily mean a slower performance.

If you are an existing runner, but new to the marathon distance, you certainly aren't alone. The number of older runners taking to the marathon has soared in the last decade. The London Marathon had 250 entrants over the age of 70 in 2008, while US statistics show that 50-plus runners make up the fastest-growing group of marathon entrants, with the quickest rate of increase in the 75–79 and 80-plus categories. An 80-year-old Canadian woman set a new marathon world record in 2008 for her age group: 4 hours, 36 minutes and 52 seconds. Proof, if you needed it, that 26.2 is perfectly possible once you are in the second half of your life.

But to make your running, and in particular your marathon training, safe and enjoyable there are a few things to bear in mind. This is particularly important if you are new to running, since you are asking a lot from your body and will need to be patient enough to allow time for adaptations to take place. If running is a new activity for you, ensure you read the advice on pages 3–4, and see your doctor for a check-up if necessary. Also heed the following points.

Smart running past 50

∴ Muscles and connective tissues become less pliable as we age, so you'll need to warm up for longer and more gently to avoid the risk of injury. Make your warm-up 10 minutes rather than 5, and incorporate some gentle stretching once you're warm, if your muscles feel stiff.

∴ Never neglect a proper cool-down and post-run stretching – since flexibility is already on the wane, you need to hold on to what you've got. A recent study found that the primary cause of older runners slowing down was a loss of flexibility and range of motion in the joints of the hip, knee and ankle, leading to a shorter stride length.

∴ Don't run daily – older runners need longer to recover, especially from tough sessions; so run on alternate days, take two days off instead of one after a hard run, and consider combining running with cross-training on an elliptical trainer, bike or in the swimming pool (good for maintaining range of motion).

∴ Think about incorporating the walk/run strategy into your regime (*see* page 134). Even Amby Burfoot, a former winner of the Boston Marathon and an editor of *Runner's World* magazine in the USA, now frequently walk/runs.

∴ Heed the signs of overtraining to ensure you aren't overstretching yourself (*see* page 78).

∴ Consider incorporating a twice-weekly resistance training programme into your regime to offset age-related muscle loss, or perform the 'Runner's strength workout' (*see* pages 61–64) on the days you don't run.

∴ Dress appropriately. No, I don't mean that Lycra hotpants are out of bounds for over-50s, just that older runners are more vulnerable to the effects of extreme heat or cold – so ensure you layer well in winter, and don't overdress on warmer days.

∴ Be particularly vigilant about hydration. Research shows that older people are less sensitive to the thirst mechanism. In one study, active healthy men aged 67 to 75 felt less thirsty and drank less voluntarily after being water-deprived than did younger men.

∴ As far as nutrition goes, the same basic rules apply to older runners as to everyone else. But it's very important to get sufficient calcium (*see* page 104). This is because calcium is a key nutrient in the maintenance of bone density, which declines as we age and may increase the risk of osteoporosis, the bone-thinning disease

that leads to frailty, loss of height and a high risk of fractures. Women are particularly vulnerable post-menopause, as plummeting oestrogen levels can cause as much as 2–5 per cent bone loss per year in the five years following the cessation of periods (*see* below).

In general, these guidelines boil down to one thing: take it easy. There are good reasons for this advice. In a study published in the *British Journal of Sports Medicine*, which tracked the running behaviour of 844 runners, being over 50 was a significant injury risk factor.

Fit to the bone

One in three women over 50 will suffer an osteoporotic fracture. But what is less well known is that one in 12 men will suffer the same fate. While running itself is protective against bone loss (because stressing bone is what makes it stronger), if you have been sedentary for many years previously, you should bear in mind that you may not have an optimal amount of 'bone in the bank' to start with (the bone-building 'window' closes at around 30 years of age). If this is the case, it is imperative that you heed the advice about not doing too much, too soon, that you consume sufficient calories and calcium, and that, if you have any of the osteoporosis risk factors outlined below, you ask your doctor about a DXA bone scan. If, on the other hand, you have been regularly active throughout your life, you have probably reaped the benefits of a healthy bone density. One study found that bone density in the femur was 5 per cent higher in runners than in non-runners, and 8 per cent higher than in completely sedentary folk. Improved body awareness, balance, co-ordination and strength – all of which stem from regular exercise – also reduce the risk of falls in later life.

Bone shakers – risk factors for osteoporosis

- Slight build
- Family history of osteoporosis
- Regular use of corticosteroid drugs
- Smoking
- Low calcium intake
- Low lifelong level of weight-bearing activity
- Excessive dieting or an eating disorder
- Early menopause or hysterectomy
- Excessive alcohol or caffeine intake (a less well-defined risk factor)

Heart to heart

If I had a pound for every occasion that someone has crowed 'Jim Fixx'[1] to me when I've mentioned I am a runner, I would be as rich as I am fit. Yes, Jim Fixx died of a heart attack while out running, but the fact remains that the biggest risk factors for both heart disease and stroke are high blood pressure, obesity, a lack of physical activity and smoking – along with a family history of these diseases. Since running helps to reduce blood pressure, as well as significantly improving the ratio of good HDL cholesterol to bad LDL cholesterol and controlling body fat, you are already making all the right moves in terms of protecting your heart, particularly if you have been active for some time. Heart health and running is one area in which you have to consider the statistics carefully. For example, a study published in the *New England Journal of Medicine*

[1]Jim Fixx was author of the best-seller, *The Complete Book of Running*. He is credited with helping start the fitness revolution in the USA, popularising running and demonstrating the health benefits of regular jogging.

Heart health: reducing the risks

❖ Always warm up and cool down – a sudden, rather than progressive, change in the level of cardiac stress is most likely to cause problems.

❖ Avoid exercising first thing in the morning when heart attack risk is higher.

❖ Be extra careful in extreme cold and heat.

❖ Do not exercise within 2 hours of a large meal, since American research shows that heart attack risk is elevated during this time.

❖ Drink tea – the flavonoids contained in green and black tea help strengthen the blood vessel walls.

❖ Stop immediately if you get chest pain, any pain that radiates into the left arm or jaw, or severe breathlessness when running.

❖ At rest, symptoms that include an irregular pulse, breathlessness, sudden tiredness and swollen ankles should also be taken seriously, since they can precipitate a cardiac event.

reported that the risk of heart attack during exercise is 56 times greater than during rest in inactive men, and five times greater in regularly active men, due to the additional demands for oxygen-enriched blood to be pumped from the heart. While 'five times greater' is a lot better news than '56 times greater', it's still enough to tempt you to swap your trainers for a pair of slippers. You have to bear in mind, though, that the overall risk of heart attack, at any time, is a whopping 40 per cent lower in habitually active men.

Running and the menopause

Most women experience the menopause between the ages of 45 and 55 – the average age is 52 years. While, in today's society, it seems to be treated more as a disease than as a life stage, the menopause is simply a signal that reproductive potential is finished.

Accompanying this is a significant drop in female hormone levels – progesterone and oestrogen – and it is this that causes the symptoms of menopause: hot flushes, vaginal dryness and, most importantly, bone loss. Another health benefit of oestrogen that we lose post-menopause is its protective effect on the heart. While men are far more at risk of coronary heart disease than women under the age of 50, the gap closes completely once a woman has undergone the menopause. This may sound worrying, but remember that, by running regularly, you are already less susceptible to heart disease than sedentary women, and that by continuing to be active and eating healthily you are maximising your chances of a long, healthy life.

Many women state that running has eased them through the menopause more gently. And there's research to back this up. In the *Journal of Advanced Nursing*, a study of menopausal women found that a year-long exercise programme helped to reduce the severity of common symptoms (such as hot flushes and mood swings). The active women also scored higher on cognitive functioning and had a more positive state of mind than non-exercisers.

Runners may also side-step one of the other, much detested side-effects of the menopause: weight gain. A University of Pittsburgh study found that, of 535 women who were randomly assigned to either a diet and exercise programme or just a weigh-in, twice as many of those who did not exercise had gained an average of 5.2 lb four years later. Those who exercised had not gained weight.

why we are here

A recent study, published in the *Archives of Internal Medicine*, tracked runners for a 20-year period and found that they stayed fit and active for longer than non-runners, and were half as likely to die prematurely.

5

sticking with it

⁝•Keeping track
HOW TO STAY MOTIVATED AND MONITOR YOUR PROGRESS

Rule number one: accept right now that there will be ups and downs in your training. Then it won't be such a shock when you experience a 'plateau', from which it seems hard to improve, or when you feel so negative about running that you can barely summon up the enthusiasm to get out the door. These fluxes in motivation, and in actual progress, are only natural, so don't be too despondent, and read on to find out how to ensure that momentary lapses or backslides don't become anything more serious.

Motivation: get it, keep it, use it!
One of the main reasons that people drop out of exercise programmes is because they don't get the results they'd hoped for. Sometimes, that's because the results they expected were unrealistic; other times it's because they were not training in the right manner to yield those much wanted results. By reading and following the advice in this book, you shouldn't fall into either of these categories. But that's not to say that there won't be days when you

wonder why you started this whole marathon business in the first place! If that happens, here are some strategies to help you get through . . .

Keep perspective
It's unlikely that anyone will get through marathon training without a busy period at work, a stinking cold, a niggling ache, a rip-roaring hangover or simply a lapse in motivation. So don't panic, or think that a couple of days off is going to ruin everything. Equally, if you do get a bit behind on your training, don't be tempted to overcompensate by doubling up when you get back on track.

Congratulate yourself
You are already among a minority in being committed enough to start training for a marathon – acknowledge that fact and be proud of it.

Don't dwell
If you are having an 'off' period at least try to enjoy it rather than skulking around feeling guilty. If you don't want to run on Sunday morning, then do something

really enjoyable instead – don't lie in bed telling your-self what a loser you are.

Enter a race

There's nothing like a deadline to focus the mind – if your marathon deadline is still too far off to feel real, try entering another, shorter-distance race that is sooner. But, remember, your finish time is not the be-all and end-all. Don't push yourself too hard, or you'll take too long to fully recover, which will have a negative effect on your true goal: attaining marathon fitness.

Add variety

Boredom is motivation's worst enemy. Avoid it by varying your training as much as you can. Don't run the same old routes every time. Go to a running camp, or visit an athletics track instead of training on the roads. If you normally run alone, go with a group – if you normally run first thing, go at dusk.

Treat yourself

The odd reward or incentive can help you feel posi-tive about training. Treat yourself to a chiropody appointment, a massage (not a sports one, but a really indulgent one with aromatherapy oils and dolphin music!) or some new kit.

Be organised

You are much more likely to stick to your plan of running if your kit is nicely laid out on the chair, your water bottle not full of stale sports drink, and your watch or heart rate monitor handily placed. Keep all your running gear in one place so you can find it easily – including socks and underwear.

Inspire yourself

Have a motivational picture on the wall/by your desk. I have a picture of Roger Bannister breaking the tape on the world's first ever 4-minute mile. You may also find that music and mantras inspire you. See pages 78 and 84 for more details.

Shift focus

Rather than simply logging the miles, try focusing on other aspects of your progress, such as the new firmness in your thighs, your ability to recover more quickly from a tough session, your lower resting heart rate, better sleep patterns or clearer skin. All gratifying reasons to keep on running.

Ask yourself why you are here

Why did you decide to run the marathon? Hopefully, what motivated you to enter is still important to you (whether it's to support a charity, to prove to your-self that you can or to regain the fitness you once had). Think about what got you started and remind yourself why it's important to see this thing through.

Create a support system

Whether it is your partner, another runner, a friend, someone from the charity you are running for or even your physio, make sure you have someone – at least one person – you can talk to about your progress, your doubts and your achievements. No man or woman is an island! The need to share our experiences is well demonstrated by the prolifera-tion of online running communities, which allow us to feel part of something even if, in reality, we are a running club of one!

Monitor your progress

Nothing is more inspiring than progress. You start off huffing and puffing around a four-mile course – now you can do six without a second thought. One of the best ways of monitoring your progress is to keep a training diary or log in which you note down the details of all your training sessions.

Your training diary can record as much or as little information as you want it to. It could simply say how long or how far you ran and at what pace, or you could include how you felt on the run, what route you took, what the weather was like, what stretches you did afterwards and what kind of mood you were in. Research shows that people who keep a training diary are more consistent about exercise than those who don't. Designated logbooks are available from specialist sports shops, or you can use a web-based log (particularly good if it enables you to download information such as heart rate or GPS data), opt for a standard diary or use a simple notebook. It may take a little perseverance at first to remember to fill it in and to find a few minutes in which to do so, but eventually it will become as much a part of your routine as running itself.

Another way of monitoring progress is to test yourself on a specific route, or repeat the 1½-mile test that you performed at the start of the programme (*see* page 5), to see whether you now fare better. There is a series of regular free 5 km races across the UK called Parkruns, which give you the ideal opportunity to compare your performance from month to month on a measured course (*see* 'Further information' (page 211) for details).

Play mind games

Your mind is as much involved in running as your heart, lungs and legs. The tips and strategies below are simple ways of persuading yourself to run when you aren't feeling fired up.

∴ Get up and put on your running kit. I have found this works a treat – I'll wake up and decide not to go for a run after all, but put on my kit, have a cup of tea and, before I know it, I'm thinking, 'hmm, perhaps I will just have a run . . .'.

> Pledge to go out just for 10 minutes. If you genuinely feel tired or under the weather, you'll want to come back when the 10 minutes are up, but the chances are, once you've done 10 minutes you'll carry on.

> Don't feel like a run at all? OK, go for a walk then, but wear your running kit, just in case, and you may just find yourself breaking into a jog.

> Forget your watch. The programme says 30 minutes at level 3. Your brain says feet up in front of the TV. So, leave your watch at home, go for a run and come home when you've had enough.

> Listen to music. Research at Brunel University has shown that, as well as providing a distraction, music can lower our rate of perceived exertion (RPE) and positively influence mood. But not any old music will do. Upbeat tunes with a tempo that fits in with the rhythm of your running work best – and, ideally, it should be music that you enjoy listening to. Even if you aren't a fan of listening to music while you are running, you can benefit from using it during your warm-up and cool down. A review study from the University of New Mexico showed that up-tempo music significantly increases breathing rate and moderately elevates heart rate, serving as a great precursor to exercise.

Train, don't strain

All these tricks and tactics to get yourself into your trainers and out the door are all very well, but if you are feeling depressed, fatigued, irritable, and if your performance seems to be taking a nosedive, you may be teetering on the brink of burnout, or 'overtraining' as the experts call it. OK, so you may not be putting in 180 km a week, like an elite distance runner, but nor does that elite runner have to fit their training in around commuting 2 hours a day, putting on a big

presentation at work, traipsing around the supermarket, caring for a sick child or wallpapering the front room. In other words, recreational runners have other stresses than running to cope with in their lives that must be taken into account. Not only that, while the elite runner may be running faster, further and more often than you, they almost certainly have a higher level of natural talent. In relative terms, you have been pushing hard, physically and mentally, and you may need to take a step back in order to recuperate. In fact, you absolutely should if you are feeling frazzled, otherwise you risk dropping out of training altogether due to burnout, illness or injury.

Signs of overtraining

:> Poor performance

:> Depression or irritability

:> Consistently raised resting pulse rate (a RHR 10 beats or more higher than usual can indicate problems)

:> Lack of motivation

:> Recurring colds, sore throats, mouth ulcers or other signs of a weakened immune system

:> Problems sleeping

:> Fluctuations in appetite

:> General fatigue

:> Irregular or absent periods (see your doctor if this persists for three months or more – this could be a symptom of amenorrhoea, which puts you at risk of weakened bones and should not be ignored)

What to do if you suspect overtraining

Rest. Take a whole week off – with absolutely no running – and ensure you get lots of sleep and rest. Eat healthily and don't overdo things. If you feel anxious about missing valuable training time, use the week to practise your mental tactics, start to plan your race strategy and the logistics of getting to the event – this will ensure you feel eager to get back on track and don't lose focus. When you venture out again, try running with no stopwatch to see how you feel. If you feel back to your old self then resume training below the level at which you stepped out. Don't try to 'catch up' by doing tougher or longer sessions.

∴ Two's company
RUNNING AND TRAINING WITH LIKEMINDED FOLK

One of the best things about running is that it is a totally independent pursuit. You don't need anyone to make it happen except yourself. Having said that, there are times when it is safer, more effective or more enjoyable to run with others – either a training partner, or with a group or club. But it isn't just motivation and companionship that you'll gain from joining a running group or club. You'll also get valuable advice and guidance, a whole load of new running routes, and a ready source of information on such things as good local races, physios and sports shops in your area.

Finding a partner

The ideal training partner is someone of pretty much the same level as you – or, so as you don't rest on your laurels, a little better. There is absolutely no point in running with your 2-hour-30-minute marathoning buddy if you are a novice, no matter what he or she says to the contrary. And don't partner up with someone who sees every training run as a competition between the two of you – it will be pretty well impossible to stick to a steady pace, or focus on quality, when you are secretly racing. And if it's your 'other half', it could quite likely lead to divorce proceedings!

Find the right person, though, and a training partner is a real asset. For a start, the sum total of motivation is twice as big, meaning that the chances of you ducking out of a training session are twice as small. It's also much easier to get through tough stuff, like intervals and hills, when you've got someone to commiserate with – or to shout encouraging words. And, on the long runs, the time passes much more quickly when you have got somebody to talk to. On a

practical level, it's also helpful to have another pair of eyes for when you are counting reps, timing an effort or following a new route. Safety is another factor to consider, particularly for female runners.

All in all, a trusty training partner – even if it's someone you run with just once or twice a week – is something every budding marathoner should aim to find. And what better place to look than your local running club?

Join the club

Before you join any running club, go along to a training session to get a feel for it – most clubs will readily allow you to do this, with no strings attached. Assess how friendly it is (is it cliquey?), whether it is a highly competitive club that expects members to race regularly, and whether there is any kind of expertise available in the way of coaching and training programmes. Some clubs are very male-dominated, or geared mainly towards a particular age group or type of running (such as sprinting). Find out as much as you can by talking to existing members. Most clubs will have specific training sessions – say, a track night and a long run – but some aren't so structured, so try to find one that suits your needs.

Find your nearest club at www.ukathletics.net or check out less formal running groups, such as Jog Scotland or Run in England (*see* 'Further information', page 211).

Sisters are doing it for themselves

Some women, especially when starting out, prefer to train in the company of other women. That's why the Women's Running Network was set up in 1999, and it now has more than 160 groups across the UK to help women of all ages and abilities get into running and continue making progress. Some groups operate dedicated marathon training programmes (*see* 'Further information', page 212, for more details).

Online clubs and forums

If you don't want – or can't find – a training partner, but you'd still like to monitor your progress, swap notes and get advice from other runners, consider getting involved with an online running community, such as Fetch Everyone or the Running Bug, or join in with the chat on a runners' forum, such as the one on the *Runner's World* website (*see* 'Further information', page 211, for more on all of these). That way you can get the lowdown on forthcoming races, get some support and feedback, but you don't have to make conversation unless you feel like it.

Running away

Until you become a runner yourself, you are unaware of the vast network of fellow runners that exists around the world. I was amazed when I first learned of marathon training camps a few years ago, but now I know that everything from weekend 'technique' clinics to point-to-point runs in exotic locations, yoga and running weekends, and warm-weather training camps are all there for the taking. It's a great way of meeting other runners, as well as getting some useful training advice and practice, and it's the kind of holiday that you can easily go on alone (*see* 'Further information', page 213, for more details).

Canine companions

For many years, my favourite training partner has been my dog, Sidney. Now that he's an old man, in dog years, he accompanies me only on recovery runs, but he still enjoys bounding along beside me, albeit a little slower than he once did. If you have a dog that is keen to run, you may find he makes the perfect running companion, providing a little extra security, fun and company. It's a valuable time-saver, too – as you won't need to find the time to take Fido for a walk as well as squeeze in a run. Special dog leads, which attach around the waist with a bungee cord, are available for running with your dog so that you can keep your arms free.

Doggie dos and don'ts

❖ Don't run with a dog younger than six months – his bones and muscles aren't fully developed yet.

❖ Don't run with a dog that is old or overweight.

❖ Remember that dogs need hydrating, too. If you aren't going to pass anywhere appropriate it's important to carry water for your canine pal. Also ensure there is a fresh bowl of water for your dog on your return.

❖ Don't take a dog running in very hot weather, since they can't regulate body temperature as well as we can. Warning signs of over-exertion include excessive panting, slowing down and a dry tongue.

❖ Don't force the dog. Start your dog off with shorter runs and stick to softer surfaces. Not all breeds are suited to running; other dogs just don't enjoy it. Breeds such as border collies, Springer spaniels, larger terriers and hunting dogs are ideally built; basset hounds are not!

❖ Speak to your vet if you are in any doubt about your dog's suitability for running.

⸭ The psychology of running
MAKING USE OF YOUR GREY MATTER TO BE A BETTER RUNNER

When elite athletes line up on the start line of a race, there's very little to choose between them in terms of their physical fitness and readiness to perform. Who wins and loses is largely down to the athletes' psychological skills and mental toughness. That's why they spend hours mentally 'rehearsing' their sport, mastering mental tricks and strategies to reduce anxiety or psych themselves up to perform, and learning how to remain focused, motivated and positive. But can common-or-garden budding marathoners benefit from this, too? You bet they can.

This section will guide you through some of the most useful psychological strategies, both for preparing for your marathon and performing on the day. But a word of warning: these techniques take practice – it's no use attempting them for the first time on race day morning. The more you practise, the more benefit you'll gain – even in the case of the techniques that are geared towards race day itself.

Tuning in versus switching off

When you run, do you think about what you're going to have for dinner, look at the window displays in the high street shops, chat to fellow runners and generally focus on anything other than your running? If so, you are what sport psychologist William Morgan called a 'disassociator', who focuses externally. If, in contrast, you naturally tune in to the rhythm of your footfall, the feel of your muscles contracting and the sound of your breathing, you are an 'associator' – someone who 'internalises' their focus and remains in tune with their body's feedback signals.

Research suggests that accomplished marathon runners are more likely to be associators, while less proficient runners are more often disassociators. But attention strategies can differ according to whether you're racing or training. In one study, 43 per cent of elite runners used just disassociative strategies when training, 21 per cent used just associative and 36 per cent used both. It's as if during the long hard days of training the athletes feel the need to tune out of the physical experience somewhat, while when it really counts, on race day, they need to remain focused internally.

So, if you feel the need to disassociate during the long months of training – distract yourself by listening to music, watching TV, chatting or exercising in a pleasant location. But don't zone out too much, or your technique might suffer, and you may miss the early warning signs of an overuse injury. As far as racing goes, try making like a pro, and practise association.

Seeing is believing

Without doubt one of the most regularly used cognitive (mental) strategies is visualisation, or mental imagery. It is now widely established that the use of mental imagery can actually enhance physical performance. It's all to do with 'seeing is believing'. In effect, the brain cannot tell the difference between something that has actually happened and a vivid mental picture of it happening. In marathon terms, if you can't picture yourself crossing that finish line, you're far less likely to put everything into achieving it, and are therefore less likely to succeed. Conversely, picture yourself doing it proficiently and it's almost as if it is a fait accompli.

Now imagine that you've just passed the 26-mile marker – you've got 385 yards to go. What will it look like, as you hit that home straight? Picture the crowds – maybe you'll have your family or friends there to watch you finish. Imagine the sounds of people cheering, announcements being made over the loudspeaker . . . Use all your senses to create a vivid image – visual, auditory, kinaesthetic (feel), taste and smell. Also try to imagine your state of mind, or mood. Think about how you would like to feel, both in terms of your body and your mind – you'll be tired, yes, but elated and delighted with your success. Put it all together into a vivid image and see yourself crossing that finish line. What does the time say on the clock? Be precise. Visualise the

figures on the clock: the hours, minutes and seconds.

Once you've achieved this, repeat it regularly. Scientists at the University of Lyon demonstrated that the more proficient the imagery skill, the greater the benefit to performance. Practise visualisation somewhere quiet, comfortable and when you are in a relaxed state. You may prefer to close your eyes. When you have finished, take a few breaths, then open your eyes and take a moment to readjust. Limit your visualisations to 1–3 minutes and repeat often for maximum effect.

Mind games on the run

Sometimes we could all use a little extra help when we're out running, to get through the tough moments. The following simple psychological techniques can be practised on the move.

Change your orientation

Instead of worrying about the outcome of the race or training run, focus on the process and the individual steps that need to be taken to get to the end. For example, think about getting to the next street corner (or mile marker in a race) or up the next hill. That way you retain focus on the 'here and now' and stop worrying about the final result.

Use a mantra

Some people find it helpful to have a mantra related to their sports performance. A mantra is simply a key word or phrase on which to focus, to prevent negative thoughts slipping in and to drip-feed your subconscious mind with positive affirmations about your abilities. It might be, 'I am a strong and capable runner' or 'I will cross the finish line with a smile on my face.' Mantras aren't just for posting up on the fridge and saying in the bath – they can be used while you're actually out training and racing, too: 'I am running fast and strong' is one I use when I'm running – it has a nice rhythm to it.

Switch strategies

If you're associating, and the focus on your body is getting too uncomfortable, try disassociating. If you're feeling unmotivated and 'not present' in your running, you are probably too disassociated, so try associating by focusing on your breathing, your arms pumping, the ground moving steadily under your feet. It sometimes helps to count your footfalls to get into an 'associated' frame of mind.

6

fuelling up

∴ Getting the basics right

THE PRINCIPLES OF GOOD NUTRITION AND HOW TO PUT THEM INTO PRACTICE

Imagine a top motor racing driver on the front row of the grid before the start of a race: he may be the best driver in the world, in the best car, but if his car contains poor-quality fuel, or if his tank is not topped up, his performance will invariably suffer. The same is true of the human body: no matter how well trained you are, and how well you have prepared, if your body contains poor-quality fuel, or not enough of it, your running won't be up to scratch.

The fuel that your body needs for normal function, daily activity and exercise comes from the food and drink that you consume. While the amount of energy you need is an important factor, the quality of your energy intake is crucial to optimal performance.

Most runners know that carbohydrate is their key fuel. However, that doesn't mean that fat and protein aren't also essential nutrients. Nor does it mean that all carbohydrate sources are as good as each other. Let's take a closer look at the main nutrients in turn, so as to determine their role in good health and great running.

Fat – is it really the bad guy?

Most of us have plenty of fat stored on our bodies – enough, in fact, to run more than 20 consecutive marathons! But is it dietary fat that we are overeating or simply calories overall? Recent statistics suggest that many people now meet the government's target of consuming no more than 35 per cent of total calories from fat, and yet more than half the population remains overweight or obese. This suggests one of two things: either that the 35 per cent recommendation is too high or that, while we are succeeding as a nation in cutting fat intake, we are still eating too many calories overall. (It's worth noting that, in the United States, recommended fat intake is significantly lower, at 30 per cent of total calorie consumption.)

I think the answer is a combination of both factors. One problem with dietary fat is that it requires less energy to be metabolised than either carbohydrate or protein, so is more likely to end up as a spare tyre than get burned off. Second, fat is a very energy-dense nutrient, containing 9 kilocalories per gram, compared to carbohydrate and protein which both contain approximately 4 kilocalories per gram.

While training can help you utilise fat as a fuel more efficiently, that isn't a reason for scoffing down lots of it. For starters, being overweight increases the risk of heart disease and diabetes. Obesity has also been associated with some types of cancer, including colo-rectal and breast cancer. Besides, when you are running 26.2 miles, you certainly won't want to be carrying more weight than you have to!

That said, fat is an essential nutrient and it does have an important role to play in a balanced diet. Certain vitamins – A, D, E and K – are fat-soluble, so can be derived only from fat sources. In addition, fat provides insulation and protection for our bodies and, for women, it enables pregnancy and lactation to take place.

How much, what type?

The UK government recommends a fat intake of no more than 35 per cent of our overall calorie intake, but you may want to consider going lower in the name of marathon training. I would recommend striving for perhaps 25–30 per cent of your overall intake. So, for example, if you consume 3000 calories per day in training, that means 750–900 calories can come from fat sources. And, since we know that 1 g of fat = 9 calories, that means 83–100 g of fat per day. Time to start reading those food labels!

Fat comes in several main forms in our diet (*see* below). All are constructed from three fatty acids attached to a unit of glycerol and, collectively, this unit is called a triglyceride. While all of them, gram for gram, have the same number of calories, they differ greatly in their roles in human health.

Saturated fatty acids

As far as your health is concerned, saturated fats are bad news, encouraging the body to produce more of the low-density lipoproteins (LDL cholesterol) and also being associated with a greater risk of some cancers. Experts recommend that no more than 11 per cent of total calorie intake should be consumed as saturated fats. Sources include meat, butter, dairy products, pastry and palm oil (often in peanut butter and processed snacks such as flapjacks).

Polyunsaturated fats

In general, polyunsaturated fats take a middle road in terms of health, since they lower LDL cholesterol and the risk of heart disease, but they also lower the 'good-guy cholesterol', high density lipoproteins (HDL). However, there are two essential fatty acids that come under the polyunsaturated umbrella: they are called 'essential' because they cannot be made by the body yet are vital to health.

Omega 6 fatty acids, or linoleic acids, come from vegetable oil, polyunsaturated margarine and products made from it. Omega 6s reduce LDL but, if consumed excessively, also may reduce HDL levels, as well as increasing the damage done by 'free radicals' linked to cancer.

Omega 3 fatty acids, or linoleic acids, have no such negative effects and are in fact positively beneficial to health, reducing the risk of blood clotting, stroke and heart disease, and controlling inflammation. They therefore can be helpful in dealing with diseases such as arthritis. The major source is oily fish but you can also get significant amounts from some nuts, including walnuts, linseed and its oils, and dark-green leafy vegetables such as kale and spinach. As a nation, we consume a lot more omega 6 than omega 3, and it is recommended that the balance is shifted the other way for better health.

Monounsaturated fats

These are distinguishable because they are liquid at room temperature, but solid when chilled (that's why French dressing, if made with olive oil, goes solid in the fridge). Studies show that replacing saturated fats with monounsaturates in the diet reduces the risk of heart disease. The beauty is that they lower LDL levels while maintaining HDL levels. They also appear to limit free radical damage. The best sources are olive oil, rapeseed oil, nut oils, avocados, nuts and seeds.

Trans fats

Trans fatty acids (TFAs) do not occur in significant amounts in nature (they are present in meat and dairy products in small quantities), but are created by adding extra hydrogen to polyunsaturated fatty acids. The chemical process this involves makes them at least as bad for health as saturated fats, increasing LDL and lowering HDL cholesterol – the perfect recipe to encourage heart disease. These fats are found mainly in processed foods, including meat products such as pies and pasties, fried fast food, biscuits and cakes – and it's only likely that your intake is hazardously high if you eat a lot of these highly refined foods. Many manufacturers are eliminating trans fats from their products, particularly margarines and spreads, as a result of TFAs' bad press, so check labels and keep intake to a minimum. The government recommends that no more than 2 per cent of total energy intake should come from trans fats.

Up your omega 3s!

A study on fat intake found that omega 3 fatty acids could enhance aerobic metabolism, improving the delivery of oxygen and nutrients to cells by reducing the viscosity of the blood and improving the condition of the red blood cells that carry haemoglobin to the cells. It may also help you recover from the rigours of training, by reducing the inflammation in muscles, tendons and ligaments associated with hard exercise. Why not make a salmon fillet part of your post-long run meal?

Get your fats right

So what does it all mean to you? Well, in general, it means cutting down on fat generally, and specifically cutting down on saturated and trans fats, so that a greater proportion of your dietary fat comes from monounsaturated and polyunsaturated sources (particularly the omega 3s). Outlawing certain foods – whatever their fat content – isn't the way to go. If you love a biscuit with your cup of tea, or if fish and chips is your favourite indulgence, then simply eat them less frequently and make healthier choices elsewhere in your diet.

Cutting out dairy products in order to trim calories isn't a wise move either, since these are the richest source of calcium, which has an essential role in muscle contraction and in metabolism. It's also vital in maintaining bone health, since calcium is a component of bone.

Protein

You don't have to be a bodybuilder or a sports scientist to know that protein is associated with muscles and strength. Dissect a muscle, and you'll find it consists almost entirely of protein. As far as your training is concerned, protein does not have a major role in energy production but it is part of the structure of every cell in the body. Sufficient dietary protein is essential for normal body maintenance, transporting oxygen around the body, regulating fluid balance, repairing tissues, and playing a role in metabolism and muscular contraction; in addition, it is a component of many of the body's enzymes, hormones and neurotransmitters. Proteins are constructed from substances called amino acids, of which there are 20, all with distinctive functions within the body. Of these 20, eight are termed 'essential' amino acids, because they must be supplied by the diet and cannot be made from other amino acids.

How much, what type?

With protein playing such a significant role in muscle tissue maintenance and repair, it follows that someone in heavy training needs more than the average Joe. For a start, the increased breakdown of protein during training needs to be compensated for, and, in addition, if glycogen stores are low (say, towards the end of your long run) certain amino acids – called branch chain amino acids – can be used for energy. While using protein as a fuel source isn't an ideal scenario, it is an essential fallback when glycogen stores are depleted. Research shows that the increased need for protein among active people is particularly significant at the outset of training, since the body has yet to become accustomed to conserving and recycling protein.

So how much is enough? The American College of Sports Medicine recommends 1.2–1.4 g per kilogram of body weight per day for active people, compared to 0.8 g for sedentary folk. This should equate to around 15 per cent of your total energy intake.

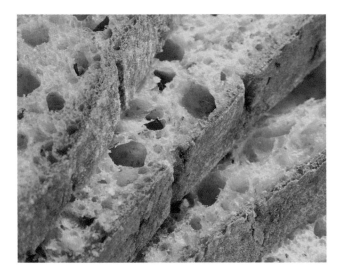

Carbohydrate

Whether you are a budding marathoner or your idea of sport is a game of darts, the majority of your energy should come from carbohydrates. So why are carbs so important? The main reason is that they provide the body's supply of glycogen, which is stored in the liver and muscles and is the fuel that powers your running. Since only a limited amount can be stored – and since carbohydrate is the only fuel your brain can use – supplies need to be constantly replenished. Too little dietary carbohydrate and you will not be firing on all cylinders. Carbs also pack a micronutrient-fuelled punch, being rich in B vitamins, iron, magnesium and chromium.

How much, what type?

A typical sedentary person consumes 40 to 50 per cent of total calories in the form of carbohydrate, but active people undoubtedly need more. Nutritionists recommend working out your carbohydrate needs in relation to body weight, rather than using a percentage of total energy intake. Recommendations vary: the American College of Sports Medicine suggests 6–10 g of carbohydrate per kg of body weight, but the upper end of this range would be too high for most non-elite athletes, who simply aren't taking in enough calories to enable them to achieve this and maintain a balanced diet; the Department of Sports Nutrition at the Australian Institute of Sport's guidelines state that 5–7 g per kg body weight is probably a better aim for recreational runners.

But what type? There was a time when carbohydrates were defined in terms of 'starches' and 'sugars'. The premise was that starches were good and sugars bad. Starches included such foods as bread, pasta and potatoes, and starchy vegetables, while sugars included sugary snacks and drinks, sweets, table sugar, fruits and fruit juices. But more recent research has revealed that the 'good and bad' argument isn't that simple. The real issue is the rate of absorption of a carbohydrate-rich food, and its consequent effect on the speed at which blood sugar levels rise, measured by the 'glycaemic index' (GI). The faster blood sugar rises, the more insulin needs to be released to carry it

out of the blood; and, since insulin acts as the 'gatekeeper' to the fat cells, the greater the chance of it being stored as fat. If you opt for foods that give a less steep blood sugar curve this will enable energy levels to be maintained and also allow the body to burn fat as a fuel more efficiently.

But bear in mind that GI is a measurement of how fast and how high blood sugar and insulin rise after you eat enough of a food to total 50 g of carbohydrate. For example, white bread and carrots have high GI scores, of 70 and 71 respectively, suggesting that both send blood sugar soaring. But, since a slice of white bread contains 18.9 g of carbohydrate and a standard portion of carrots (80 g, or a handful) contains 3.1 g of carbohydrate, you would have to eat 16 handfuls of carrots to get 50 g of carbohydrate, whereas you would only need to eat 2½ slices of bread to get the same amount.

The other point that is often overlooked is that we rarely eat foods on their own, and there are many factors that mitigate the effect on blood sugar levels, such as the presence of fibre, acid and protein.

So how can you determine a food's GI? Well, in general, less refined foods and wholefood varieties have a lower GI than their more processed cousins. For example, brown rice is better than white, wholemeal bread is preferable to a sliced white loaf, but the only really accurate way of knowing is to look the food up on a GI reference table. You will find that many runners' staples – bagels, baked potatoes, pasta, rice and breakfast cereal – have a moderate to high glycaemic index, but research suggests that highly active, fit people have a less pronounced response to high GI foods and don't have to worry so much about their effects on blood sugar. That said, opting for mainly wholegrains, wholemeal bread, pasta and rice, pulses and beans, and eating a wide range of fruits and vegetables, will ensure a sustained energy supply as well as a nutrient-rich diet.

What to eat before and after a run

If you haven't eaten since lunchtime and are running straight after work or early evening, you'll need something to tide you over and provide the fuel necessary for your workout. Why? To prevent low blood sugar (hypoglycaemia), which could leave you feeling tired, dizzy and lightheaded, and certainly won't contribute to good performance. This is where high GI foods can come into their own, providing you with readily accessible fuel. A slice of malt loaf, a sports drink, or half a bagel with banana and honey an hour before your run should do the trick. If, however, you are watching your weight, then opt for a lower GI snack a couple of hours before you run. Fruit and yoghurt, a smoothie or a few Ryvitas with peanut butter all provide a good mix of carbohydrate and protein, taking the edge off hunger and making you feel alert and psyched up for a run. Research

in the *Exercise Immunology Review* also found that taking carbohydrate on board before exercise helps to mitigate the decreased immune function associated with heavy training.

Once your run is over, a carbohydrate-based snack will help replenish your glycogen stores. Research suggests that there is a window of opportunity in the first half hour post-run, when glycogen stores are particularly receptive, so if you wait too long you miss this opportunity. However, think carefully about whether you need to top up your glycogen levels. Have you done a long run (more than 90 minutes)? Was it a particularly demanding session? Will you be running the next day? Given time, the body will replenish depleted energy stores of its own accord – it's only if you've performed a particularly tough session (including a long run) or intend to run again within the next 24 hours, that you need a post-run snack; otherwise, it's simply excess calories. If the answer is yes, then aim to eat 1 g of carbohydrate for every kg of your body weight to optimise refuelling, and take some protein on board with your carbs to optimise absorption. For example, a cheese or tuna sandwich, or pitta bread with hummus or a flavoured milk drink. Also try to eat some fruit to provide antioxidants, which help offset the damage caused by training. After long runs, or runs on hot days, a salty food, such as pretzels or rice cakes, helps to restore electrolyte balance as well as stimulating thirst. Regardless of how hard or long your run is, always ensure that you rehydrate afterwards. (*See* page 96 for more information on hydration.)

∴ A question of calories

WORKING OUT HOW MUCH ENERGY YOU NEED TO MAINTAIN, LOSE OR GAIN WEIGHT

Now that we've looked at the basics of good nutrition, you might be wondering whether you are eating enough – or too much – to optimise your performance. There's a very simple equation when it comes to maintaining your body weight: calories in = calories out = steady weight.

If 'calories out' exceed 'calories in', you'll lose weight; and if 'calories in' exceed 'calories out', you'll gain weight. Simple, huh? But how do you know how many calories you need and, indeed, how many you are expending through your training and other activities? Thankfully, it's not too difficult to find out. Read on to find out more . . .

How much do you need?

How much energy you need is determined by three things: your resting metabolic rate (RMR), which is the minimum number of calories needed to survive, even if you stayed in bed all day long; the 'thermic effect of food', which is the energy needed to digest what you eat; and, finally, energy for daily activity, whether that be washing the dishes or walking to the bus stop. To get a rough idea of how many calories you use, grab a calculator and do the following sums.

1 My weight in kilograms (1 kilogram = 2.2 lb)	
2 *Females* I am 18–30 years old: weight x 14.7. Answer + 496 = RMR *or* I am 31–60 years old: weight x 8.7. Answer + 829 = RMR *Males* I am 18–30 years old: weight x 15.3. Answer + 679 = RMR *or* I am 31–60 years old: weight x 11.6. Answer + 879 = RMR	*My estimated RMR*
3 *Take this figure and multiply it by the number below most closely representing your typical daily activity level (exclusive of running)* I am sedentary (sit or stand most of the day) *1.4* I am moderately active (some walking each day and regular active leisure time activities) *1.7* I am very active (physically active each day) *2.0*	*My result*

Now let's think about the calories you expend running. A very broad guideline to the number of calories expended through running is 100 calories per mile. Remember, though, that running uphill and off-road on soft or uneven surfaces uses more calories.

If you want a more accurate picture of the energy you burn through running, use the following calculation:

Body weight in kg x average weekly distance in km x 1.036 [Ans]/7 (in order to get a daily amount)

In terms of marathon training, if you are running, say, 30 miles a week, you will expend around 3000 calories more than if you were sedentary. That breaks down to 430 calories per day extra needed, assuming that you are a stable weight and happy with that weight. Ensure that the extra energy you take on board is good-quality food and drink, rich in carbohydrate, and not chocolate bars and biscuits. Remember, too, that if you use sports drinks you may already be supplying a significant amount of these extra calories.

But I want to lose weight!

If you embark on a serious marathon training programme and do not increase your calorie intake you will almost certainly lose weight, but there's a fine line between shedding unwanted pounds and failing to provide your body with all the energy it needs to fuel training and recovery. Do not attempt to follow a strict calorie-controlled diet and marathon train simultaneously. You'll end up feeling exhausted and depressed, your running will suffer and you'll put yourself at risk of illness and ill health through a lack of vitamins and minerals, as well as possible dehydration.

The following tips will assist your weight loss efforts.

:> Cut down on high-fat and processed or highly refined foods, particularly saturated fats, manufactured snacks, cakes, crisps and biscuits, hard cheese, fatty cuts of meat and alcohol.

:> Add resistance training to your running regime to increase muscle mass and, therefore, metabolic rate.

:> Ensure you stay hydrated, otherwise you may mistake thirst signals for hunger.

:> Make liquid foods a regular aspect of your diet; research from Penn State University showed that these are more filling than drier foods of the same calorie content. For example, thick carrot soup instead of raw carrots, a fruit smoothie rather than a banana.

:> Only use energy drinks, gels or bars on or after long runs – not as routine.

:> Keep healthy snacks at the ready – if you come in from a run feeling ravenous, you'll want something to munch on quickly, so ensure you have a range of healthy choices.

why we are here

Running gives us the opportunity to face the elements, breathe fresh air and see greenery, fulfilling an innate need to immerse ourselves in nature that ecopsychologists call 'biophilia'. Studies show that this boosts serotonin levels, making us feel more calm and content, and that it promotes healing.

⋮ Fluid thinking
THE IMPORTANCE OF HYDRATION BEFORE, DURING AND AFTER RUNNING

Sixty per cent of human body weight comprises water. It bathes and nourishes every cell, transports nutrients, cushions and protects organs and joints, and generally keeps us alive and kicking. Even if you barely lifted a finger, your body would need 2 to 2.5 litres of fluid per day for normal function, so it quickly becomes evident that, as a marathoner in training, your needs are even greater.

Maintaining fluid balance

Strenuous exercise – like running – generates 20 times more heat than when you are at rest. We have to dissipate that heat somehow, to regulate and stabilise body temperature. The body's favoured method of losing heat is through sweating, which, of course, causes water loss through the skin. Typical sweat rates for an endurance runner range from 0.4–1.8 litres per hour of exercise – and if this fluid isn't replenished, dehydration will set in, causing a raised heart rate, increased blood pressure, a far higher rate of perception of effort and, ultimately, a decline in performance. To offset fluid loss resulting from exercise, you need to think about drinking before, during and after training sessions and races.

But how much should you drink? And what should be in your bottle? The American College of Sports

Medicine (ACSM), an internationally recognised authority on sport science, revised its guidelines on fluid intake and exercise in 2007, completely removing recommendations to drink specific volumes of fluid. It did this in the light of increasing evidence showing that individual fluid needs vary so greatly that it simply isn't possible to suggest a 'one size fits all' volume. With this in mind, it's important that you become familiar with your own fluid needs by monitoring your intake during training and finding out what works for you. The ACSM report suggests a possible starting point for marathon runners of somewhere in the region of 0.4 to 0.8 litres per hour – with the higher rates for faster, heavier individuals competing in warm environments, and the lower rates for slower, lighter runners competing in cooler environments. In training, try to experiment with fluid intakes within these guidelines, so you are more confident about how much you will need to consume on race day. But if you feel you need slightly more or slightly less, that's fine – everyone is different.

The ACSM recommends pre- and post-exercise weighing to assess fluid loss (see the 'Weigh in' panel on page 98). The amount of weight lost after a training session gives a good indication of how much water the body has sweated out (yes, it's all water, not fat!).

In an ideal world, you would consume the same volume of fluid that you lost through sweating, but research from Aberdeen University suggests that replacing 80 per cent of what we've lost is sufficient to leave performance unaffected.

There are two other simple ways of monitoring your fluid needs. It used to be believed that thirst was not a good indicator of hydration status, but experts now believe that it is perfectly reasonable to consider how thirsty you are when deciding whether or not to take a drink. Trying to stay one step ahead of your thirst can lead to overhydration,

which we'll look at in more detail on page 100. In a study from the University of Cape Town, cyclists who were forced to replace their actual sweat loss with fluids drunk performed worse than when they drank according to what they felt they needed.

Another useful indicator is the colour – and volume – of your urine. A normal volume of pale-coloured urine indicates good hydration, while scant volumes of dark-coloured urine suggest you may be dehydrated. However, be wary of using urine colour as your only hydration assessment if you take vitamin supplements, as these can make you produce unusually dark urine and mistakenly lead you to believe you are underhydrated.

The final consideration worth bearing in mind is your common sense. If you have been drinking lots of fluids in the lead-up to a race and taking water on board little and often, it's unlikely that you are dehydrated. If, on the other hand, you've been running at a fairly hard pace on a hot day, and have been sweating profusely, you may need to consider drinking a little more.

Drinking on the run

Your hydration strategy for running should begin long before you put on your trainers. If you start a training session or race underhydrated, you'll be fighting a losing battle trying to compensate later – even a level of dehydration equal to a 2 per cent loss of body weight could add minutes to your marathon time. The ACSM report is very clear on the importance of 'pre-hydrating' several hours before activity, to allow time for fluids to be absorbed and for urine output to return to normal.

But think about drinking 'little and often' rather than glugging down huge volumes all at once, which will not only cause your stomach to feel uncomfortable but will also increase your chances of having to take a mid-run pitstop.

Weigh in

Weigh yourself naked before and after (towelled down to remove excess sweat) a training run of a measured time (30 or 60 minutes is ideal, as it makes the maths easier!). Do not drink any fluid during the run. The amount of weight you lose represents water loss – each gram lost equates to 1 ml of fluid. So, for example, if you lost 0.6 kg (600 g) after an hour-long run, this would equal 600 ml of fluid per hour. You could then aim to drink 120–150 ml every 15 minutes during future runs, to offset your losses (this represents 80–100 per cent of your fluid loss). Remember to factor in the weather conditions and your exercise intensity when you're performing this test – you'll sweat more in hotter weather or if you're running faster.

And, guys, be warned: research by world fitness organisation IDEA shows that men are more likely to be dehydrated at the start of a workout than women.

Beginning your session well hydrated stands you in good stead for getting the most out of your training. But what about fluid consumption on the run? Well, how much, what and, indeed, if, you need to drink depend greatly on how far and how fast you are running, as well as the temperature. On a half-hour run, for example, you don't really need to drink at all, unless you really want to – the duration isn't really sufficient for the effects of dehydration to take hold. But once the duration of a run goes up, fluid replacement becomes more important. Think of it this way: with a 'typical' sweat rate of 1 litre per hour, a 60 kg runner would lose only 0.8 per cent of their body weight in half an hour, which is unlikely to have a detrimental effect on performance. But double that run time to an hour and the fluid loss would equal 1.6 per cent of body weight, more likely to have an effect. (Notch it up 2 hours, and you're looking at a significant 3.2 per cent loss in body weight.)

As we've learned, there is no set volume of fluid that can be recommended for every runner, but whatever your individual needs, drink the fluid in small amounts when you are running. Many runners find it helpful to break down their estimated fluid requirement into smaller volumes, which they drink on a schedule. For example, a runner with an estimated fluid need of 0.6 litres per hour might drink 150 ml every 15 minutes, or 100 ml every 10 minutes. This is a good way of ensuring you are meeting your fluid needs. But use your head, too: if you feel thirsty, drink. If your stomach is already sloshing around with water, don't.

While water is perfectly adequate for runs under an hour, it is well worth swapping the H_2O for an isotonic sports drink on lengthier sessions. One study of 98 marathon runners compared the effects of a sports drink and a placebo, consumed at the rate of 1 litre an hour during a marathon: the runners who got the real thing were able to work at a higher heart rate, especially during the last 10 km of the race (when most people begin to slow down). The other benefit of imbibing sports drinks during exercise is that they can hasten recovery for subsequent exercise sessions. In a study published in the *International Journal of Sport Nutrition and Exercise Metabolism*, a group of cyclists performed an 80-minute ride while ingesting either plain water or a carbohydrate-containing drink. They then had to perform a 10 km time trial on the bike, as fast as possible. The cyclists performed better in the time trial when they received the carbo-fuelled drink during the 80-minute ride compared to plain water.

The International Marathon Medical Directors Association (IMMDA) suggests drinking sports drink on all runs longer than 30 minutes. 'The added carbohydrate and electrolytes speed absorption of fluids and have the added benefit of energy fuel and electrolytes,' says their report, 'Fluid recommendations for runners and walkers'. This suggestion may be due to the fact that the risk of hyponatraemia (*see* 'Too much of a good thing', below) is lower when sports drinks, rather than plain water, are consumed. You may be inclined not to follow this advice if you are trying to shed excess pounds though – given that water is calorie-free and the average sports drink has 200 calories per litre. But a study published in the journal *International Sports Nutrition* found that exercisers who drank sports drink consumed fewer calories over the rest of the day compared to water drinkers. Again, see what works for you.

Post-run hydration

Don't forget about hydration the minute you hit 'stop' on your sports watch. Rehydration is one of the most important components of recovery. The body can't

What to look for in a sports drink

- ❖ For use during exercise, you need an 'isotonic' formula, which has a 6–8 per cent carbohydrate content (any higher, and it is an 'energy' drink, which won't provide enough energy quickly enough to utilise during the run itself).

- ❖ It should also contain electrolyte salts including sodium, potassium and chloride. Research shows that isotonic sports drinks are absorbed into the bloodstream as quickly as water, delivering energy and replenishing the electrolytes lost through sweat, as well as helping you rehydrate.

- ❖ It's important that you like the taste of your sports drink – studies show that this has an influence on how much you'll consume.

- ❖ If you don't want to fork out for proprietary drinks, make your own. Mix 200–250 ml of squash (not sugar-free) with 800 ml of water and add a quarter teaspoon of salt.

replenish glycogen stores when it is in a dehydrated state, as it needs to stash 3 grams of water for every gram of carbohydrate. Plain water is a perfectly valid way of quenching your thirst if you haven't run very far or fast, won't be running the next day or if you are watching your calorie intake. But if you've completed a demanding session, you can speed up your recovery by replacing lost salts and carbohydrate. Research suggests that taking a little protein along with carbohydrate in a recovery drink works better than carbohydrate alone. Many proprietary 'recovery drinks' contain both nutrients, but a natural and convenient alternative is milk or a flavoured milk drink. The American College of Sports Medicine also states that consuming salt (sodium) during the recovery period can help retain ingested fluids and stimulate thirst. The 'little and often' rule applies yet again with recovery hydration – gulp down litres all at once and you'll simply pee it out. Don't worry if it takes a little while for your urine to return to its normal, healthy, pale colour – this can take time.

Too much of a good thing

There's been a lot of media coverage regarding the issue of consuming too much water during endurance events, following a number of cases of 'hyponatraemia', a potentially fatal condition in which the sodium concentration in the blood drops excessively due to too much water in the bloodstream. Endurance athletes have become so used to hearing the 'drink, drink, drink' message that many have unwittingly overdone it. The tragic death of a runner in the 2007 London Marathon stands testament to this, along with an increasing number of reported

What's your tipple?

The 2 litres, or 'eight glasses a day', mantra is one that most of us are familiar with when it comes to water intake. But many nutrition experts now refute this, pointing out that at least a third of our daily fluid requirements are met by solid food, juice, milk, soft drinks and, yes, even tea and coffee. Professor Ron Maughan, one of the UK's top hydration researchers, says, 'Caffeine is a diuretic, but the fluid provided in the drink is enough to offset its diuretic effect. Take 60 mg of caffeine and add it to a cupful of water and milk, and you'll likely end up more hydrated than if you hadn't drunk it.' In fact there may be some positive benefits to taking caffeine on board before a training run or race, which you can read about on page 105.

cases at other marathons and triathlons. So who is most at risk of hyponatraemia?

Well, nobody is immune to exercise-associated hyponatraemia. But it is true to say that some people are more susceptible than others and that some activities – including marathon running – are riskier than others. Running a marathon entails running at a moderate intensity for a long duration, usually with ample access to fluid, which is why it is riskier than a sport like tennis or football – in which the opportunities for drinking are greatly reduced – or shorter-duration, higher-intensity running events like 10km races.

The pace at which a marathoner runs is also a factor – though this could be simply because the longer you're out on the road, the more opportunities and time you have to take fluids on board. Research published in the *New England Journal of Medicine* on hyponatraemia in marathon runners found that those most likely to suffer problems were runners who took more than 4 hours to finish the race – particularly those who consumed fluid at every mile, taking on more than 3 litres throughout the race.

The study also found that those with a low body mass index, a higher proportion of body fat to muscle or a small body size were at greater risk than larger athletes, which has led to the suggestion that women are more vulnerable than men, as reported in the *Clinical Journal of Sports Medicine*. There's also limited evidence to suggest that overuse of non-steroidal anti-inflammatories, like ibuprofen, can increase the risk of hyponatraemia by affecting kidney function.

Research indicates that your fitness level and your acclimatisation to the conditions in which the race is run can also influence your susceptibility to hyponatraemia. The sweat glands of athletes who are used to exercising in warm environments have an increased capacity for holding on to sodium, while less fit or unacclimatised runners are more likely to excrete sweat containing high sodium concentrations. If this is combined with a high sweat rate (i.e. the *amount* of fluid lost in sweat) it can result in large amounts of sodium being lost, elevating the risk of hyponatraemia. That's why getting to know your own individual fluid requirements is so important.

Without discounting all this, don't get too worried about the risks of hyponatraemia. The fact is that dehydration is a far more likely scenario. If you drink sensibly, you shouldn't suffer from either condition. If, however, you feel unwell during or after a long run or race, it's essential to seek medical help immediately. The faster and lower blood sodium falls, the greater the risk, so the sooner your situation is assessed, the better.

Safe drinking tips

:: Get to know your fluid needs in training and abide by them during the race.

:: Use sports drinks, which contain small amounts of sodium, instead of water on long runs and races.

:: If you are a slower runner, consider running the marathon with a salty snack, such as pretzels, to consume after a couple of hours.

Dehydration alert

Common signs of dehydration include:

:> fatigue

:> headache

:> poor performance

:> dizziness

:> lack of urination

:> muscle cramps

:> confusion.

:: Adjust the rate of fluid intake to suit your race pace: slower race pace = slower drinking rate.

:: Don't drink if you're not thirsty.

:: Do not feel compelled to drink at every drink station, nor to drink the entire contents of a cup or bottle that you have picked up.

:: Don't copy other runners' drinking habits – their fluid needs are probably very different from your own.

What about alcohol?

While you don't see many runners puffing away on cigarettes after a race, quite a few will be heading for the local pub for a drink. And that is absolutely fine, but there are a few points to bear in mind. First, alcohol is calorific. A pint of bitter weighs in at 175 calories, a 440 ml can of premium lager at 260, and a 175 ml glass of red wine (the standard pub measurement) at 115 calories. And even if the drink itself isn't a calorie issue for you, a study in the *American Journal of Clinical Nutrition* found that in 52 volunteers, a single pre-lunch wine or beer resulted in an increased calorie intake over the next 24 hours.

Second, alcohol cannot be used directly by the muscles – it travels straight into the bloodstream from where it has to be metabolised before the body can make use of more preferable fuel sources, such as carbohydrate or fat. Consume it too regularly and it will suppress fat oxidation and promote fat storage – the exact opposite of what you want. Alcohol is also a diuretic, causing your body to lose water and increasing the likelihood of dehydration.

However guilty you feel, don't run with a hangover. It affects your capacity to exercise, causing palpitations, interfering with body temperature control, dulling reflexes and increasing perception of effort. Equally, it's not wise to drink alcohol straight after a heavy training session or race: alcohol has been shown to interfere with muscle repair and recovery.

why we are here

Running is one of the best ways of staying in shape for life. A study from Arizona State University found that highly active women over 35 years old had a far higher resting metabolic rate than their sedentary counterparts.

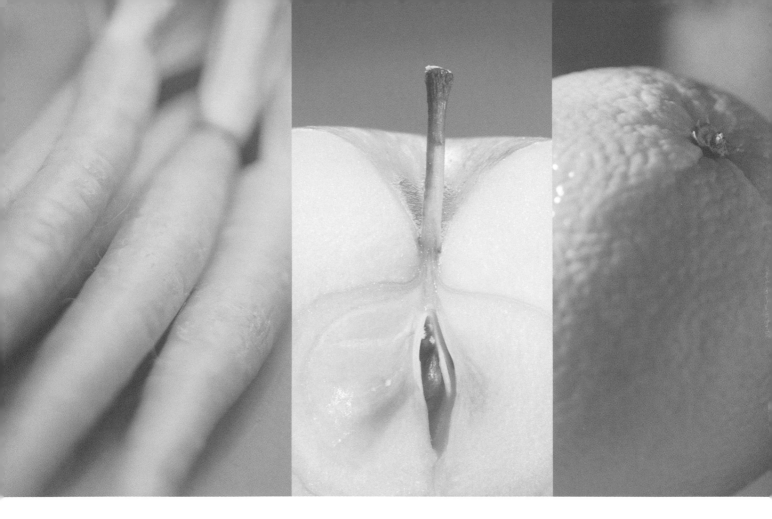

⁖ The extras: vitamins, minerals and the rest

WHO NEEDS EXTRAS? WILL SUPPLEMENTS HELP YOU RUN FASTER?
PLUS SPECIAL DIETARY CONSIDERATIONS

We'd all be rattling if we took the myriad pills, potions and powders that are allegedly going to help us run faster, from vitamins and minerals to ergogenic aids and dietary supplements . . . But what does the evidence say? And if your diet isn't 'normal', are there further considerations to bear in mind?

Vitamins and minerals

Provided that you are eating a healthy balanced diet, following the principles outlined in this section, you should be getting sufficient quantities of vitamins and minerals in your diet. In fact, a study from Columbia University points out that given that your overall calorie intake may be higher than that of the average population (to meet your higher energy needs), you are *more* likely to be ticking all the right boxes, provided you are eating a wide variety of healthy, nutritious foods. And, as far as performance is concerned, the 'if some is good, more must be better' argument doesn't seem to work. Although iron, zinc and B vitamins are all essential components of a runner's diet, research demonstrates no

Calcium

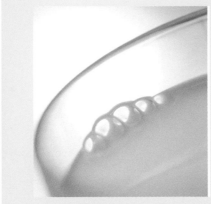

Calcium is best known for its role in bone building, and there is no doubt that calcium deficiency is bad news for anyone who is regularly running, and putting the skeletal system under stress.

But calcium also plays an important role in muscular contraction, neural function and maintaining a normal heart rhythm. Women in particular should be vigilant about calcium intake, since a third of women post-menopause are affected by osteoporosis, a condition in which the bones become thin and fragile (*see* page 71 for information and advice). The recommended daily allowance in the UK is 700 mg (compared to 1000 mg in the United States), but women who are breast-feeding and anyone who has been diagnosed with osteoporosis needs more: 1200 mg per day. The major source of calcium in the diet is dairy products – those who avoid dairy should seek out calcium-enriched alternatives, such as fortified cereals and soy products, lentils and beans, nuts and seeds, or dark green leafy vegetables. Fish with bones in (such as canned sardines or salmon) are also good sources. Research suggests that upping calcium intake through diet is more effective than taking supplements.

Iron

Iron is an essential mineral in the human body – it is involved in the formation of red blood cells and the transportation of oxygen to all the body's cells. Insufficient iron can hamper athletic performance by allowing haemoglobin to fall below optimal levels and, according to research from Cornell University, can lessen adaptation to endurance training (meaning you don't reap the benefits of all your hard work). But you don't have to be anaemic to have low iron levels – a study in the *American Journal of Clinical Nutrition* found that iron deficiency without anaemia occurred in 12 per cent of pre-menopausal women in the United States, and that iron supplementation improved aerobic performance significantly.

All runners should ensure that their iron intake is sufficient. Research suggests that iron turnover is greater in distance runners due to something known as 'footstrike haemolysis' – the loss of iron from red blood cells as a result of repeated impact. But the runners who are most at risk of iron deficiency are women (due to menstruation), those on low-calorie diets (who are more at risk of deficiencies of any type), vegetarians and vegans. The latter two are susceptible because 'haem' iron sources from meat and fish are better absorbed than plant-derived sources. Men should consume 8.7 mg of iron a day, women 14.8 mg per day. Do not take iron supplements without medical advice, however – overconsumption of iron can have adverse health effects.

Antioxidants

Strenuous physical activity increases the level of oxidative stress on the body, leading some to suggest that it should be avoided, due to the damaging effects of the so-called 'free radicals' that result from it. However, research from Harokopio University in Greece suggests that while prolonged endurance exercise does indeed raise oxidative stress, it also elevates the body's ability to deal with it. That said, a diet rich in antioxidants will help your body repair exercise-induced damage and support your immune system. Vitamins A, C and E, along with the mineral selenium, all act as antioxidants, and fruit and vegetables are the best source (brazil nuts and mushrooms are good sources of selenium). Generally, the more colourful the food, the more likely it is to be rich in antioxidants. For example, red grapes are better than white ones, pink grapefruit is better than white grapefruit, and sweet potatoes are better than standard spuds. The jury is out as far as taking antioxidant supplements is concerned. A recent review from the University of Florida states that there is limited evidence that dietary supplementation with antioxidants will improve performance.

benefit of supplementing them unless a pre-existing deficiency has been established. That said, if you exclude certain food groups (for example, if you are a vegetarian or vegan), if you don't eat at least five portions of fruit and vegetables per day, or if you regularly skip meals and rely on ready meals and takeaways, a good-quality multi-vitamin and mineral supplement may be of benefit. The panel opposite shows three micronutrients that you certainly don't want to be going short of . . .

Ergogenic aids

Surveys suggest that half of all runners use nutritional supplements, but the evidence supporting many of these is scant to say the least, and such supplements may serve only to decrease your bank balance rather than increase your performance. In a lot of cases, there are as many studies to refute a supplement's efficacy as there are to support it. For example, the use of glutamine has, in some cases, been shown to assist recovery and support the immune system in athletes, while other studies have found that although supplementation elevates levels of glutamine in the body, this does not bring about any specific health or performance benefits.

Similarly, many sportspeople (me included) have latched on to the idea of taking glucosamine sulphate (GS) to help prevent the breakdown of cartilage and stimulate new growth, thereby lessening joint pain and the risk of osteoarthritis. Research on the efficacy of GS supplementation is mixed. For example, a study published in the *British Journal of Sports Medicine* found that 2000 mg taken for 12 weeks provided pain relief and improved function in 88 per cent of subjects with knee pain. However, a study from Belgrade that looked at GS's effect on the recovery of athletes who had suffered knee injuries found that 1500 mg, taken for 28 days, did not reduce pain or swelling – although it did improve mobility in the joint.

In a 'meta-analysis' (combination of the results of several studies) of 15 studies on glucosamine supplementation, published in the *Journal of the American Medical Association*, effectiveness of treatment was rated on a scale of 0.2–0.8. The average score was 0.44 and 0.5 was the marker for 'moderate' effectiveness, suggesting that, in some cases, it does have at least some benefit. This same equivocal story is repeated when you look at many popularly used ergogenic aids. But there is one nutritional supplement that, as an endurance runner, you will almost certainly benefit from . . .

Caffeine

Studies have shown quite conclusively that endurance exercise performance can be enhanced by caffeine use. It was initially believed that this was due to it promoting fat utilisation, thereby sparing glycogen for later in the session. But recent research suggests that it improves contractile force in muscles and reduces rate of perceived exertion, enabling us to go for longer without succumbing to pain and fatigue. A study from Loughborough University also found that it improved mental focus and concentration during exhaustive exercise.

So how much do you need to get a performance benefit? Canadian researchers have found that a dose of 1–3 mg per kg of body weight offers perform-ance benefits, although the journal *Sports Medicine* reports safe benefits from higher doses, up to 6 mg/kg. Not surprisingly, research also suggests that non-habitual caffeine users get more of a benefit than coffee addicts (abstaining from caffeine for seven days prior to the race is one way around this). As a guideline, a can of Red Bull contains around 80 mg of caffeine; a single espresso, 65 mg; a large latte, 130 mg. Take your caffeine dose (remember, caffeine comes in the form of energy gels and pills as well as in beverages) 60–90 minutes before your run. And always test your strategy out in training before trying it in a race. Potential detrimental side-effects include gastric upset, sleep disturbance and interactions with other dietary supplements.

While caffeinated drinks get a bad press for their dehydrating and diuretic effect on sportspeople, the American College of Sports Medicine states that there is no evidence to suggest that caffeine consumption prior to exercise either increases urination or dehy-dration, possibly due to high levels of adrenaline inter-fering with the usual effect on the kidneys.

It seems that caffeine may also have a benefit in recovery. A study published in the *Journal of Applied Physiology* found that glycogen was replenished more quickly post-exercise when carbohydrate was combined with caffeine. Cyclists who added caffeine to their carbohydrate-based recovery drink had 66 per cent more glycogen in their muscles 4 hours after finishing an exhaustive session compared to when they consumed carbohydrate alone.

Special diets

There are a few added challenges related to eating healthily during marathon training if you follow a restricted or special diet – one that excludes certain foods or food groups. While it is beyond the realms of this book to go into great detail about specific diets, here are some areas that particular groups should be especially aware of.

Vegetarians

Vegetarians are, in general, less likely to suffer from heart disease and cancer than meat eaters, but avoiding meat and fish could lead to sub-optimal iron and zinc intake, and to low levels of omega 3 fatty acids, which are important for the heart and in damp-ening down inflammation in the body. It also means that you need to think more carefully about your protein sources, since only animal-derived foods (including dairy products) can offer the full range of essential amino acids. Here are a few other tips to ensure you don't fall short of your optimal training diet:

- consume vitamin C-rich foods with non-haem iron sources to optimise absorption
- avoid drinking tea with non-haem iron sources, since this reduces absorption
- eat lots of wholemeal bread, eggs, nuts and seeds, to ensure sufficient zinc intake
- top up omega 3s with linseed, rapeseed oil, walnut and walnut oil, and pumpkin seeds.

Vegans

All the above advice applies to vegans, too, although there is the added challenge of achieving a balanced healthy diet without dairy products and eggs. The most important issue of concern is calcium. A UK study of more than 34,000 adults found that vegans had a higher risk of bone fracture than meat eaters, fish eaters and vegetarians, due to a low calcium intake. You'll need to ensure you get sufficient calcium (*see* page 104) from non-dairy sources or from supple-mentation. Iron is also in short supply in a vegan diet, so consume plenty of fortified breakfast cereals, pulses and green leafy vegetables (kale and broccoli are the best sources), and consider having your ferritin and haemoglobin levels assessed by your doctor if you are feeling fatigued or weak and showing pallor. To get your full complement of amino acids (protein) on a dairy-free diet, you need to combine two different plant-based foods, such as serving lentils with rice, peanut butter with wholemeal bread, or a soya food with pasta. Another micronutrient that you may fall short of is vitamin B12, abundant in milk and dairy products, meat and fish, but also soya products, fortified cereal and yeast extract. A vitamin B complex supplement is recommended.

Low-carb diets

Regardless of their enduring popularity, I advise giving low-carb diets a wide berth during marathon training. Why? Because carbohydrate is the essential runner's fuel – without it, you simply won't perform to the best of your ability. A landmark study demonstrated that people on a low-carb diet who were asked to cycle until exhaustion on an exercise bike managed only one hour, while those on a moderate-carbohydrate diet did 115 minutes and those on a high-carb diet clocked 170 minutes. A study from the University of Connecticut also suggests that a high-protein diet makes you significantly more dehydrated during exercise than does a normal balanced diet.

- Run in areas where there are other people, and at times of the day when there are more people around; avoid poorly lit areas in the evening and early morning. Vary your routes and times. If you always go the same way, at the same time, it's just possible that someone might notice that fact.

- Consider taking a self-defence class to improve your knowledge of what to do should you ever be attacked.

- Think about investing in a lightweight personal alarm. If the worst should happen and you were to be attacked, the piercing noise it emits is likely to give you a few more seconds to act before the attacker recovers.

- Carry a slip of paper in your shoe or shorts pocket with your name, telephone number and blood type on, plus any other relevant medical information (allergies, etc.)

Be safe, be seen

Personal safety when running also means being vigilant about traffic. The golden rule is to be seen, but never to assume that you have been – even in daylight. Bright yellow or orange kit helps make you stand out, but at night, reflective panels and strips are visible from a greater distance. For maximum effectiveness, wear reflective gear on your 'moving parts' (the arms and legs), rather than on your trunk, to make you easier to spot.

Avoid doing speed work or timed sessions on routes that involve crossing roads or you may be tempted to run out without looking for oncoming traffic. Be particularly careful about cars backing out of drives and cyclists riding on pavements. If you're running on country roads, face the oncoming traffic unless you are approaching a blind bend, and keep well in.

Four-legged friends and foes

Most runners have a 'dog story' to tell, so it is unlikely that you will complete a few months of marathon training without some kind of 'run in' with Rover, or his owner! Even though most dogs are harmless, it can be alarming when one decides to chase you, jump up or bark as you approach. If you are passing a dog that is off its lead and showing a little too much interest in you, it is advisable to break into a walk, or call out, 'Is he OK with runners?' as you approach. Try to give some warning of your arrival, since surprising the dog (not to mention its owner) is likely to have negative consequences. What if the owner is nowhere to be seen? Give the dog as wide a berth as possible and walk, don't run, past. If he approaches you in a less-than-friendly fashion, don't make eye contact or attempt to kick out or throw anything at the dog – say 'NO!' or 'DOWN!' in a firm, loud voice.

As for the other animals you may encounter while running, believe it or not I've been pursued by horses, cows, sheep and even geese on my off-road meanders! If you are running off-road – always follow the Countryside Code, shutting gates, keeping your dog on its lead where specified and respecting rights-of-way signs. As with dogs, don't surprise livestock, but make a noise so that they know you are coming. Stick to field borders, rather than going straight across the middle, to avoid alarming them, particularly if you are running with a dog. If large animals – including deer – have young ones, you may have to find a different route altogether. It isn't wise to come between a cow and its calf or to approach a deer with fawn.

OK, so ticks don't have four legs (four pairs of legs, actually), but they can pose a threat to runners training in long grass or undergrowth. Consider wearing long pants rather than shorts, to avoid the risk of picking up a tick. These nasty little creatures bury their heads under your skin and feed on your blood – they can also cause Lyme disease. Always check yourself (and your dog) for signs of ticks when you return home – if you find one, use tweezers to carefully twist it out, being careful not to leave behind the mouth parts. Special 'hooks' are available from outdoor shops for tick removal.

Whether the weather is fine or foul . . .

Feeling hot hot hot!

Nearly double the number of people dropped out of the 2007 London Marathon compared to the previous year. The fact that midday temperatures exceeded 21ºC is almost certainly a factor. But while we can't control the weather, there are a few sensible precautions to take when you are running in the heat.

- Drink more: since you sweat a lot more in hot conditions, you need to drink more fluids to prevent your body from overheating.

- Consider running very early or late to avoid the heat of the day. In temperatures above 26ºC, accompanied by humidity, it is advisable to give running a miss.

- Wear as little as possible – shorts and vest, and a sun visor.

- Sports sunglasses filter out UVA and UVB rays. Running consistently without protection can increase the risk of glaucoma and cataracts. Go for orange, brown or mirrored lenses to combat glare and bright light.

- Don't forget about sun protection. You need a minimum of SPF 20, and it needs to be a sweat-resistant brand. When applying, remember the tops of your ears (your head, if you have a bald spot or thinning hair), the backs of your ankles and sides of your neck.

- To prevent getting overheated in hot weather, consider taking a dip in a cold bath, the sea or a swimming pool before you begin running. Researchers from Charles Sturt University in Australia found that 'pre-cooling' enabled exercisers to run 4 minutes longer on a treadmill than those who did not take the icy plunge.

Baby, it's cold outside

There are bound to be days during your training when the weather is looking less than inviting. That's no reason to stay inside, but you should consider the following points.

- Spend longer warming up in cold weather, to prevent muscle tears and strains, and to allow your cardiovascular system to adapt gradually.

- Ensure your trainers have good traction on wet pavements and anywhere icy.

- Eat – don't run on empty. Cold days mean you need to insulate yourself before you set off.

- Protect your extremities. In icy weather, blood is shunted to vital areas such as your internal organs, while blood vessels near to the skin surface close to prevent heat loss. Your fingers, toes, ears and nose are vulnerable to frostbite when it's really cold, so wear a hat and mittens or gloves, and perhaps even a scarf.

- Dress in thin layers to trap heat, rather than thick, heavy clothing.

- Do drink. The cold weather can fool you into believing you aren't thirsty or sweating much.

- Avoid speed work that involves long rest periods, since you will get cold very quickly.

- To make getting out the door that bit easier, put your clothes on the radiator or in the tumble dryer to make them toasty before you put them on.

∷ Dealing with injuries

HOW TO STOP NIGGLES BECOMING LONGER-LASTING PROBLEMS

According to a report on running injuries published in 2004, up to 70 per cent of runners experience injury in any given year. I hope that, by heeding the advice and following the exercises in the 'Body maintenance' section (page 59), and sticking to the realistic and achievable training programmes in this book, you won't suffer the same fate. But no runner is immune to injury, so it is as well to take a look at what to do if you do experience something more than a niggle, and at some of the more common injuries that runners have to contend with.

Injuries can be divided into two categories: acute injuries, in which something happens 'suddenly', such as when you fall and twist your ankle; and chronic injuries, in which the problem comes on more gradually. In runners, chronic (or 'overuse') injuries are far more common. According to a study from California State University, the main factors are training errors (such as doing too much, too soon), which account for more than 60 per cent of all running injuries, and biomechanical or anatomical shortcomings, such as poor running technique, overpronation or a leg length discrepancy.

First aid

So what should you do if you get injured? For acute injuries (such as a hamstring tear), the first port of call is the RICE strategy – an acronym for **R**est, **I**ce, **C**ompression and **E**levation. See the panel opposite for how to 'RICE' an injury effectively. Depending on the severity of the injury, you may want to see a doctor or sports medicine expert for a proper diagnosis and treatment advice. Don't take anti-inflammatories for the first 48 hours, because the body needs its 'inflammatory response' to protect the injured area. After

two days, start to gently mobilise the injured area, with gentle stretching and movement through the greatest possible range of motion that you can manage comfortably. Don't be tempted to continue not to use the injured part, otherwise it will seize up. As the injury continues to heal, ensure that you work on regaining both flexibility and strength. You may need to get advice on a specific rehabilitation programme.

As for chronic injuries, such as a nagging pain behind the kneecap or along the bottom of the foot, the important parts of the RICE strategy are the first two: rest and ice. Given that the principle cause of such an injury is overuse, it is imperative to use the injured part as little as possible for a couple of days, to allow inflammation and soreness to subside. Don't be tempted to keep 'testing out' your sore bit, to see if it has got better yet!

Another useful treatment for chronic injuries (particularly those that involve swelling, redness or heat) is a non-steroidal anti-inflammatory drug, such as ibuprofen or aspirin. Take them regularly for three to seven days, but do *not* use drugs to enable you to continue training without pain.

After a proactive rest period (in other words, using ice and drugs where appropriate), start to mobilise the injured area with gentle stretching and non-weighted movement. If the pain has gone, you could try a short run, but don't overdo it, and stop if you feel the pain returning. If the problem is lingering, go and see a sports medicine expert for further investigation. This is particularly important if you are in the middle of your marathon training and up against a deadline. Don't waste too much time hoping the problem will improve on its own.

It's worth bearing in mind that overuse injuries

don't come out of nowhere. If you upped your mileage a little too much or bought a new pair of training shoes and suffered as a result, fine. But if you weren't really aware of having done anything differently and got injured it is worth taking a closer look at your training regime, your running technique and your shoes for clues as to why the problem occurred.

Make the most of your appointment

When you consult a physiotherapist, or other sports practitioner, ensure that you come away clear about what your problem is, what the likely cause is and what action you need to take, both to hasten recovery and to prevent it happening again. In particular, if you are given exercises or stretches to do, ensure you know exactly how to do them, and how often. Don't be afraid to take notes or ask for diagrams, if it helps. Also get an idea of how long you will be out of the running, and how many appointments the practitioner anticipates that you will need. Be wary if your treatment seems to be going on and on, without any signs of the injury improving. Either they haven't found the true cause, or they are keeping you coming back by withholding either information or treatment. Also, do what you're told! There is no sense in paying good money for expert advice if you don't heed it.

A final thought: many injuries are recurring ones, suggesting that while the problem appeared to be resolved, the underlying cause was not identified. If the same old injury plagues you time and again, it's well worth investing in an appointment with a specialist – a physiotherapist, biomechanist or podiatrist – to determine what's causing it, and what can be done to solve it once and for all.

Healing alternatives

> Arnica – available in gel, cream or pill form – is a popular homeopathic remedy for bruising, inflammation and swelling.

RICE in action

> Rest: put as little stress as possible on the injured part.

> Ice: use crushed ice (not cubes) or bags of frozen peas, which can be moulded around the injured area. Don't put ice directly on to your skin – it will burn; protect your skin with cling film, muslin or a tea towel. Ice massage can also be useful for smaller areas of soreness. Aim for 8 minutes every 2–3 hours. When I did the Himalayan 100-Mile race my most cherished possession was my supply of instant cold packs – bags full of crystals with a pouch inside containing a chemical that, when you burst it, makes the crystals turn icy cold. The cool lasts for 30 minutes and then you have to dispose of the bag.

> Compression: use an elasticated bandage or sleeve to compress the area surrounding an acute injury, to help reduce blood flow and swelling.

> Elevation: in the case of acute injuries, elevate the injured part above your heart.

Continue with RICE measures for three to five days.

> Avoid alcohol, which will exacerbate inflammation and delay healing by increasing blood flow.

> *Don't* apply heat to injuries. You might feel like consoling yourself with a long, hot bath but the heat won't help your injury.

> Be positive: research shows that a positive outlook on recovery can speed up the process.

> A TENS unit can provide relief for chronic or acute pain through electrotherapy, administered via pads that you attach to the appropriate injured site of the body.

The hit list

These are some of the more common injuries that runners encounter. I've included symptoms and risk factors to help you identify what the problem might be, but don't use this as a replacement for professional advice.

Achilles tendinitis

Inflammation of the Achilles tendon along the back of the lower leg.

What it feels like

Pain, stiffness and tenderness at the back of the lower leg and heel, particularly in the morning, when rising on to the toes and during running, especially when you start out.

Risk factors

Overpronation, tight calf muscles, an excessively stiff forefoot in your running shoe, sudden increase in mileage, too much hill and/or speed work.

Case notes

When the initial pain and inflammation subsides, practise exercise 9 on page 64 to regain eccentric calf strength and flexibility.

Iliotibial band friction syndrome

The iliotibial band is a fibrous tissue that extends from the hip to just below the knee – it is actually a very long tendon that is attached to the tensor fascia latae muscle in the hip. In iliotibial band friction syndrome, the band becomes over-tight and inflamed, causing it to rub against the surrounding structures. It accounts for more than 10 per cent of all running injuries.

What it feels like

A sharp pain or friction on the lateral side of the knee (either towards the top or bottom edge of the kneecap), and even a 'catching' sensation as the band slides over the bony prominences of the thigh bone or shinbone, where it attaches.

Risk factors

Inexperience, lots of downhill running, excessive pronation, hip abductor weakness (particular gluteus medius), a tight lower back, frequent running on cambered surfaces or an athletics track.

Case notes

Research in the *Clinical Journal of Sports Medicine* suggests that weakness in the hip (particularly the gluteus medius muscle) makes runners vulnerable to IBFS. Do exercises 6 and 7 on page 63 and the Thomas stretch on page 58 religiously. Using a tennis ball or foam roller to massage along the side of the thigh can also help to loosen off a tight ITB.

Ankle sprain

What it feels like

There's a difference between 'turning' your ankle, after which you may be able to continue running (a grade 1 sprain) and a full-blown sprain, which entails a fully or partially torn ligament, swelling and bruising (grades 2–3).

Risk factors

Not looking where you are going! Running on uneven ground. Weak ankles.

Case notes

Apply the RICE strategy immediately. See a doctor to ensure no bones are broken. Do not begin running again until you can move the ankle freely in all directions and hop continuously without pain. A wobble board can help strengthen the muscles of the lower legs and prevent reoccurrence.

Muscle strains and tears

Excessive strain on, or rupture of, muscle fibres. These are most likely to occur in muscles that pass over two joints, such as the upper calf or hamstring. A strain will cause pain, and perhaps tightness and swelling, but only minimal tearing of muscle fibres. An acute tear usually occurs as a result of a sudden movement in an extreme range, such as during explosive drills or sprinting. Any tear is obviously accompanied by sudden pain, and may show as bruising or even a 'trail' of bleeding in the muscle. RICE is the first line of treatment and should be maintained for 48 hours, but get yourself to a specialist quickly. As soon as you can, following the first 48 hours, begin gentle stretching and strengthening exercises for the injured area.

Risk factors
Failing to warm up, previous strain or tear in the same area with inadequate rehabilitation, over-training, poor flexibility.

Case notes
Strains and tears often return because a build-up of scar tissue hampers smooth muscle contraction, and the pain causes you to alter your biomechanics. Sports massage can help dissipate scar tissue, while a programme of appropriate stretching and strengthening can prevent reoccurrences.

Piriformis syndrome
The piriformis muscle is a deep hip rotator and plays a very important role in stabilising the pelvis and allowing for correct gait. It can be a little oversensitive, however, and in the presence of swelling can switch off or go into spasm.

What it feels like
Piriformis-induced problems are varied, so the symptoms are diverse. A deep, dull ache in the buttock is a common sign, as is a shooting or persistent pain down the hamstring (this is because the sciatic nerve runs close to or through the piriformis muscle).

Risk factors
Poor pelvic stability, weak hip abductors or hamstrings, tight adductors, hip flexors and lower back. Overpronation, causing the hips to internally rotate, can also be a factor.

Case notes
If the piriformis goes into spasm, a 'trigger release' technique can bring almost instant relief – see a sports massage therapist or physiotherapist. Try the exercises for pelvic instability on page 62 and the hip rotator stretch on page 56, holding it for up to a minute and then repeating. Sit on top of a tennis ball to work into the painful areas. Avoid running down hills while you resolve this problem.

Plantar fasciitis
Inflammation of the plantar fascia, a sheath of connective tissue that runs along the entire bottom of the foot and fans out to all the toes.

What it feels like
Pain under the front of the heel (where the plantar fascia originates). It is often at its worst first thing in the morning. If you palpate the heel, you'll probably find an area of acute tenderness.

Risk factors
Abnormal running gait, tight calf muscles, weak foot muscles, high arches, excessive mileage.

Case notes
A golf ball or tennis ball under the sole of the foot can be used to massage the tight, sore area. Ask a physio about exercises to strengthen the 'lumbricals' – the deep foot muscles. Avoid walking or running barefoot while you are suffering.

Runner's knee
More correctly known as 'patellofemoral pain syndrome', this is generally caused by the kneecap maltracking, causing pain and inflammation, and possibly degeneration of the cartilage.

What it feels like
Persistent, throbbing or stabbing pain behind the knee cap, a sensation of heat in the joint. Particularly bad on going downstairs and after long periods of sitting. It is estimated that 60 per cent of knee

injuries are a result of the kneecap maltracking (*see* page 60).

Risk factors

Weak vastus medialis muscle (the innermost quadriceps), tight lateral structures around the knee joint, weak pelvic stabilisers, overpronation, flat feet.

Case notes

Exercises 7 and 8 on page 63 can help prevent runner's knee and strengthen weak areas to help prevent it in future.

Shin problems

Shin problems are often given the umbrella term 'shin splints', but there are distinct conditions affecting the area. Medial tibial stress syndrome (MTSS) is the official name for conditions where there is inflammation of the connective tissue or 'fascia', which attaches to the main shinbone (the tibia).

What it feels like

Pain along the inner side of the lower leg (medial tibial stress syndrome), just where the muscle and bone meet. The top layer of bone, the periosteum, can get inflamed in some instances. Unlike stress fractures, the exact area of soreness in MTSS can't be determined – it's a more generalised tenderness.

Risk factors

Being a beginner, overtraining (particularly on hard surfaces), overpronation, worn out or inappropriate shoes, an imbalance between the strength of calves and shin muscles.

Case notes

Massage along the sore area with ice or an anti-inflammatory gel. Stretch and strengthen the calf and shin muscles (see pages 54–56 and 64). Also read 'Stress fractures', below, to rule this out as an underlying cause.

Another shin condition, known as compartment syndrome, is characterised by generalised shin pain that always comes on at the exact same time or distance into your run. This is because compartment syndrome is caused by the muscles swelling within the sausage-skin-like 'fascia' of the shin, with a resultant increase in pressure to the point at which the structures are pressing against the shin bone and blood flow is compromised. The symptoms include pain, a feeling of tightness in the area, unusual nerve sensations (paresthesia) and, occasionally, muscle weakness.

Risk factors

A sudden increase in training volume.

Case notes

RICE will not help with compartment syndrome, although anti-inflammatories will. Modify your training until the problem subsides. If the pain persists, see a sports medicine expert.

Stress fractures

A stress fracture is a tiny hairline crack in the bone, caused by repeated impact. The most common sites in runners are the shin and bones of the feet.

What it feels like

A very specific point of tenderness upon the bone. The pain will not ease off during running, and may return at night.

Risk factors

Training too much on hard surfaces, building up mileage too quickly, inadequate rest, wearing worn-out trainers, excessive pronation, being amenorrhoeic, being an older runner.

Case notes

Do not run on a suspected stress fracture – or you may cause a full-blown fracture. It takes around six weeks for a stress fracture to heal – non-weight-bearing cross-training is the only sensible option during this time.

❖ Occupational hazards
PREVENTION AND CURE OF COMMON RUNNING AFFLICTIONS AND TROUBLES

Athlete's foot

Athlete's foot is a fungal infection that loves damp, sweaty places, so it isn't any wonder it attacks runners' feet. If you are prone to this painful and itchy condition, try dabbing tea tree oil between your toes after you have thoroughly washed and dried them, and wear flip-flops if you are in public, wet areas, such as shower blocks or gym changing rooms. An attack can be curbed by using an anti-fungal product such as Lamisil or Daktarin, but remember that your trainers may be harbouring the culprit: soak your trainer insoles in a tea tree oil solution or spray with an anti-fungal spray.

Blisters

Blisters are a build-up of fluid between the upper and lower layers of the skin, caused by friction between you and your shoes or socks. Hardly life-threatening, but they can cause untold misery to runners who are prone to them. If you are one, avoid cotton or seamed socks and ensure your shoes fit perfectly. If you get a blister, protect it from further friction with a blister plaster, moleskin or even surgical tape. You need to pop it only if it feels painful. If you do opt to pop, then use a sterilised needle heated in a flame, and pop it close to the unblistered skin to drain the fluid. Dab antiseptic lotion on and then cover with a blister plaster for at least 48 hours before leaving the area bare. Always have a stash of blister plasters handy. Look for those that create a 'second skin' between the blister and your footwear, such as Compeed, to cushion the skin. These are also breathable and waterproof, so your blister won't fester or get sore.

Black toenails

Black toenails are the result of bruising and blood blisters under the nail, normally caused by your toes repeatedly hitting the front of your shoe. Shoes that are too tight, or too big, can cause this – as can running downhill. If the toenail just looks ugly and doesn't hurt – leave it alone. It will either grow out or, more likely, fall off. If, however, there is a soreness and pressure behind the nail, you may need to drain the blood blister by piercing the nail. A podiatrist or doctor can do this for you or, if you are brave, you can do it yourself, using a sterilised sharp object such as a safety pin. Once the blood has drained, bathe with antiseptic and tape the nail in place.

Cramp

Exercise-associated muscle cramp (EAMC) is an involuntary, sharp contraction of muscle that happens either during or immediately after exercise. The cause of cramping is not well understood – it is often put down to dehydration or an imbalance of electrolytes, but research from the University of Cape Town found no connection between either of these factors and the incidence of cramp in a group of 72 runners. Fatigue, however, does seem to be a contributing factor, which is probably why 67 per cent of marathon runners have experienced cramp. It seems that fatigue can hamper muscular contraction, causing muscles to contract or relax at the wrong time. Cramps most often occur in muscles that span two joints, such as the calf or hamstrings.

If you get cramp, the South African researchers suggest stretching as the first port of call. And while they found no connection between cramp and electrolyte status, researchers at the University of North Carolina found that cramp sufferers fared better in hot conditions when they drank electrolyte-containing sports drinks compared to other fluids, so it's worth considering what, and how much, you drink.

What about prevention? A thorough warm-up is essential. It is also important to maintain good flexibility and posture.

Rashes

A heat rash anywhere on the skin, or a sweat rash under your arms, under the breasts or in the groin area is an unpleasant, but surprisingly common, running affliction. Minimise the risk by always showering immediately after running, wearing sweat-wicking breathable fabrics, not wearing dirty kit, and by using petroleum jelly or Bodyglide to prevent chafing. If you do get a rash, treat it with an anti-fungal lotion or cream – preferably one combined with hydrocortisone – to reduce redness and itching.

Stitches

Most runners get a stitch – or exercise-related transient abdominal pain (ETAP), as the science bods call it – at some point during training or racing, but still we don't really know what causes them. Research from Australia suggests that younger and less experienced runners are more susceptible than veterans of distance running, and that both genders are equally likely to get stitches. It used to be thought that the jolting action of running was to blame, but this seems unlikely, given that athletes in non-impact sports such as cycling also suffer from ETAP. Recent theories implicate fatigue of the diaphragm muscle (the dome-shaped muscle just beneath the lungs) or irritation of the peritoneum, a double-layered, fluid-filled sheath surrounding the abdom-

inal cavity. There are two possible mechanisms behind this latter theory: first, that the pain is caused by a reduction in the amount of fluid separating the two layers as a result of blood being diverted to the working muscles and dehydration; second, that a bloated stomach pushes against the inner layer. If either is the case, then the following measures should help: ensure you warm up thoroughly, maintain good core stability, stay hydrated, but don't glug down too much fluid at once and leave a reasonable gap after eating. What you drink could also play a part; research in the *International Journal of Sports Nutrition and Exercise Metabolism* found that fruit juice caused more bloating and stitches than did a proprietary isotonic sports drink. You may find that changing the rhythm of your breathing to match your footfall helps alleviate the pain when a stitch strikes, but in my experience, walking for a few moments while kneading the painful area is the most effective solution.

Tummy trouble

Half of all runners have experienced some kind of bowel or stomach problem during training or racing, whether it is abdominal pain, heartburn, nausea, diarrhoea or sickness. Among the many and varied possible causes are dehydration, sensitivity to a particular food, reduced blood flow to the intestines (perhaps due to eating too close to running) and the jolting action of running. Beginners tend to be more blighted by the 'runner's trots' than more experienced runners. If you can identify what caused your tummy trouble, so much the better – avoid the trigger when important training runs or races are approaching. If, however, you aren't sure what's causing the problem, keep a 'food and toilet' diary for a few days, being particularly aware of the following common irritants.

> Caffeine: can irritate the gastrointestinal tract (which is why it often makes us 'go' in the morning).

> Alcohol: a high intake of alcohol the day before can affect your stomach the day after.

> Sugar: highly concentrated sugar solutions – such as energy and sports drinks – can cause gastrointestinal distress in some people. That's why it's vital that you experiment with sports drinks in different concentrations in training to see what works for you. A 6–8 per cent carbohydrate solution should be OK, but some people find they need to dilute sports drinks with water.

> Fibrous foods: prior to a race or training run is the rare time when you don't want to opt for fibrous foods, since they take a long time to digest and absorb a lot of water, making you feel bloated and heavy.

> Dairy products: some people find dairy products hard to digest.

> Fruit: can cause stomach cramping.

> Aspirin and ibuprofen: non-steroidal anti-inflammatories can cause stomach upsets and even bleeding if taken too often or on an empty stomach.

- Will you be able to serve me breakfast early? (You'll need to eat at least 2 hours before the start time, preferably 3 hours.)

- Will you be able to provide me with something appropriate for breakfast? (A whopping fry-up is out of the question!)

- Will I be able to get an alarm call? (Just to be sure you don't sleep through your big day!)

If you aren't staying away from home the night before the race, and have a journey to contend with in the morning, it's essential that you have your route well planned. Are you sure you can park there, or, if you're travelling on public transport, will you definitely be able to get a taxi from the station or depot to the start area? Remember that many local roads may be closed. Allow plenty of time for unexpected traffic, getting lost, train delays or, the worst of all eventualities, breaking down.

Get familiar

You should be able to see a map of the course either in the race literature or on the internet. Study it properly – don't just glance at it. Where are the hills? What landmarks are there that you can set in your mind and keep an eye out for? Where are your supporters going to stand? How will they get to that point, and from there to the next vantage spot? Remember to say which side of the road you want your fans to stand on – be very specific, and ensure they also have a copy of the route map and that they have an idea of what time you'll be where.

If at all feasible, try driving or cycling the marathon course so that you are aware of what's in store. Try running some of it, too, perhaps the last few miles, so that you can practise visualising the finish and yourself running strongly towards it. However, don't

do this the night before the race, when you should be resting, and when it may serve to make you anxious rather than more prepared.

What to pack

What you need to take with you is obviously an individual decision, and depends on where you are going, how long for and whether you'll be staying on after the race. Let's start by looking at race kit.

Even if it's been grey and miserable for weeks – or relentless sunshine – you should pack different kit options for different weather conditions – you just never know. It's a good idea to put all your kit on before you pack it to ensure you haven't forgotten something essential, like your race socks or sports bra. For more vocal support on the way round the course, write or print your name on to the front of your race vest or T-shirt. It gives spectators something to shout out and you'll be amazed how encouraging it is to hear your name being called.

Kit checklist

- Race number

- Safety pins to attach your number to your top

- Your timing chip (if you've been given one)

- Running shoes and spare laces

- Running socks

- Comfortable underwear

- Shorts or bottoms

- Sports bra

- Vest or T-shirt

- Waterproof top (gilet or sleeved, depending on what you are used to)

- Bin liner and disposable warm clothes to keep

you warm and dry when you are waiting for the race to start

:> Hat and gloves for races in cooler climes

:> A visor works well for hot days, protecting your face from the sun without making your head hot

:> Sunglasses – not just to shield your eyes from the sun but to keep out grit and flies, and to give you 'anonymity' and an internal focus

:> Hair ties or a hair band to keep long or unruly hair out of your face

:> Warm, comfortable clothing (including socks and underwear) to put on after the race to travel back from the finish.

That's the race kit sorted. But what else might you need with you? I certainly recommend taking the race information you've been sent, in case you need to check anything at the last minute. Here are a few of the less obvious things to consider packing.

:> Sunscreen: even if it's not clear skies and sunshine you can still get sunburned, so it's worth protecting your skin with a sweat-resistant sunscreen.

:> A local road map of the town or area where you're headed, in case you have trouble finding the start area.

:> Nail scissors: cut your toenails straight across and shorter than the tips of your toes to avoid them ending up black and bruised.

:> Mobile phone and charger: you may need it to help you find relatives and friends at the finish area.

:> A basic first aid kit: it's worth packing Immodium for upset tummies and ibuprofen or another NSAID for any muscular aches or pains.

Travelling overseas to race

If you are travelling overseas for your race, arrive in plenty of time to allow yourself to get over the fatigue of the journey. Pack your running shoes, kit, timing chip and race information in your hand luggage, just in case.

If you are travelling to a different time zone, you may need to build in a couple of days to adjust – this is particularly the case if you are travelling east, which tends to trigger more severe jet lag than westward journeys.

Minimise the effects of a long plane trip by staying well hydrated, avoiding alcohol, getting up to move around frequently and setting your watch to the new time zone as soon as you leave the ground. When you arrive, try to stay awake until it's officially bedtime. Stick to familiar food and drink in the days prior to the race and don't exhaust yourself with sightseeing and shopping.

If possible, take a day or two after the race to recover and appreciate the sights of where you are. A long plane journey immediately after a marathon is likely to be pretty uncomfortable.

:> Petroleum jelly: smearing it liberally on to all moving parts is one of the best ways of avoiding chafing and soreness, such as jogger's nipple or raw inner thighs. Though if you are really susceptible to chafing in a particular area, it is worth covering it with either a plaster or adhesive moleskin.

:> Blister plasters: if you are worried about blisters, you might want to run armed with a blister plaster or two in your pocket.

:> Any 'special' foods or drinks that you might want for before, during and after the race. This might include your favourite breakfast cereal or spread, as well as race-specific fuel such as jelly babies, energy drinks or gels.

- Tissues/toilet paper: if you get caught short and need to make a pitstop, don't expect the toilets (if there are any) to be fully equipped. It's useful to have your own.

- Money: since you are separated from all your possessions for the duration of the race, it can be useful to have some cash stashed in your sock or in your shorts pocket for eventualities, such as a taxi, if you have to bail out, or fail to meet up with your friends and family at the finish for some reason, or for phone calls, food and drink.

- A pace band (*see* page 126).

- Drinks bottle: you don't have to take one, since there will be regular drinks stations en route, but you may prefer to carry your own.

∴ Winding down

WHY, HOW AND WHEN TO TAPER YOUR TRAINING FOR BEST RESULTS ON RACE DAY

With three weeks to go until the marathon, you may feel this is your last chance to get in some decent training. Wrong! This is the time to start winding your training down. Performing well on marathon day isn't just a matter of peaking in your fitness, it's also about ensuring you are fully recovered from the rigours of training, so that you can do your best and feel fresh and ready on the day. Now is the perfect time to devise your race strategy, since you will have a good idea of your capabilities and aspirations.

Devising your race plan

'Get to the finish line in one piece' does not constitute a race strategy. You must stand on the start line with a target finish time in mind, and an idea of your 'split times'. Split times are simply the amount of time it takes you to complete any given section of the course – it could be each mile or kilometre, every 10 km, or the first and second half of the race. Having a goal race pace ensures that you don't go off too quickly, or, indeed, run slower than you need to. While experienced marathoners can normally predict their finish time within a few minutes, novices can be as much as an hour out – largely because they don't spend any time figuring out what their goal race pace should be.

To determine your goal race pace and estimated finish time, look closely at the times and speeds you have accomplished in your training. If, for example, you have run 18 miles at a speed of 9 minutes per mile in your training (and felt shattered afterwards), let's face it, it is unlikely that you'll be able to run a further 8 miles at the same speed on race day. But slowing your pace by an extra 30 to 60 seconds a mile will make the race far more comfortable, and your likelihood of success far greater. If this is your first marathon, be conservative in your target – the idea is to complete, not compete.

Another useful way of gauging your likely finish time is to use your performance times over shorter distances, such as 10 km races or half marathons, as a basis. As a very general guideline, doubling your half marathon time and adding 10–20 minutes gives an estimated marathon time. A slightly more accurate approach is to use a race pace calculator, which you can find on many running websites. These calculators are based on mathematical formulae – they don't simply multiply your time by the increased distance you'll be racing at.

Once you have established your target time, calculate what speeds you should run at to get consistent split times for each mile, and when the start gun sounds try to achieve this pace immediately – your goal should be to try to run the 26th mile at the same pace as the first or, better still, a little faster! Haile Gebrselassie broke the 10 km world record by varying his pace by less than 1 second per lap for 23 of the 25 laps – he even sped up on the last two. Of course, he didn't have thousands of other runners jostling for space with him in the opening kilometres, which is why marathoners often aim for a 'negative split', in which you run the second half of the race slightly faster than the first. Whether you go for a negative split, or even splits, you certainly don't want to be slowing down as the miles pass. See over the page for how to work out your split times.

How to work out your splits

Simply convert your target time to minutes, then divide by 26.2. You'll end up with a 'decimal' number, which you then need to convert to minutes and seconds to give you a split time for each mile.

Example

Target time: 3 hr 40 min = 220 min
220 divided by 26.2 = 8.40
8.40 = 8 min 24 sec per mile

The next stage is to work out the accumulative time for each mile.

Example

8 min 24 sec per mile means that at mile 3, your watch should read 25.12

Take your split times with you on race day. 'Pace bands' are often available at large race registration expos, or you can download them from some running websites. These give you your splits for each mile, based on a set finish time, such as 3 hours 45 minutes or 4 hours 20 minutes, and save you having to do the maths yourself. Another option is to write your key split times upside down on your race number, so you can glance at them with ease. Do use your split times. They are there to enable you to make any necessary adjustments to your pace, not as decoration!

The taper caper

As you now know, running causes muscle damage, to which the body has to adapt. It also expends energy and depletes carbohydrate stores in muscle. To maximise your recovery and optimise the chances of a great race, you need to give the body plenty of time to repair the muscle damage, replenish carbohydrate stores and rest weary limbs. The decrease in training volume leading up to a big event is called the taper. A proper taper will give you some mental drive, too, so that you line up at the start feeling raring to go.

How to taper

As you will see in the training programmes on pages 169–189, the last long run takes place three weeks before race day; after that, run training volume is steadily reduced. Research undertaken at Ball State University found that this is the optimum amount of time between the last hard effort and the race itself – some coaches even recommend doing your final long run four weeks before race day. Whatever you do, though, don't be tempted to squeeze in another long run beyond three weeks out.

While you could be forgiven for worrying that you will 'lose' your fitness during the taper, bear in mind that many of the adaptations that have taken place are enduring ones, such as an increased number and size of mitochondria in the muscle cells, an increased volume of red blood cells, and stronger muscle fibres. Research shows that, by reducing your training volume to a third of your highest level, you would be able to maintain your cardiovascular fitness for around eight weeks, so don't worry about a mere three weeks causing a decline in your potential. In fact, one study found that a good taper yielded a 3 per cent improvement in race time. That equates to knocking 9 minutes off a 5-hour marathon. If you are tempted to cram in extra running, remind yourself that there is very little to be gained in the way of endurance, speed or strength now.

It is not unusual to feel suddenly lethargic and heavy during the taper. This is partly because your glycogen stores are full (since you aren't continually depleting them with training), and each gram of glycogen stores with it 3 grams of water. Your body has also become accustomed to a large volume of activity, and removing this from the equation can leave you feeling as if you could barely run a mile, let alone a marathon. Don't see this as a sign to go out for a gruelling training run; simply ensure that you aren't overeating and that you are well hydrated, and have confidence in the training you've done.

That said, one of the most important, and often overlooked, aspects of a taper is that while you are reducing overall volume, you should not be reducing intensity. For example, you may still include an interval session but instead of doing six 4-minute reps, you might only do two to four reps. Keeping some pacier work in your schedule helps you to maintain your speed and strength. One study from the University of East Carolina found that athletes who reduced their overall training volume by 70 per cent but still included daily race-pace intervals knocked an average of 29 seconds off their 5 km run time. I'm not suggesting you do daily interval sessions, but you get the picture!

It's worth sticking to grass and other more forgiving surfaces on your taper period runs, to reduce the amount of impact and muscle damage. But be extra vigilant on uneven ground.

A sports massage in the final week (perhaps after your last long run the week before the marathon) can help alleviate any tightness and encourage blood flow and recovery in the muscles. Don't leave it to the day before, though, as it may leave you feeling low on energy – and don't have one if you have never had one before. Remember the rule: never try anything new at this late stage of the game.

Try to get plenty of rest during the last few days, too. Avoid spending more time than you have to on your feet, or engaging in tiring activities such as gardening or DIY. Even if you don't sleep well the night before, you will be fine so long as you are well rested in the lead-up to the event.

Pace groups

A common feature of larger and big city marathons these days are 'pace groups'. These are set up with 'leaders' whose role is to run the race at a constant pace to achieve a set time, say 4 hours. Pacers are normally advertised well in advance of the race, so check the pre-race details to see if they will be present at your marathon, and where to find them at the start. There's no obligation to stay in the group just because you start with them – but doing at least the first few miles with a pace group can help prevent you overdoing it in the early stages of the race and blowing your chances.

Adjusting your diet

Your training isn't the only thing you need to taper in these final weeks – food and fluid intake need addressing, too. You will have become accustomed to eating more than usual for a few months but, now that you are not training so much, you need to make sure you don't take too many calories on board. And, because of the importance of carbohydrate to your running performance, you need to maximise your glycogen stores by increasing the carb content of your diet in the days leading up to the race (*see* the 'carbo-loading' panel). That doesn't mean you need to eat pasta for breakfast lunch and dinner, but it does mean that you should ensure you have carbo-hydrate at every meal. Equally, remember that carbohydrate means cereal, pasta, potatoes, rice, bread products, bananas, dried fruit and starchy vegetables – not pastries, biscuits, cakes, pizza, flap-jacks and crisps!

The taper period is the ideal time to do a 'meal-time race rehearsal' – in other words, have your pre-race supper the night before, and your pre-race breakfast the morning before one of your final training runs, to ensure that it all feels comfort-able and nothing repeats on you or causes gastrointestinal distress.

Research suggests that plenty of vitamin E and C

Carbo-load wisely

Carbo-loading is one of those phrases that has made its way into the public domain, but what does it really mean? Well, the original strategy was to deplete glycogen stores by cutting out carbohydrate from the diet (and running) for three to four days. Then, a few days before a race, you would pile on the carbs, in the hope that your 'hungry' glycogen stores would snap them all up and overcompensate by taking on more than they would have done previously. While this strategy can work, it can also leave you feeling sluggish, or bloated and heavy. And research now indicates that you can fare just as well when you skip the depletion phase and simply increase your carbohydrate intake over the three to seven days leading up to the race, while simultaneously reducing mileage. According to sports nutritionist Nancy Clark, a gain of 2–3 lb of weight indicates successful carbo-loading.

in the weeks prior to the race will reduce muscle damage and aid recovery. Step up your intake of vitamin C- and E-rich fruits and vegetables. But if you are susceptible to the runner's trots, avoid high-fibre foods for 48 hours before the race.

The final 24 hours

The race is just 24 hours away now! You may well be spending much of this day travelling. If not, then make the most of it and relax. Get out some uplifting DVDs (*Chariots of Fire*, anyone?) and relax in front of the TV, read an absorbing book or go for a gentle stroll in the fresh air. This is also the ideal time to do your final check of all your kit and race instruc-tions, and revisit the mental strategies on page 83. Many coaches recommend a short run the day before the race (but make sure you have had a complete rest day the day before that). The benefits of running the day before are probably more mental than phys-ical, but it's a good idea to remind your legs what running feels like! Don't overdo it, though: a 20-minute jog, with a few short bouts at your marathon pace, is perfect.

Make sure you are hydrating well in the final 24 hours, by sipping fluids little and often. Don't be afraid to have the odd cup of tea or coffee if you usually do, but don't go overboard on the caffeine, and avoid eating or drinking anything that you are not used to.

A lot of emphasis is placed on the 'last supper', what with pasta parties and carbo-loading strate-gies, but ideally the largest meal on the eve of race day should be eaten earlier in the day, and just a light snack taken in the evening. Why? Well, a heavy meal won't help you sleep well, and it may also mean you wake up feeling sluggish. If you don't fancy a big lunch – or can't practically arrange to eat at lunchtime, at least have your evening meal early to allow plenty of time to digest the food. Talking of digestion, there is more information on gastric upsets on page 118, but you may want to avoid gas-producing foods in your last pre-race meals – such as cabbage, Brussels sprouts, beans, pulses and high-fibre cereals. Drinking alcohol isn't advisable the night before your marathon, but one glass of wine or beer shouldn't hurt if it will help you to relax. Remember to balance it out with lots of other non-alcoholic fluids, too. Finally, don't go to bed feeling hungry. If you're peckish, have some toast or cereal to take the edge off.

Although in theory you ought to go to bed early to get plenty of rest, many people end up lying in bed thinking about the day ahead. Don't get stressed if you find yourself wide awake at 3 o'clock in the morning – it's your muscles, not your brain, that benefit most from sleep and you'll still be able to run well even if you have spent most of the night staring at the bedroom ceiling! A milky drink before bed and a warm (not hot) bath may help you relax and feel sleepy enough for bed. Interestingly, a study by the Social Research Issues Centre in Oxford found that runners in the London Marathon who had sex the night before ran, on average, 5 minutes faster than those who abstained. The researchers weren't sure why, but there's a good chance that it could help to dispel pre-race tension and aid sleep.

why we are here

Regular runners have a lifetime heart attack mortality risk some 70 per cent lower than sedentary people.

⁖Seeing success
MENTAL STRATEGIES TO GET YOU IN THE RIGHT FRAME OF MIND FOR THE RACE

With race day fast approaching, you may suddenly be feeling as if your stomach is tying itself in knots, and doubting whether you really can achieve this goal of yours. Don't worry, these feelings are normal, and they can be used to your advantage, to get you into the right state of readiness for the race – what sports psychologists call your 'zone of optimal functioning'.

Psyching up – or chilling out
When we talk about stress we normally mean it in a negative way, but stress, physiologically speaking, isn't necessarily a bad thing: it's simply our body's way of preparing to deal with an oncoming challenge or situation.

What is more relevant, in performance terms, is the *level* of stress, or 'arousal', that you experience prior to performance. The signs of arousal are both physiological and psychological: the former include raised heart rate, muscle tension, breathing rate, blood pressure, clammy palms, 'butterflies' and general sweating. Psychological telltale signs are feelings of anxiety, fear and self-doubt. You often hear people talking about getting psyched up to perform, but there's a fine line between being primed for performance and being too hyped to focus properly. The ideal level of arousal differs from person to person, and it's important that you learn what your ideal level is so that you can prepare adequately for your marathon. Some runners will thrive on the tension that builds before a big race, while others will be in and out of the loo, their stomachs in knots. So what about you? Do you like to get pepped up to perform, or do you feel the need to remain calm and keep a hold on your nerves?

One of the best ways to determine which of these sounds like you is to look back to how you felt prior to other big events in your life. Ideally, these would be other races, but anything that presented a big challenge will do. Did you feel like sitting on your own, collecting your thoughts, or did you want to tear the phone book in half and let out an animal roar? These signs indicate whether you need to look at psyching up or chilling out to get in the zone. Once you've decided which is you, follow the guidelines suggested below to find some useful strategies that should help you get your butterflies flying in formation.

Me, nervous?

Here are some of the less obvious signs of anxiety and stress:

- feelings of fatigue
- nausea
- flushed skin
- yawning
- voice distortion
- desire to urinate
- 'cotton' feeling in mouth
- trembling muscles/muscular tension.

Strategies to psych up

Play it again
Before a training run or race, listen to tunes that fire you up. Research by sport psychologists at Brunel University found that music can positively affect your mood, elevate your heart rate and reduce anxiety. Ideally, the music should match the heart rate at which you plan to work, give or take a few beats. The songs should make you feel good and increase your energy levels – so don't just pick something with 155 bpm that you actually detest, like thrash metal. The researchers found that exercisers were more likely to get in the zone when they rated the music being played highly. You may want to listen to music on your way to the race, or take an MP3 player to listen to while you warm up.

Activate!
Self-activation is an umbrella term that covers all manner of weird and wonderful ways athletes psych themselves up. Tennis player Jimmy Connors used to slap himself on the thigh prior to a match; many athletes make use of the crowd, encouraging them to make a noise and get excited, in order to get themselves in the right state of mind. While you might have trouble with the latter strategy ('Who's that nutter shouting at us over there?'), bantering with club mates, playing with your dog or kids, or firing off some brisk 'strides' might help.

Make a picture
Visualisation can be a great way of priming yourself for a race or training run. Use your visualisation skills to create a picture of yourself running comfortably and steadily – passing those who set off too fast and are now tiring. Feel how ready your muscles are for the challenge, how your feet are itching to get moving, your heart rate already elevating in anticipation.

Strategies to chill out

Say 'om'
Learning to meditate can be a valuable tool in your marathon survival kit, particularly if you get very

nervous before a race. By focusing on a single thought, sound or object, or simply your breathing, you will be able to quieten your mind and switch off from niggling worries and fears. Research shows that meditation can alter the pattern of alpha waves in the brain and invoke a relaxation response. There are many different types of meditation, including transcendental meditation, in which you have your own personal mantra to focus upon.

Take a breather

Utilising a longer exhalation than the length of the inhalation induces a feeling of calm. Breathe in for a count of four, allowing the abdomen to swell as your diaphragm rises. Hold for a count of four, then exhale for a count of six, pulling belly button to spine as you expel the air slowly.

Tune in

Just as music can psych you up before a race, it can also be used to calm and soothe nerves. Brunel University researchers found that Japanese classical music increased alpha activity in the brain, associated with relaxation. It doesn't have to be classical, but if you're opting for folk or love songs, make sure that the music you select doesn't have any negative connotations.

Reframe the situation

What we perceive of a situation and the reality are often very different. Imagine, for example, that you are scared of house spiders, and there is one on the bedroom wall. While the objective situation is that there is a small, harmless creature in your bedroom, your perception is likely to engender fear, anxiety and revulsion. However, the process of cognitive restructuring is used to 'reframe' the situation in a more positive light. Here's an example that might relate to your race-day nerves. You are lining up for the race, and your heart's racing, your tummy tumbling and your skin tingling – the accompanying thought might be, 'God, I'm nervous.' This could be restructured as, 'All my body's signals say it's raring to go. I am ready to perform.'

Give yourself a talking to

'I'll never make it. What if I get a stitch? I bet I hit the wall and have to drop out or walk the rest of the way . . .'. Sound familiar? These are some classic examples of negative self-talk. You might think talk is cheap but there's a lot of evidence that the way you talk to yourself has a profound effect on your self-esteem and confidence, and can influence your behaviour. Positive self-talk is associated with improved performance while negative self-talk can be detrimental. Your subconscious is listening . . .

Pre-performance rituals

Research suggests that mental state prior to performance affects mental state *during* performance – so it's essential to go in to your race with the right mindset. While the psyching up and chilling out strategies will certainly help you achieve this, creating a 'pre-performance ritual' for yourself is a highly effective way of priming you for the race.

A pre-performance ritual is simply a routine that you practise in training, and always do before a race. Once the pre-performance ritual is complete, it acts as a mental 'trigger' that tells you, 'OK, time to race.' Pre-performance rituals practised by sports stars are as diverse and numerous as the athletes themselves, and there is no point in copying what someone else does. Experiment with a few different strategies along the way, but ensure that you end up with an easy-to-follow, consistent routine.

Another great way to get geared up is to create a 'circle of excellence'. This is a technique derived from NLP – neurolinguistic programming – and its purpose

is to create a 'virtual toolbag' of all the positive resources you may need for your marathon. For example, let's say you feel you need confidence, determination, discipline and focus. Start by drawing an imaginary circle on the floor (big enough to stand on). Stand close by, and think back to a situation when you felt totally confident. Remember, using all your senses, what it felt like. As soon as you can feel it, step into your circle to deposit it there, stepping out again as the feeling fades. Repeat this sequence with the other

attributes you need until you have all your required resources in the circle. Then simply 'pack your circle' away in your pocket, behind your ear or under your watch, until the big day, when you will unpack it and step inside, until you are glowing with excellence . . .

A winning vision

'In the last two or three days before race day, visualise yourself at various points in the race – particularly focus on crossing the finish line. When I won the London Marathon I found myself daydreaming on the last few long runs of pulling away from the pack and crossing the line with my arms raised. On the day it worked out just like that and I had the confidence to make my move 4 miles from the end because I really believed I could win.'
Mike Gratton, winner of the London Marathon, 1983

why we are here

Running makes you more resilient to stress. Volunteers subjected to extreme cold, excessive noise or unpleasant pictures were less stressed by the experience after they had been running than they were after sitting quietly.

⁝ The last resort

A SURVIVAL STRATEGY FOR COMPLETING THE RACE WHEN TRAINING HASN'T GONE TO PLAN

You may have been struck down with flu for a month, you may have been given a huge project with a hideous deadline at work, or you may simply have failed to pull your finger out – whatever the reason, you haven't managed to get the training in, and you are now wondering whether you can make it to the finish line.

Well, you have two options: you pull out of the race, and perhaps defer your entry to next year (not all races will allow this), or find another event later in the calendar; or you adjust your goals ('Oh well, I'm probably not going to win this year . . .') to something that befits the amount of training you have achieved.

If you haven't managed to run 15 miles in training, I don't recommend trying to run the marathon. There is simply too much uncharted territory to take on. But you could walk/run it, and this is where my 'last resort' plan comes in.

The 'last resort' is a walk/run programme that should get you round the course in one piece, if not, perhaps, as fast as you had first envisaged. Having said that, many people have successfully used a walk/run strategy to help them improve their finish time, not just get round the course. According to Jeff Galloway, a leading proponent of the walk/run protocol, the average improvement made by veteran marathon runners who adopted the strategy instead of running continuously was 13 minutes. 'Mentally, [the walk/run sessions] are a way to break up the marathon into segments that are doable,' he says. 'Physically, they allow the muscles to recover before they hit the wall.' Galloway also insists that many sub-3-hour runners have successfully used a walk/run race plan.

Before we look at how to put the last resort plan into action, a word about injury. This plan is not designed for people to 'get round' the marathon while still battling with an injury. If you are still rehabilitating from an injury (in other words, if the problem has not yet been resolved), it is not advisable to take part.

Rule 1

Walk/run from mile 1. Not from when your legs begin to feel a bit tired, but from the very beginning. What should the breakdown of walking and running be? It depends on how far you progressed with your long runs.

:: If you didn't make it beyond 13 miles, then walk for 1 minute after every 5 minutes of running.

:: If you managed a run of 14–16 miles in training, run until you hit each mile marker and then walk for 2 minutes.

:: If you got close to 17–18 miles, I suggest walking for 1 minute after passing each mile marker.

If you feel self-conscious about walking, particularly in the early stages of the race, pretend to be adjusting your race number, taking a drink or stretching. Ignore spectators urging you to get running again! 'The most important walk breaks are the early ones,' says Galloway. If you feel absolutely great by mile 22, then you could risk cutting the walk breaks to 30 seconds, or even doing away with them altogether; but *don't* be tempted to do this earlier in the race.

Rule 2

Try to practise your walk/run protocol at least a few times in training before race day to get an idea of how it feels, and to determine your exact walk/run breakdown.

Rule 3

Use sports drink instead of water to rehydrate. Not only because it will provide you with extra energy, but because you are more at risk of hyponatraemia at a very slow pace, and the salts contained within an isotonic drink will help prevent it.

Rule 4

Remember to body scan. Don't be afraid to stop and stretch out anything that feels tight or tense – you aren't racing the clock now.

Rule 5

Read the mental strategies on pages 130–133 to help your brain get you round the course, and check out the race tactics on pages 141–142.

Rule 6

This is a last-resort strategy – but it isn't infallible; if you are feeling really terrible on the way round, you may have to consider dropping out.

race day success

:: The practicals
LAST-MINUTE PREPARATION AND CONSIDERATIONS

What will probably be one of the most memorable days of your life – one way or another – has finally arrived. The key to making it memorable in a good way is to be meticulously prepared, both mentally and physically, and to have the common sense to be flexible enough to adapt your plans. Preparing properly means adopting a strategy for the day – not just the race – so that you can approach your marathon with quiet confidence.

Breakfast time
Research suggests that eating 2 to 4 hours before you run gives you the best chance of topping up fuel stores without causing gastrointestinal discomfort. It's down to personal taste, but make sure you've given this important final meal a try in your race rehearsal. The ideal pre-race meal should include a little fat and protein and a lot of carbohydrate. It could be porridge, breakfast cereal with milk, toast with scrambled or

boiled egg, or a bagel with peanut butter and banana. Avoid high-fibre foods if you are susceptible to tummy upsets. If you usually have a cup or two of tea or coffee in the morning, by all means have them. (It helps many a runner go to the toilet, which is one thing you then won't have to worry about!)

What if you feel too nervous to eat?

It really is advisable to eat something; you need to top up the calories your body has burned through sleeping. In a study on cyclists, a 400-calorie breakfast 3 hours before a ride to fatigue enabled them to go for an average of 27 minutes longer than when they just had water. If you can't face solids, then have a liquid breakfast – an energy drink that you are familiar with, a smoothie or even a meal-replacement drink.

What to wear

There isn't anything magical about race kit – it's simply the training kit that you feel most comfortable and happy in, and that suits the conditions you'll be racing in. Take a close look at the weather forecast for race day, and plan accordingly, but have contingency kit for all weather options – you never know what might happen on the day (see pages 42–45 for more information). If it's a morning race, the start is almost certainly going to be during the coolest part of the day. The ubiquitous dustbin liner, with holes cut out for your head and arms, will help conserve body heat and keep light rain off, too. It can easily be discarded once the race is under way.

Even if race morning is a little chilly, don't be tempted to wear too much clothing – you'll be out there a long time, and the chances are that the temperature will increase as the day progresses – not to mention your own body temperature, which will rise as you get into your stride.

Once you leave your accommodation (or home) there'll be no going back for things you've forgotten. It's advisable to have a list of essentials (use the checklist on pages 122–124 as your basis) on which you can tick off items as you put them on, or in your bag.

Peace of mind

There's no way of guaranteeing that things won't go wrong on race day, but being well organised certainly minimises the chances. Think of things that have gone wrong before, either in training or racing, and be prepared for such eventualities should they occur. For example, if you had to make a dash behind the nearest tree because of runner's trots, taking an anti-diarrhoea remedy such as Immodium on race day is a wise precaution. If you got freezing cold waiting for the race to start, make sure you have plenty of warm clothing. If you spent ages wandering around, stiff and tired, post-race because you hadn't made a clear arrangement with friends and family about where to meet, make sure that the plan is set in concrete this time round!

:• Race day: on the run
MAKING IT SUCCESSFULLY TO THE START LINE – AND THE FINISH LINE

The start

You've made it to the start! Congratulations. Take comfort in the fact that London Marathon statistics show that 98 per cent of those who make it to the start line will make it to the finish line.

If you are well organised, you will have time to kill once you reach the start area of the race – there are still a few tasks to do, such as dropping off your baggage, making final kit choices, visiting the loo (quite possibly, more than once) and warming up. The order in which you do these things depends on whether you are alone or with supporters, your frame of mind and what the weather is like (you don't want to be standing around shivering in your race kit, for example, because you got rid of your baggage too early). In the final hour, top up your energy levels with a sports drink, or a high GI snack, such as an energy gel or bar, jelly babies or Jaffa cakes (whatever you have practised in training) along with some water.

Don't warm up too long before the race begins or you'll only get cold again. You don't need to do much in the way of warming up anyway, as it isn't as if you are going to set off at top speed. And since the first mile is likely to be slow (at least in mass-participation events) you can use that time to gradually pick up the pace. Do some gentle mobilisations, and jog for 5 to 10 minutes – then stretch if you want to. Don't, however, start doing stretches that you've just spotted another runner doing – you shouldn't be doing anything that isn't a tried and tested part of your routine.

On your marks

- :• Get into your start area with plenty of time to spare, and keep moving to avoid getting cold or stiff.

- :• Be prepared to take a few minutes to cross the start line if you are taking part in one of the big city marathons. You don't need to panic about time ticking away, most races now use chip timing, so your personal time starts only when you cross the start line mats.

- :• Be vigilant about other runners and the myriad clothing, binliners and fluid containers that inevitably litter the ground. This is not a time to take a tumble!

- :• Check your shoelaces are fastened.

- :• Check that your stopwatch is ready for the off, if you are wearing one, and remember to start it when you begin running.

- :• Chat to other runners if it helps you relax, or focus internally if you find that more calming.

- :• Do not set off too fast. It will be tempting – the cheering crowds, the mass of fellow runners, the sheer relief of having made it this far . . . but avoid a fast start at all costs. Studies suggest that when marathon runners begin the race at a pace that is just 2 per cent faster than the pace they have practised in training, they struggle in the final 6 miles of the event.

One final tip: *enjoy yourself!* There will never be another first marathon for you, so enjoy it to the max. Don't be too hung up over your finish time (whatever it is, it will be a PB!), and soak up the atmosphere as much as possible.

spectators, and give a confident stance rather than one that looks as if you're slowly wearing yourself into the ground.

∴ Once you are on the final few miles, pick out a runner and try to catch them up. Even if you don't manage it, it gives you something to focus on as you dig deep into your final reserves of energy.

Fuel on the run – what, when and how much?

It used to be illegal to drink during a marathon race – now, the medical profession is somewhat wiser and recommends that every runner should drink regularly throughout. Even a 2 per cent level of dehydration can reduce performance by as much as 5 per cent, so drinking correctly is as important to getting a good time as it is to safeguarding your health.

As you approach a drinks station, try to make eye contact with someone holding a drink out so that they know you are going to take it from them. This saves you missing out, or having a drink extended in front of you that ends up down your T-shirt. Some runners can drink and run at the same time – there's a bit of a knack to it that involves taking sips while 'closing' the epiglottis, before allowing the liquid to go down the throat. Others prefer to slow to a walk – or even stop – to prevent a choking fit, and to ensure they actually get some of the liquid down their gullet! If you are going to stop to drink, don't park yourself in front of the drinks station itself, but move on and stand to the side.

Water or sports drink?

The research certainly falls in favour of sports drinks when looking at an endurance event as long as the marathon. It's worth researching whether sports drinks are going to be provided at your chosen race, so you can then try out that particular brand and see how you get on with it.

If you can't stomach sports drinks, you'll need to rehydrate with water alone, but you could consider taking on extra fuel in the form of easy-to-digest snacks. The amount you should drink is dependent on the weather, the speed with which you are likely to finish the race and your personal hydration habits. If there are drinks stations at every mile, you won't need to stop at them all, but you should certainly be aiming for a drink every 15–30 minutes.

Should you eat during the race?

When you exercise, blood flow to the digestive system is greatly reduced. Anything solid you consume will take a long time to digest, and could end up causing stomach problems, as well as taking a while to boost your energy levels. If you do decide to take a snack on the run, choose something that is high in carbohydrate – particularly foods high on the glycaemic index – and easy to stomach. Jelly babies or wine gums fit this category; be wary about eating the ubiquitous orange segments that are frequently on offer – orange is a high-fibre food and may cause stomach problems. As with sports drinks, try eating on the run in training first, not just on race day. A final consideration as far as food is concerned is salt. This is particularly important if it is a hot day, you are a slower runner or if you aren't using isotonic sports drinks. A salty snack, such as mini-rice cakes or pretzels, can help you maintain sodium levels and reduce the risks of hyponatraemia.

The finish line

As you turn on to the home straight of your race, with the finish line in sight for the first time, it can be a very emotional experience. It's quite common to find a sudden surge of energy that has you almost sprinting the last few yards rather than jogging. That's why it is a good idea to familiarise yourself with the race route – so that you know when it's safe to use up every last drop of energy. (In my first ever marathon, I saw the 26-mile marker and sprinted. I forgot that there was still another 385 yards to go and, believe me, they hurt!) If there's a camera at the finish taking souvenir photos, ensure you look up at it, smile and don't obscure your race number with your arms. As you cross the line, stop your watch and keep moving. Don't come to a complete halt too quickly, since this might make you feel dizzy or nauseous. As you make your way to the reuniting point or baggage area, use the foil blanket, if you are given one, since your body temperature will drop quickly. Soak up the atmosphere and allow your accomplishment to sink in – you are a hero!

Dropping out

There are times in most people's marathons when the thought of dropping out pops into their heads. This is a tough physical and mental challenge, and you aren't necessarily going to be smiling the whole way round. If it's general fatigue rather than a specific problem that's putting you off, dig deep into your mental and physical reserves to keep going (*see* the strategies on page 83). If, however, you feel incapable of making it to the finish, and believe that to try to do so would be detrimental to your health, it is wise to live to fight another day, rather than push yourself beyond your limits and end up ill or badly injured. If you suffer from repeated diarrhoea or vomiting on the way round, feel dizzy or faint, or get chest pain accompanied by severe breathlessness, stop at an aid station for medical assistance.

Dropping out of your marathon is bound to be a difficult decision to make – months of training and hard work, possibly with the added burden of sponsorship money, are inevitably big incentives to continue, but you must heed your body's warning signs if you are feeling unwell. Once you've taken the decision to pull out, make sure you let someone involved in the race organisation know, and seek assistance to get back to the finish area (or start). Some marathons arrange buses or trains to help runners who have had to stop, but this isn't always possible at events where there are fewer runners and miles of open roads. This is when that money in your sock may prove invaluable.

⠿ The road to recovery

HOW CAN YOU ASSIST THE RECOVERY PROCESS?
HOW LONG BEFORE YOU SHOULD START RUNNING AGAIN?

It's all over – you've done it. Whether it was 26.2 miles of torture, or – I hope – a triumphant journey that will stay with you for the rest of your life, it's important to give some thought to a proper strategy for recovery, both to make it through the rest of the day on a high note and also so that normal life can resume as quickly as possible.

Post-race survival

Get into some warm, dry clothes as soon as you can. The hours following the completion of a marathon are one time when stretching isn't particularly advisable, since the muscles are already likely to be inflamed and damaged. If possible, though, keep moving for 10 to 15 minutes after your run as a cool-down, rather than throwing yourself on to the nearest flat surface, which will only serve to stiffen you up further. There is some evidence that an ice bath can help reduce muscle soreness after hard exercise, but it's unlikely that this will be either convenient or appealing so soon after the race.

Your priority now should be to rehydrate and refuel. A sports drink is a good start, as it provides fluid, carbohydrate and electrolytes, but frankly, you may be sick to death of the taste of them by this stage. Water, along with a salty snack, will help to replace fluid and electrolytes, but get some carbs in swiftly, too – within 20 to 30 minutes is ideal as this is when those depleted glycogen stores are most receptive.

Aim to take in 1 g of carbohydrate for each kg of your body weight, along with 10–20 g of protein, to support muscle repair. A cheese or tuna sandwich might fit the bill, or you could opt for a milk-based drink. Research from Northumbria University found that chocolate milk was an effective post-exercise recovery aid. Alternatively, a proprietary recovery drink, a banana smoothie or even a skinny latte will provide the same nutrients. Also try to eat some fruit in the first couple of hours post-race, to boost your antioxidant levels. Continue to sip fluids throughout the day – dehydration will further lower your immunity, which will already have been compromised by the physical endeavour of running a marathon.

You may be in the mood to celebrate (and rightly so), but try to avoid alcohol for a few hours at least, until you've started to rehydrate and your urine output has returned to normal.

Give some thought to your post-race meal. Oily fish, rich in protein and omega-3s, will help muscle repair and dampen inflammation, while a good carbohydrate source, such as potatoes, rice or pasta, will help to restore your energy. Add plenty of fruit and vegetables for vitamins, minerals and antioxidants.

Making a quick recovery

For the first few days after the race you will almost certainly feel battered and sore – all those ground forces will have taken their toll on your skeleton (you'll have temporarily shrunk by 1 to 2 cm), while the repeated muscular contractions will have caused substantial microtrauma – tiny tears and bleeding within the muscle itself – which builds up pressure and causes pain. Ask any experienced marathoner when this is at its most severe, and they will tell you that two days after the race is the worst time, which is why the condition is known as delayed onset muscle soreness, or DOMS. During this time, simple activities,

like walking or going downstairs, can cause much agony, but are a great source of amusement to observing friends and family!

So is there anything you can do to minimise the symptoms? The evidence is equivocal. A study from the Queensland Academy of Sport in Australia looked at massage, ice baths, stretching, cooling down and plain old rest, and found that doing nothing worked just as well as all the other practices. However, other research published in the *International Journal of Sports Medicine* found that gentle activity aided lactate removal and improved later sports performance better than complete rest (although this was not after a marathon.)

Recovery aids

Sleep and rest Perhaps the most important recovery aid of all is rest. As you know, it is during rest that your body repairs and regenerates, so your need for rest is currently greater. Try to get plenty of sleep, and restrict yourself to gentle, low-impact activities.
Ice Paula Radcliffe is well known for her regular ice baths, but what does the evidence say about 'cryotherapy'? Queensland Academy research suggests that the effect is just analgesic – as in it numbs you to your pain, rather than actually alleviating it – but not all experts agree with this, saying that constricting the blood vessels is a good thing when there is so much inflammation in the body. The study found that contrast bathing – alternating hot and cold – was more effective than either cold-water or hot-water immersions. The easiest way to achieve this is to alternate the temperature of a shower from hot to cold. This is 30 seconds of each, three times. If there is no hot shower then use cold jets interspersed by rubbing with a towel.
Compression tights These tight-fitting garments assist with venous return (blood flow back to the heart) and studies have shown that they can help to accelerate recovery. Research last year, published in the *Journal of Sports Science and Medicine*, found that they worked by enabling faster cell repair. Look for tights that have 'graded' compression – in other words, the compression should be greatest at the bottom and exert less pressure further up.
Anti-inflammatories Drugs that fall into this class include ibuprofen and aspirin – they will help to reduce inflammation and soreness. The herbal remedy arnica has also been shown to act as an anti-inflammatory.
Echinacea Research has shown that in the first 48 hours after a marathon, your immune system is vulnerable, meaning that you are more likely to come down with anything that is going in the way of viruses and infections. Echinacea is a herb that can help support immunity.
Massage A sports massage will help rid the muscles of waste products and stimulate blood flow to assist repair and reduce stiffness. But save the massage until two to four days after your race, since it is likely that your muscles will be too sore before that.

What won't help your recovery, I'm afraid, is a hot bath. It might feel good, but heat is the last thing your muscles need right now. Alcohol, too, will hamper the body's ability to combat inflammation and soreness.

While general aches and pains are par for the course after a marathon, anything more specific should be looked at by a sports medicine specialist as soon as possible.

Mental recovery

One thing that is often overlooked in the post-marathon period is how you might feel psychologically. People are constantly saying, 'You must feel so proud', or 'I bet you are over the moon.' And yet, often, all you feel is a huge sense of anticlimax. It's not surprising – this race has taken over a great deal of your life for the last few months, and now it is all over, leaving one big empty space. As one runner so eloquently put it: 'Once over the line, the pounding and the pain may stop, but the aching exhaustion doesn't. Then the loneliness sets in, the anti-climax of finishing a marathon. The endless minutes of pain and emptiness when the crowds have disappeared, the challenge has been completed and you have no idea what to do with yourself!'

To come back to earth with less of a bang, it's a great idea to have something planned in the days following the race – a few days away, a celebratory gathering or dinner, or something else pleasurable to focus on. It will be a little while before you are back to any serious running, and then, of course, you can set your sights on another race.

Race review

In the meantime, one of the most valuable uses of your time is to do a race review. Think about every aspect of your performance and preparation to glean as much information as you can to put to future use.

What went right in your race? What went wrong? How was your choice of kit? Did your hydration strategy work? Did you have supporters at the places where you needed them most? And what about the training? Did you feel tired cardiovascularly, or was it your muscles that fatigued first? Do you think you should have done more long runs? Did you taper enough? Write down all your feedback – and when you come to do your next race, factor it in to your preparations.

When can I run again?

My recommendation is to lay off running for a full week, no matter how long the race took you. Not only because this optimises recovery, reduces your risk of contracting a virus due to a compromised immune system, and allows minor afflictions such as blisters and chafing to heal, but also because it gives you time to re-attune to normal life, spend some time with your family and friends, and take a genuine break from running. Studies show that people who rest for a whole week after the marathon actually perform better in subsequent training than those who attempt to run in the first few days. The body needs this time to replace energy stores and repair tissue damage, and there is no likelihood of any fitness being lost in such a short space of time. But the decision is yours.

If you feel up to it, you could do some gentle swimming or cycling towards the end of the week.

For some, it may be closer to a fortnight or a month before they feel recovered enough to take to the streets. When you do next decide to go for a run, do not have a particular goal in mind – simply run while it feels good and stop if it doesn't.

How long before I can race?

If you have been bitten by the racing bug as a result of your marathon journey, it probably won't be long before you are itching to enter another race. But don't be too quick to sign up for anything – racing demands a lot from the body and you need to allow plenty of time for recovery. An oft-quoted rule of thumb is to take one day for every mile you raced before entering another race. But when you've undertaken something as challenging as a marathon, a 26-day recovery is not sufficient. (Think of it this way, most elite marathoners only do one or two races per year.) I recommend leaving at least two to three months, preferably longer, before you sign up for another 26.2 or, indeed, something even more challenging! In the meantime, you could work on improving your performance over a shorter distance, such as 10 km. There is more information on events and races in Chapter 10.

10 the ultimate race guide

᪥ Choosing your event

HOW TO PICK A WINNING RACE

Marathon running is a sport the world just can't seem to get enough of. In 2007, a record number of marathons worldwide – 19 races – boasted more than 10,000 finishers, with ten events clocking more than 20,000. Globally, the number of marathon runners has increased by more than 10 per cent in the past decade. In addition, the number of women participating in marathons has rocketed from 10 per cent in 1980 to 40 per cent in 2007 (almost a third of runners in the 2008 London Marathon were female).

While the leading marathon runners are getting faster and faster, smashing world records for the marathon distance, the average finish time is getting slower. But that doesn't mean our running ability is diminishing, just that more and more 'recreational' runners are getting involved, who don't have lofty aspirations about sub-2.30 finish times. In 1980, the average American man finished a marathon in 3 hours 32 minutes. By 2007, that time had slowed to 4 hours 20 minutes. That's good news for marathon virgins, since it means you'll be in good company, even if you're closer to the back of the pack than to the leaders.

When you first consider running a marathon, it's usually the major, world-famous races that spring to mind. The top contenders read like a tour of the world's fashion epicentres: London, New York, Paris . . .

But while these races may be the biggest and best known, it doesn't mean they are the only marathons worth entering – so don't be despondent if you haven't managed to secure a place in one of them. There are still plenty of worthwhile events out there at which you can put all that training to good use. Besides offering diverse marathon experiences, some of the lesser-known and smaller races are easier to get into, have fewer organisational hassles and may even yield a faster finishing time, thanks to less crowding.

Picking your perfect race

There are many factors to consider when choosing the right race for you – from time of year to location, the size (and ability) of the field and the route itself. Do as much research as you can, asking other runners, looking at race reports and surfing the net – if you're in doubt about something, contact the race organisers to ask.

When thinking about timing, you need to consider the likely weather conditions at that time of year, as well as how long the date leaves you for training. Most marathons are held in spring and autumn, to increase the chances of good running conditions (most runners perform best at temperatures ranging from 10–12ºC), but there are some in which the inclement weather is all part of the challenge.

Think carefully about location when you are selecting a race. Are you willing to travel a long distance to make your marathon debut? And, if so, have you factored in how you might deal with travel

fatigue or jet lag? (You may need to build in more time to your travel plans.) Do you have willing friends or family to accompany you? It's not wise to race somewhere where you have no one to support you on the way round or offer assistance at the start and finish. If you decide to make your race part of a longer holiday, I recommend planning for the majority of the time to be post-race, otherwise it can hang over you and spoil your enjoyment.

It's definitely worth considering booking a race package if you are opting for an overseas race – this will include your race entry fee, along with accommodation and travel, and takes away the stress and uncertainty of turning up in a foreign place and not knowing what to do.

As far as race size is concerned – there's a lot to be said for the electric atmosphere of the huge city races like London and New York. But there are fewer hassles involved in getting to the start, dropping off baggage and picking up your race number in smaller events. (In fact, many smaller races send your number out to you in the post, so no registration is required.) That said, be wary of small local races, where there is likely to be little crowd support and a stronger, more experienced field.

Finally, consider the route. If you want to achieve a PB, you need to look for flat races without too many twists and turns, little wind and wide roads. Many of the big city marathons – including London, Berlin and Chicago – are pancake flat, which makes life a little easier. But if you do choose a hillier course, make sure you train for it. Other terrain issues to consider are the quality of the surface underfoot (London's tarmac is said to be easier on the joints than New York's concrete), the altitude (Madrid boasts Europe's highest city marathon), and the width and straightness of the course. You can download route maps for the majority of marathons from the event websites. Another factor to consider is the view. More than 45 per cent of people in a survey said that the scenery was an important consideration when choosing a race, so it's worth a second thought. While Rotterdam is renowned as one of the fastest marathons in the world, it's certainly not scenic, for example. And, depending on your point of view, routes that cover the same lap more than once can be motivating . . . or soul destroying.

More points to bear in mind before you sign up

:: What is the race cut-off time?

:: Do you have to register before race day? (You need to factor this in to your travel plans.)

:: How many drinks stations are there? Can you get sports drinks, or just water?

:: What time of day is the race held? (This may have a bearing on the time you need to get up as well as the weather conditions.)

:: Will it be easy for your supporters to make their way to different points along the course?

:: Will you get a decent medal?

:: What are the logistics like for getting to the start and, more importantly, from the finish?

Over the page, you'll find the lowdown on some of the biggest and best marathons around the world, as well as a few of the lesser-known alternatives to consider.

⠶ The world marathon guide

A GUIDE TO SOME OF THE MAJOR MARATHONS AROUND THE GLOBE, PLUS SOME QUIRKIER RACES TO CONSIDER

Berlin

Official name?
The Real Berlin International Marathon

When is it?
End of September

How many people run it?
There are more than 30,000 participants – including plenty of first-timers and overseas runners, though, interestingly, only a fifth are women; it's the third biggest marathon in the world.

What's the course like?
It's flat and fast – the scene of Haile Gebrselassie's world records in 2007 and 2008. The race starts and finishes in the same park and takes you past all the major landmarks in the former east and west areas of Berlin, finishing at the Brandenburg Gate. The cut-off time is a generous 6¼ hours – power walking is allowed, but Nordic walking poles are not permitted.

Why run it?
There's a good chance of achieving a good time, not just because of the course, but because of a fast and well-organised start. The million spectators and the sounds of 70 live bands along the route should help spur you on, too. The race might also appeal to those with a sense of history. In 1990, some 25,000 runners took the opportunity to run through the Brandenburg Gate, just three days before German reunification took place. There is a famously lively post-race party, and free massage at the finish!

Any downsides?
A pricey entry fee.

How can I find out more?
www.real-berlin-marathon.com

Testimonial
'Berlin is probably Europe's most exciting capital city and running the marathon is a great way to experience it. The start and finish are both in the Tiergarten, in the centre of Berlin, and are in strolling distance of central hotels. When I ran it in 2006 the weather was great and there was no need to leave kit at the start. The looping course also means it is great for spectators and we were cheered loudly all the way. The finish through the Brandenburg Gate is spectacular, and we regrouped on the steps of Germany's historic parliament building – the Reichstag. Organisation is slick, as you might expect, and free massages and beer at the finish were a bonus. The inline skaters marathon the day before on the same course, and the decent expo created a marathon buzz throughout the weekend.' *Jeff Pyrah, Guildford and Godalming Athletics Club*

Boston

Official name?
Boston Athletic Association Boston Marathon

When is it?
Held annually on the third Monday in April, which is Patriot's Day, a state-wide holiday in Massachusetts

How many people run it?
Over 20,000 – the strict age- and sex-related qualifying times mean they are the swifter runners, although if you enter via one of the accredited UK agents (*see* below), you don't need to meet the qualifying standards.

What's the course like?
Challenging, but scenic. It is a point-to-point undulating course finishing in the city centre, unlikely to produce a personal best. Although primarily a downhill race, there are plenty of climbs in between. Most notably, the suburb of Newton hosts seven hills, culminating with the infamous Heartbreak Hill. Though most of the hills are not particularly steep, the fact that they are later in the race makes them both physically and psychologically draining. The difficulty of the downhill sections also takes many runners by surprise, since the steep descents of the late miles torture their quads!

Why run it?
Boston is the oldest continuously held marathon in the world – first run in 1897. It's not the fastest marathon course, nor is it the most difficult, but it is arguably the most prestigious, thanks to the challenging qualifying times and the high calibre of international athletes. It is also renowned for great organisation. With over 500,000 enthusiastic spectators, Boston has a very special atmosphere.

Any downsides?
Not PB material. Challenging qualification times (for example, male age 18–34, 3 hr 10 min; female age 18–34, 3 hr 40 min) will exclude many runners. In 2007, 64 per cent of participants finished in under 4 hours.

How can I find out more?
Visit www.bostonmarathon.org or go via 209 Events or Sports Tours (*see* 'Further information', page 213).

Chicago

Official name?
The Bank of America Chicago Marathon

When is it?
Second Sunday in October (register from February)

How many people run it?
Around 30,000 finishers, with a good male/female split; it historically attracts a strong elite field, including runners such as Paula Radcliffe, but that's not to say it's not an event for beginners, as the course and organisation make for a smooth debut.

What's the course like?
The flat, single-loop course is recognised as one of the world's fastest, run along broad, uncongested streets with cityscape views. There are no significant hills on the course: the highest elevation is 24 feet and there is one slight incline in the final mile. The race starts and finishes at Grant Park on the shores of Lake Michigan, just 10 minutes from the city centre, and travels through 29 historic and diverse neighbourhoods on every side of the city. Runners have 6 hours and 30 minutes to complete the course, and those who have not finished will be required to use pavements adjacent to the course, and to obey all traffic signals and signs.

Why run it?
Event organisation is impressive, particularly at the start, where runners set off along the ten-lane Columbus Drive. Runners from 100 different countries participate, supported by more than 1.5 million spectators. Nike pacing teams pledge to get you round in anything from 3 hours to 5 hours 45 minutes. Gatorade and water are provided at drinks stations – bananas are on offer later on the course. A new, colour-coded event alert system (EAS) keeps participants up to date with the status of course conditions leading up to and on race day. The levels range from low (green) to moderate (yellow) to high (red) to extreme (which signals event cancellation) based on a variety of factors, including weather conditions.

Any downsides?
An uncivilised start time of 7.30 am. No option of deferring entry in the event of illness or injury.

How can I find out more?
Visit www.chicagomarathon.com or phone + (312) 904–9800 for entry details.

Testimonial
'The last few miles are probably the least populated crowd-wise so go out slow as there's little moral support to bring you home if you are struggling. There are fewer costumed folk as well – there are more serious runners. So if you feel like going as part of a six-man centipede you'll probably make more of an impact at a fancy dress-heavy event like the London Marathon.' *Shane Starling, Brighton & Hove Athletics Club*

Edinburgh

Official name?
The Albert Bartlett Edinburgh Marathon

When is it?
Late May/early June

How many people run it?
12,500 run the full race, with a further 4000 in four-person relay teams – making it the second biggest UK marathon after London.

What's the course like?
It's a point-to-point route, starting in the city centre, heading out past Arthur's Seat and then heading east along Portobello Promenade beside the Firth of Forth. You bypass the finish at around 8 miles, continuing east for a further 10 miles before doubling back on yourself to return to the finish at Musselburgh racecourse. From start to finish, it's slightly downhill.

Why run it?
The race was rated the fastest marathon in the UK by *Runner's World* magazine and it takes place in one of Europe's most beautiful cities. A comfortable 6½-hour cut-off time with a third of all participants being charity runners. Pleasant temperatures likely: around 17°C. Lucozade Sport provided at three drinks stations, water every 2–3 miles.

Any downsides?
Getting back to the city centre from Musselburgh has involved long delays in the past. The finish area can get a bit congested, although the race organisers have made changes to alleviate this for future races. Unpredictable Scottish weather!

How can I find out more?
Visit www.edinburgh-marathon.com. Entries open in September of the preceding year.

Testimonial
'Despite driving rain at the start, the streets were lined with umbrella-wielding spectators and there was a great atmosphere – but, further on, the race was less well supported, partly because it's difficult for spectators to follow the route on public transport. The course twists and turns a bit for the first few miles but once you're on the waterfront it's as straight as a die, good for getting into a rhythm. As far as PB potential is concerned, I ran an almost identical time at Edinburgh and London.' *Sam Murphy, East London Triathletes*

London

Official name?
The Virgin London Marathon (as from 2010, when Virgin takes over from Flora as the race's main sponsor)

When is it?
Mid-April

How many people run it?
Approximately 35,000 – roughly one third are women; world-class runners compete along with many club runners and 'fun runners'.

What's the course like?
Mostly flat (except a slight incline in the first quarter) and fast. It's a point-to-point course, starting on Blackheath and finishing in The Mall in central London.

Why run it?
It's the biggest mass-participation sporting event in the UK. There are 23 water stops, 6600 marshals, 440 feet of urinal troughs, 1400 St John Ambulance staff and 47 medical stations. London landmarks along the course include Canary Wharf, the *Cutty Sark*, Buckingham Palace and the Tower of London. For most runners it is the one million spectators and entertainers around the course that help to keep them on the move – it's been described as one long street party, rivalled only by New York's marathon for atmosphere. The emphasis on raising money for charity also means it has a high proportion of people in outlandish costumes running the race. Lucozade Sport is on offer at aid stations every 5 km, with water at every mile.

Any downsides?
It's notoriously tough to get in – many people try for years on the trot to get a place. The ballot entry system is now online only and registration opens the day after the race of the preceding year.

How can I find out more?
Visit www.virginlondonmarathon.com. Many people get their entries through charities, via the Golden Bond scheme. Approach individual charities or see the race website for details of the year's chosen causes.

Testimonial
'Every runner should "do London" once – it's especially good for beginners as it is superbly organised, from the day you get your acceptance to the moment you cross the finish line. The atmosphere and crowd support is so good, it's almost impossible to consider walking, or dropping out.' *Neil Shires, North Devon Road Runners, Lynton*

New York

Official name?
The ING New York City Marathon

When is it?
First Sunday in November

How many people run it?
Approximately 38,000 – New York has now taken the top spot as the world's biggest marathon with 38,607 finishers in 2007, including runners from 105 different nations, with the UK being particularly well represented.

What's the course like?
It runs through the streets of New York's five culturally and ethnically diverse boroughs: Staten Island, Brooklyn, Queens, the Bronx and Manhattan. The course starts on Staten Island and finishes in Central Park, where entertainment, food and drink are laid on. Hills, particularly in the last five miles, bridges and turns all add to the challenge.

Why run it?
The original big city marathon, New York was the model for many others around the world. There are hydration and fuel stations, medical support, music, baggage handling, security and the most enthusiastic race spectators anywhere – reputedly 2 million of them – creating an electric atmosphere. The mean average temperature for the time of year is a comfortable 11ºC, although that does mean you need extra gear to keep warm at the start.

Any downsides?
Recent reports suggest that organisation has become less efficient as the race continues to grow in size, with gridlock-style queues to and from the baggage drop-off and queues for transport to the start. There can be a long wait in the holding complex before the start of the race, due to the inordinately early hour at which the bus drops competitors off. Low PB potential.

How can I find out more?
Visit www.nycmarathon.org or contact UK agents, Sports Tours or 209 Events (*see* 'Further information', page 213).

Testimonial
'Running New York gave me the biggest buzz I could ever imagine getting, in the absence of running out on to the pitch at Twickenham or Wembley. Having done various other marathons and mass-participation events, I cannot think of one that comes close to NYC in terms of atmosphere, though the tough course means that, unless this is your first marathon, you are unlikely to set a PB. And be prepared: the logistics of getting nearly 40,000 runners to Staten Island make for a cold, long morning. The waiting around at the start, following your 6 am bus ride from Manhattan, can get pretty tedious – but it is soon forgotten as you ride the wave of emotion of 2 million New Yorkers shouting and cheering you round. The route takes you through parts of town that you would not normally see, before finishing in the stunning autumn beauty of Central Park. Enjoy!' *Peter Bovill, Serpentine Running Club*

Paris

Official name?
Marathon International de Paris

When is it?
Early April

How many people run it?
Approximately 20,000 – 16 per cent female.

What's the course like?

It's a swift course, with few undulations, that starts along the Champs-Elysées, passes through the Place de la Concorde, along the banks of the River Seine, and past Notre Dame and the Eiffel Tower. A gentle descent leads you to the finish at the Arc de Triomphe on Avenue Foch.

Why run it?

With over 150,000 spectators, it's reasonably lively, although there are a number of quieter areas towards the end. Apart from the prospect of combining it with a weekend of gastronomy and shopping, Paris is a good option because it's not too far from the UK to get to, and it's virtually at the same time of year as the London Marathon, which means that you can take advantage of UK training camps, races and seminars. As far as the race itself is concerned, it's known for being well organised from start to finish. Aid stations placed every 5 km offer water, dried fruit, oranges, bananas and sponges. The race puts on pacers for six different target times (from sub-3 hours to 4½ hours) – you'll be given a colour-coded bib based on your target time.

Any downsides?

It's not a good bet for slower runners, with one of the highest proportions of sub-3 runners of any big race. The time limit is 5 hours and 40 minutes. All runners need to provide a doctor's certificate, issued within the 12 months preceding the race, to be allowed to take part.

How can I find out more?

Visit www.parismarathon.com or, for package deals including race entry, travel and accommodation, contact Sports Tours or 209 Events (see 'Further information').

Testimonial

'Paris was the most beautiful city I'd ever visited, and the course the most scenic I'd ever run. There was not a dull kilometre on the route! Starting in the shadow of the Arc de Triomphe on Champs-Elysées made a picture-perfect start as thousands of athletes flooded down the straight, tree-lined avenue through the heart of Paris.' *Cameron Burt, Hares & Hounds Running Club, Glasgow*

Stockholm

Official name?
Stockholm Marathon

When is it?
End of May

How many people run it?
18,500 people enter the race – more than 8500 are from overseas.

What's the course like?
The scenic two-lap course starts and finishes at the 1912 Olympic Stadium and runs through central Stockholm's 14 islands, along beautiful waterways, through the woods of the Royal Park, and past the sights of the city, including the Royal Palace, City Hall, Houses of Parliament and the Royal Opera House. The elevation from start to finish is just 29 metres. There's a 6-hour cut-off point.

Why run it?
Considered by many to be one of the best marathons in the world, the Stockholm Marathon is ranked number one by the *Ultimate Guide to International Marathons*. Top marks were given for course beauty, race organisation and appropriateness for first-timers. There are pace groups for runners from 3 hours to 5½ hours. The atmosphere is excellent, with hundreds of thousands of spectators offering encouragement on the way round, and beers and hot dogs on offer at the finish! If the weather is hot (18ºC is typical), a few shower stalls are located along the course. A very civilised 2 pm start time. Convenient to start and finish in the same place.

Any downsides?
Like other Scandinavian countries, Sweden can be expensive. It can be hot for marathon running in May. Lap races can be a little less interesting than single-loop courses.

How can I find out more?
Visit www.stockholmmarathon.se, call +46-8 545 66 440 or go via UK agents (*see* 'Further information', page 213).

❖ And a few less obvious races to consider . . .

Loch Ness

When? Early October

Who? Around 6000 runners

What? The Baxters Loch Ness Marathon follows a spectacular point-to-point route through stunning Highland scenery, along the south-eastern shores of Loch Ness (offering a monster-spotting distraction), and then crosses the River Ness to finish in Inverness Queens Park Stadium.

Visit www.lochnessmarathon.com

Tresco

When? The same day as the London Marathon (April)

Who? 125 runners

What? Seven and a half undulating laps of the beautiful island of Tresco, one of the Isles of Scilly, positioned off Cornwall in the Atlantic. Caught in the Gulf Stream, the island boasts palm trees, cacti and white beaches. Runners must pledge to raise £500 for cystic fibrosis charities.

Visit www.tresco.co.uk/about-tresco/marathon/Tresco-Marathon.asp

Safaricom

When? Late June

Who? 750 runners – locals plus a large number of UK and US participants

What? A marathon that raises funds for conservation, education, healthcare and community development projects in northern Kenya. The two-lap marathon is run on dirt roads through the Lewa Wildlife Conservancy, and is billed as one of the ten toughest in the world due to its altitude, climate and harsh terrain. Armed vehicles keep a lookout for hostile wildlife!

Visit www.lewa.org

Tokyo

When? Late March

Who? It's already grown to a field of 25,000 since it began in 2007

What? One of the newest big city marathons on the block, with a great sightseeing route, of which the first 5 km are downhill.

Visit www.tokyo42195.org

Great Wall of China

When? May

Who? Around 1700 take part (some in the half marathon)

What? A challenging race, including a staggering 5164 steps to conquer and ups and downs of 10 per cent gradient! Only part of the course is on the wall itself, the remainder travels through nearby villages and fields, on gravel and tarmac. Expect humidity and high temperatures.

Visit www.great-wall-marathon.com

Marathon du Medoc

When? September

Who? 8500 runners vie for places; many race in fancy dress

What? A high-spirited race among the beautiful vineyards of the Medoc, passing 50 chateaux. Forget water stations – here you'll be able to seek refreshment from all manner of 'gourmet stands' offering wine, oysters, ham, cheese and ice cream. And, when you finish, you'll get one of the best goodie bags known to man: including not just a medal and T-shirt but also a bottle of Medoc wine and other refreshments! Just don't expect a PB . . .

Visit www.marathondumedoc.com

❯ Taking it further
ALL ABOUT ULTRA RUNNING, MOUNTAIN MARATHONS AND MULTI-STAGE RACES

When you first started your marathon training, you were probably convinced that running 26.2 miles was the extreme edge of human endeavour. Well, you might be surprised to know that there are a growing number of people out there who class themselves as 'ultra runners', and take part in races and events longer than 26.2 miles. Even 27 miles would count, but ultra marathons are most commonly 31 miles (50 km), 62 miles (100 km) or 100 miles (160 km). Ultra marathons, such as the 53-mile Highland Fling in Scotland, often combine road and off-road sections, although some, such as the Comrades Marathon (56 miles) in South Africa, are solely on the road. Ultras are usually about getting from A to B in the allotted time (for example, runners in the West Highland Way race get 35 hours to cover 95 miles). Rarely, races are based on time, with runners attempting to cover the greatest possible distance (frequently in the form of multiple laps) in the time allotted (often 24 or 48 hours).

Now, before you write off ultra running as a sport for loonies, consider the fact that most participants do not run the whole way. They walk when the terrain or incline demands it; they stop for food and drink, as well as to change kit or shoes, consult the route map or even take in the view. It's all par for the course when you are on the move for what amounts to a working day. And, because the terrain and topography vary so much from race to race, it's virtually impossible to make meaningful comparisons between your finish time in one race and another, so the focus is more on reaching the finish line than competing against the clock. As ultra runner Alistair Bryan-Jones says, 'the camaraderie and spirit of these events is very different to typical road races. The fields are generally smaller and people get to know each other through the racing scene. Also, the slower pace means it is much easier to chat to other competitors.'

Multi-stage races
For the real die-hards, there are multi-stage ultra races, such as the gruelling Marathon des Sables, a 240 km event run in six stages through the Saharan desert in searing heat, the stunningly scenic five-day Himalayan 100-Mile Stage race, with an altitude of 12,500 ft to contend with and, perhaps the daddy of all ultras, the Ultra trail du tour du Mont Blanc, which requires you to cover 163 km in less than 46 hours, starting in Chamonix. Only 40–50 per cent of starters make it to the finish.

Making the jump
You have already proved that you can complete the marathon distance. If you are considering ultra running, the two main points to bear in mind are that you will be running for longer and at a significantly slower pace (at least a minute slower per mile than your marathon pace). Time on your feet is essential, so long, slow runs – and even walks (or walk breaks within your long runs) – are key. Allow plenty of time to train for your chosen event – there are no shortcuts when you are running these extended distances. As the event draws nearer, you may want to consider doing two long runs on consecutive days in a week to (a) maximise your mileage and (b) get used to running when you are already tired. This will also help you develop mental toughness – an essential attribute for ultra runners. You

will undoubtedly go through bad patches and question your ability to carry on, so developing the mental skills to deal with this in training will help.

Don't make the mistake of doing all your runs at 'ultra slow' pace, though, or you will lose speed. Long intervals, hills and threshold runs are all useful sessions to supplement your long running.

I dipped my toes into ultra running with a 50 km event, but most experienced ultra runners recommend gunning for something a good bit further than a standard marathon. A good place to start looking is the Vasque series of ultra races, which are spread across the UK (see www.runfurther.com).

Get accustomed to carrying not just fluid but energy snacks and food on your long runs – your body will need to refuel on the move if you are to make the distance. Different things work for different people, so you'll need to experiment with a variety of foods.

For details and websites on ultra running *see* 'Further information' (page 213).

Mountain marathons

Mountain marathons are a UK institution. The oldest one, the OMM (Original Mountain Marathon), has been running since 1968. Then there is the well-established Scottish LAMM (Lowe Alpine Mountain Marathon) and the Saunders Lakeland Mountain Marathon. What all these events have in common is that they entail two days of running up and down hills, far away from well-trodden paths, finding your own route to a number of 'checkpoints' on the way to the overnight campsite, where you (hopefully!) get some brief respite before doing it all again the next day. Participants work in teams of two and each pair carries their own tent, fluid, food, sleeping bags, clothing and first aid supplies. There is a range of courses aimed at different levels of fitness/experience – the longest typically cover around 50 miles across the two days, with a huge amount of ascending and descending. Road running will only help so much in training for an event of this kind. Your aim should be to get out to the hills (running both up and down), practise some long runs carrying a backpack and perfect your navigation skills. Knees and ankles can take a battering from terrain that might include deep heather, tussocky grass and rocks, so strength training can help. Deciding what kit to wear and carry is also a steep learning curve. The most experienced runners will manage to pare their gear down to less than 5 kg, while the average runner will be struggling with significantly more weight.

Adventure racing

Adventure racing is a fast-growing pastime among runners who are keen to test their sporting prowess in other areas, or inject a little variety into their training. Adventure races range from extremely demanding multi-day events, such as the 520 km-long Raid in France event, which demands climbing, walking, rafting, horse riding and mountain biking, as well as more beginner-friendly events like the city-based Urban Rat Race series.

One very positive aspect of adventure racing that you don't get so much from running is teamwork. Many races welcome – or insist upon – team entries, which not only makes the whole thing more fun but also allows each member to play upon their own strengths. See 'Further information' (page 213) for more details.

∵ Running for charity
THE MARATHON TASK OF RAISING MONEY TO EARN YOUR RACE PLACE

Many runners find their way to a marathon start line via a charity place – that is, a guaranteed entry to a specific race, in return for raising a specified sum of money for the charity holding the place. One benefit in taking this route is getting access to races that are difficult to get in to, including London and New York. But perhaps even more valuable is the support package that comes with the marathon place, since it takes the organisational headache away. Your race package could simply be a fundraising pack, T-shirt with logo and a post-race party, or it could include flights and accommodation (for foreign races), regular group training sessions and post-race massage. Some charities operate a 'tier' system in which the more money you raise, the more benefits you get.

However, raising £2000 or more can be just as challenging – and time consuming – as training for the marathon itself, and you may find it too much of a pressure, particularly if you are anxious about your ability to raise the specified amount of money, or are worried about fitting in the training. If you do decide to go for a charity place, pick up a copy of *Runner's World* magazine, where numerous charities advertise the races they hold places for, or visit the 'charity directory' on the *Runner's World* website. Alternatively, contact the charity of your choice directly, to see whether it holds marathon places.

Of course, not everyone who runs for charity does so as a way of getting a much-in-demand guaranteed race entry. Many run for their chosen charity because they believe passionately in the cause, to support someone they know is in need and/or to raise awareness about an issue they feel strongly about. You can run for any charity you like, but it is best to let them know of your intentions – most have fundraising packs, or at the very least sponsorship forms, which will make your money-raising task a little easier.

Through the efforts of charity runners, the London Marathon has become the world's largest single fundraising event – by 2007, it had raised £361.5 million for charity since its inception in 1981. There's no doubt about it, charities benefit greatly from runners' help. But think carefully before you take on such a challenge: the added incentive of raising money may be just the impetus you need; on the other hand, the last thing you want is to be worrying about fundraising when you need to focus on your training. For some, it may be wise to leave your charity run until you have already got a marathon under your belt and know what you are taking on.

If you intend to run for charity, read the money-spinning tips below to help you maximise your fundraising potential.

Make it easy on yourself

∵ Run for something you believe in, not just the charity giving away the best T-shirt or race package. It will help you 'sell' your cause to others if you care about it yourself, and it will also make you feel more inclined to put in the necessary effort.

∵ Be an opportunist! Tell everyone you meet what you are doing and why (if, for example, you are supporting a particular charity because it's related to an illness someone close to you has suffered). You never know who might feel the same as you – from your hairdresser to the GP receptionist, to your solicitor or business colleague. Take your sponsorship form and supporting information about your chosen charity everywhere you go – in case you meet someone who will sponsor you. Go through your home and work address books to see whether there are contacts you have forgotten about that you could approach.

❖ Be – or do – something different. Running the marathon is a fantastic feat in itself but millions have done it, and potential sponsors may be suffering 'marathon fatigue'. If, however, you are dressing up in an outlandish outfit, pledging to do something wacky on the way round, or if you set up a system in which the more feats you do, the more money they have to give, then people are more likely to take an interest.

❖ Get some help from friends and family. Most charities can provide you with multiple sponsorship forms so that others can help raise funds for you. If you are enlisting help from your kids, set them a 'target' to aim for, and reward them when they achieve it.

❖ Set up your own web page at charity donation website Justgiving (www.justgiving.com). Since it began in 1999, more than £3.5 million has been raised for over 6000 different charities via this easy-to-use service. Justgiving enables friends, family and colleagues to sponsor you online (saving the need to traipse around with a sponsorship form) and pay the money directly into your Justgiving account via credit or debit card. Through your own personal web page, your sponsors can stay up to date with your progress towards your goal and send messages of support. The service has been particularly valuable to smaller charities, as it cuts their costs, but charities of all sizes benefit.

❖ If you work for a large company, try to get its support too, perhaps by running in branded clothing with its logo on. See whether it will match the amount you raise – some companies offer this kind of scheme. Use your company's noticeboard, newsletter or internal email to publicise your plans.

❖ Ask your chosen charity for fundraising ideas that have worked for others, and for material to support your cause, such as information leaflets, badges, baseball hats, stickers, etc.

❖ It's the oldest trick in the book: get the first person who signs your sponsorship form to pledge a reasonable sum. Then others will feel less able to pledge £1.

❖ Bear in mind, though, that not everyone will be able to offer money, so be ready to suggest that they help you in another way if they can. For example, they could help you design and make a fancy dress costume to run in, or assist you in doing a car boot sale.

❖ Take the money when it's offered to you. While officially you should wait until you have run the race before collecting sponsorship, there will be people you may not see for a while, or who might have lost interest by the time you get around to asking them for the money they have pledged. If the worst comes to the worst, and you don't run (or complete) the race, most sponsors will still allow you to give the money to your charity.

Organising a fundraising event

From car boot sales to a quiz night at your local pub, from a cake baking contest to a sponsored head shaving, there is no end to the possibilities when it comes to fundraising ideas. But there are a few points to bear in mind, such as what is and is not legal, how to make the event safe and how to guarantee success.

First, think about your 'market' when you are planning what your event should be. There's no point in organising an event that your nearest and dearest won't be interested in, or one that will cost so much to put on that the net profit you make is not worth the time and effort invested. Sometimes the simplest of ideas, which are easy to set up and run, are the most effective. Come up with a list of suggestions and take a straw poll among your friends and family.

Once you have decided what to do, get planning. Choose the date, time and venue for your event carefully and ensure you have long enough to organise and publicise it. Is it convenient for the type of people you want to attend? Will it clash with a major sporting event? Would it be better on a weekday, or in school holidays?

Draw up a simple budget, including a rough idea of how much you will need to outlay (for publicity, prizes and refreshments, for example) and where the income will come from (ticket or goods sales, or donations, for example). You'll also need to enlist help to keep things running smoothly on the day, although you should be able to persuade a few friends and family members to give their help for nothing.

Stay on the right side of the law!
As far as the law is concerned, if an event is to be held in a public place, you need to inform the police and local council of what you propose to do. You may also need to consider public liability insurance, as well as facilities such as toilets, signage, first aid and refreshments. That's why the simpler events are sometimes the most effective fundraisers.

You cannot collect money for charity in a public place without a Street Collection Licence from the local authority or council. Only a limited number are issued each year, and you will need to apply at least a month before the date of your collection. A 'public place' is any location where the public has unrestricted access, and includes car parks and shop entrances. For door-to-door money collecting (which you can do only for a registered charity), you need to apply for a House-to-House Collection Licence (sometimes a single-use certificate is issued instead of a licence). This also covers collecting money inside pubs. Again, contact your local authority in good time and ensure that you abide by the conditions outlined in the licence agreement.

Finally, ensure that you include the registered charity number of your chosen charity on all your printed materials (including posters, letters and tickets) – this is a legal requirement.

Be a media darling!
You don't need to hire top writers, but it is essential that your fundraising antics and events are well publicised. Send press releases to local radio and newspapers to get some free editorial space or air time, including any 'human interest' angles, such as why you chose to support that particular charity, and any unusual information about yourself, such as the fact that you only took up running at 50 after a lifetime of debauchery! Local papers will sometimes do a weekly column on your progress, while a local radio station might ask you to come into the studio both before and after the race to give the story an 'ending'.

If your fundraising event is for the general public (such as an auction or pub quiz night), ensure you have maximised exposure: think about putting up posters in shop windows, libraries, leisure centres and on office noticeboards; put flyers on car windscreens and get your friends to tell their friends. Send emails and texts to everyone in your address book.

Start your publicity campaign well in advance – you can never have too much publicity!

around the 26.2-mile course. It still includes some quality training – you'll just be performing fewer sessions overall.

Before you decide which programme suits you, bear in mind that the real beauty of these programmes is that they have been designed to be interchangeable, right up to week 12 (beyond this, you can still swap some sessions but not the long run/race schedule for the last four weeks). This unique flexibility enables you to move from one programme to another, as long as you stick to the appropriate week. So, for example, you may have done five weeks in the *Perfect World* and suddenly hit a busy patch at work, so you can switch to the *Real World* for a fortnight, or even permanently. Similarly, if you are following a 'first-timer' programme and finding it too easy, you can switch to the 'experienced' version on the same, or a different, programme. This should help you fit in your training, and provide the progression and variety that a good marathon training programme needs.

Rather than simply photocopying the programmes and following them religiously, get out your diary and schedule your runs in now. Not only does this help you determine what kind of realistic training commitment you are able to make, it also turns your runs into appointments that you are likely to keep, rather than something you just 'hope' you'll fit in around your normal life.

Ready to get started?

Training notes

- Each week's training begins with a long run, which many runners perform on a Sunday. When you know the date of your race, work back from it to determine the appropriate dates for each session. You don't have to do the sessions on the days stipulated. However, it is important to follow the 'hard/easy' format – in other words, spread out the tougher sessions, rather than do them on consecutive days.

- When strength training is stipulated, consider using the Runner's Strength workout on page 61. For cross-training options, see pages 66–68.

- The programmes build progressively, week on week – but there are a few weeks where the overall mileage decreases, in order to assist recovery. Don't ignore these and try to cram in more training.

- Some races are scheduled along the way as progress markers – if you can't find a race on the day suggested, it's fine to do it the week before or after, or do a time trial with friends, alone or even on the treadmill. Don't be tempted to race too often during your marathon build-up – this will hamper the development of your long run.

- Some sessions that denote time are rounded up to the nearest 5 or 10 minutes.

- The runs on the beginners' programmes are given in time, rather than distance. I think it's important not to get too hung up on mileage when training for your first marathon, although you can, of course, log mileage too, if you use a GPS or speed–distance monitor. The programmes for more experienced runners use a mix of time and distance to enable you to gauge your mileage more accurately and get a better idea of your race pace.

- A recommended effort level is denoted for each session. See the panel below to get a feel for each of the different effort levels. Don't simply run as fast as you can for every session!

- If you have to skip some training sessions for any reason, try to at least maintain the weekly long run and one of the quality sessions (such as intervals, hills or threshold training).

⠆ Remember, you can always use a walk/run strategy on your long runs (*see* page 134). This is an invaluable way of breaking through mental barriers about how long you are able to be out there 'on your feet'.

⠆ The final three weeks of training are significantly lower in volume. This is your race taper. Do not be tempted to continue training hard up to a week or two before the big day. You will not be optimally recovered. Read more about tapering on page 126.

⠆ Finally, these and all other marathon training programmes are not set in stone. If the programme says 'long run, 120 mins' and your muscles are shrieking 'No!', then listen to your body and adapt, or skip, as necessary. I'm not suggesting you should cop out whenever things get tough, but to avoid injury and get the maximum enjoyment out of your training, it's important to keep it all in perspective.

Pace yourself

Easy
Use the lower end of this pace range (60–65 per cent) for recovery runs, the 'recovery' sections of your interval training, hills and fartlek. Your long runs, particularly if you are a beginner, should also fall into the 'easy' category, equating to 65–70 per cent of heart rate reserve (*see* page 14).
RPE rating 5–6 out of 10: 'I could do this for hours.'

Steady
This pace is for your steady runs, and some long runs (to ensure you don't only become accustomed to doing longer runs at a very slow pace). Equates to around 70–80 per cent of heart rate reserve.
RPE rating 7 out of 10: 'I'm working, but I feel comfortable.'

Challenging
Use this pace on your threshold runs and longer intervals and hill training. Equates to 80–85 per cent of heart rate reserve.
RPE rating 8.5 out of 10: 'Hmmm, I seem to have stepped outside my comfort zone.'

Tough
Use this pace, which is above your lactate threshold, for shorter intervals. Equates to 85–95 per cent per of heart rate reserve.
RPE rating 9–10 out of 10: 'When can I stop?!'

perfect world
marathon training programme
for first-timers

1
Sunday:	Long run 60 mins easy
Monday:	20 mins easy
Tuesday:	40 mins steady (ideally off-road) with 6 x 1 minute hill repeats
Wednesday:	Rest
Thursday:	Strength training 30–45 mins
Friday:	Rest or low-impact cross-training
Saturday:	30 mins steady

2
Sunday:	Long run 70 mins easy
Monday:	20 mins easy
Tuesday:	45 mins steady (ideally off-road) with 6 x 1 minute hill repeats
Wednesday:	Rest
Thursday:	Strength training 30–45 mins
Friday:	Rest or low-impact cross-training
Saturday:	30 mins steady

3
Sunday:	Long run 80 mins easy
Monday:	30 mins easy
Tuesday:	45 mins steady (ideally off-road) with 8 x 1 minute hill repeats
Wednesday:	Rest
Thursday:	Strength training 30–45 mins
Friday:	Rest or low-impact cross-training
Saturday:	40 mins steady

4
Sunday:	Rest
Monday:	30 mins steady
Tuesday:	45 mins off-road run with 8 x 1 minute hill repeats steady
Wednesday:	Rest
Thursday:	Strength training 30–45 mins
Friday:	Rest or low-impact cross-training
Saturday:	40 mins easy

5
Sunday:	Long run 90 mins easy (last 20 mins steady)
Monday:	30 mins easy
Tuesday:	45 mins off-road run including 10 x 1 minute challenging/1 minute easy
Wednesday:	Rest
Thursday:	Strength training 30–45 mins
Friday:	Rest or low-impact cross-training
Saturday:	30 mins easy

6

Sunday:	10 km race (or time trial)*
Monday:	30 mins easy
Tuesday:	45 mins off-road run including 10 x 1 minute challenging/1 minute easy
Wednesday:	Rest
Thursday:	Strength training 30–45 mins
Friday:	Rest or low-impact cross-training
Saturday:	30 mins easy

*Use your 10 km time to predict your marathon time using an online race pace prediction calculator

7

Sunday:	Long run 100 mins easy
Monday:	30 mins easy (last 10 mins at predicted marathon pace)
Tuesday:	45 mins off-road run including 10 x 1 minute tough/1 minute easy
Wednesday:	Rest
Thursday:	Threshold run 40 mins (3 x 8 mins challenging, 2 mins easy, 5 minute warm-up and cool-down)
Friday:	Rest or low-impact cross-training
Saturday:	30 mins easy

8

Sunday:	Long run 120 mins easy (last 20 mins of each hour steady)
Monday:	30 mins easy
Tuesday:	45 mins off-road run including 10 x 1 minute tough/1 minute easy
Wednesday:	Rest
Thursday:	Threshold run 40 mins (3 x 8 mins challenging, 2 mins easy, 5 minute warm-up and cool-down)
Friday:	Rest or low-impact cross-training
Saturday:	30 mins easy

9

Sunday:	Long run 140 mins easy (last 40 mins steady)
Monday:	30 mins easy
Tuesday:	45 mins off-road run including 10 x 1 minute tough/1 minute easy
Wednesday:	Rest
Thursday:	Threshold run 40 mins (2 x 10 mins challenging, 2 mins easy, 8 minute warm-up and cool-down)
Friday:	Rest or low-impact cross-training
Saturday:	30 mins steady (last 3 mins tough)

10

Sunday:	Rest
Monday:	30 mins easy
Tuesday:	45 mins off-road run including 6 x 2 mins challenging/2 mins easy
Wednesday:	Rest
Thursday:	Threshold run 40 mins (2 x 10 mins challenging, 2 mins easy, 8 minute warm-up and cool-down)
Friday:	Rest or low-impact cross-training
Saturday:	30 mins easy

11

Sunday:	Long run 150 mins easy (last 30 mins steady)
Monday:	30 mins easy
Tuesday:	45 mins off-road run including 6 x 2 mins challenging/2 mins easy
Wednesday:	Rest
Thursday:	Threshold run 50 mins (2 x 12 mins challenging, 2 mins easy, 11 minute warm-up and cool-down)
Friday:	Rest or low-impact cross-training
Saturday:	30 mins easy

12

Sunday:	Long run 180 mins easy (last 20 mins of each hour steady)
Monday:	30 mins easy
Tuesday:	45 mins off-road run including 6 x 2 mins tough/2 mins easy
Wednesday:	Rest
Thursday:	Threshold run 50 mins (2 x 12 mins challenging, 2 mins easy, 11 minute warm-up and cool-down)
Friday:	Rest or low-impact cross-training
Saturday:	30 mins easy

13

Sunday:	Half marathon or 10 mile race (or time trial)*
Monday:	30 mins easy
Tuesday:	45 mins off-road run including 6 x 2 mins tough/2 mins easy
Wednesday:	Rest
Thursday:	Threshold run 50 mins (2 x 15 mins challenging, 2 mins easy, 8 minute warm-up and cool-down)
Friday:	Rest or low-impact cross-training
Saturday:	30 mins easy

* Use your half marathon (or 10 mile) race time to predict your marathon time using an online race pace prediction calculator

14

Sunday:	Long run 180 mins easy (last 20 mins of each hour at marathon pace, as predicted by your half marathon/10 mile race)
Monday:	30 mins easy
Tuesday:	45 mins off-road run including 6 x 2 mins tough/2 mins easy
Wednesday:	Rest
Thursday:	Threshold run 50 mins (2 x 15 mins challenging, 2 mins easy, 8 minute warm-up and cool-down)
Friday:	Rest or low-impact cross-training
Saturday:	30 mins easy

15

Sunday:	Long run 70–90 mins easy (last 20 mins at marathon pace)*
Monday:	30 mins easy (last 3 mins tough)
Tuesday:	30 mins off-road run including 4 x 2 mins tough/2 mins easy
Wednesday:	Rest
Thursday:	Threshold run 30 mins (1 x 20 mins challenging, 5 mins warm-up and cool-down)
Friday:	Rest
Saturday:	30 mins at marathon pace

* Use this session as a dress rehearsal for kit and nutrition strategies

16

Sunday:	45 mins easy
Monday:	Rest
Tuesday:	Threshold run 15 mins (1 x 5 mins challenging, 5 mins warm-up and cool-down)
Wednesday:	Rest
Thursday:	20 mins at marathon pace
Friday:	Rest
Saturday:	20 mins easy (last 5 mins at marathon pace)
RACE DAY!	

perfect world
marathon training programme
for experienced runners

1
Sunday: Long run 8 miles easy
Monday: 30 mins easy
Tuesday: 40 mins steady (ideally off-road) with 8 x 1 minute hill repeats
Wednesday: Rest
Thursday: Threshold run 40 mins (10 min warm up and cool down and 5 x 4 mins challenging pace with 90 seconds easy)
Friday: Rest or cross-train
Saturday: 30 mins steady

2
Sunday: Long run 9 miles easy
Monday: 30 mins easy
Tuesday: 45 mins steady (ideally off-road) with 8 x 1 minute hill repeats
Wednesday: Rest
Thursday: Threshold run 40 mins (10 min warm up and cool down and 5 x 4 mins challenging pace with 90 seconds easy)
Friday: Rest or cross-train
Saturday: 30 mins steady

3
Sunday: Long run 10 miles (last 3 miles steady)
Monday: 30 mins easy
Tuesday: 45 mins steady (ideally off-road) with 10 mins Kenyan hills
Wednesday: Rest
Thursday: Threshold run 40 mins (10 min warm up and cool down and 4 x 5 mins challenging pace with 90 seconds easy)
Friday: Rest or cross-train
Saturday: 45 mins steady

4
Sunday: 10 km race*
Monday: 30 mins easy
Tuesday: 45 mins steady (ideally off-road) with 10 mins Kenyan hills
Wednesday: Rest
Thursday: Threshold run 40 mins (10 min warm up and cool down and 4 x 5 mins challenging pace with 90 seconds easy)
Friday: Rest or cross-train
Saturday: 40 mins easy
* Use your 10 km time to predict your marathon time using an online race pace prediction calculator

5
Sunday: Long run 100–120 mins off-road easy
Monday: 30 mins easy
Tuesday: 45 mins fartlek session including 6 efforts of 30–180 seconds at tough pace
Wednesday: Rest
Thursday: Threshold run 40 mins (10 min warm-up and cool-down and 2 x 10 mins challenging pace with 90 seconds easy in between)
Friday: Rest or cross-train
Saturday: 30 mins steady

6

Sunday:	6 miles steady
Monday:	30 mins easy
Tuesday:	50 mins fartlek session including 8 efforts of 30–120 seconds at tough pace
Wednesday:	Rest
Thursday:	Threshold run 40 mins (10 min warm-up and cool-down and 2 x 10 mins challenging pace with 90 seconds easy)
Friday:	Rest or cross-train
Saturday:	30 mins easy

7

Sunday:	Long run 15 miles easy
Monday:	30 mins easy
Tuesday:	50 mins fartlek session including 8 efforts of 60–180 seconds at tough pace
Wednesday:	Rest
Thursday:	Threshold run 45 mins (10 min warm up and cool down and 2 x 12 mins challenging pace with 90 seconds easy)
Friday:	Rest or cross-train
Saturday:	30 mins easy

8

Sunday:	Long run 140–160 mins off-road easy
Monday:	30 mins easy
Tuesday:	Rest or cross-train
Wednesday:	50 mins fartlek session including 8 efforts of 60–180 seconds at tough pace
Thursday:	Rest
Friday:	Rest or cross-train
Saturday:	30 mins easy

9

Sunday:	Half marathon or 10 mile race*
Monday:	30 mins easy
Tuesday:	10 min warm-up 4 x 1 km tough with 2 mins easy, 10 mins cool-down
Wednesday:	Rest
Thursday:	Threshold run 40 mins (10 min easy, 20 mins challenging pace, 10 mins easy)
Friday:	Rest or cross-train
Saturday:	30 mins steady (last 3 mins tough)

* Use your half marathon (or 10 mile) race time to predict your marathon time using an online race pace prediction calculator

10

Sunday:	Long run 18 miles easy (last 3 miles steady)
Monday:	30 mins easy
Tuesday:	10 min warm-up 4 x 1 km tough with 2 mins easy, 10 mins cool-down
Wednesday:	Rest
Thursday:	Threshold run 40 mins (10 min easy, 20 mins challenging pace, 10 mins easy)
Friday:	Rest or cross-train
Saturday:	30 mins steady

11

Sunday:	6 miles at predicted marathon pace
Monday:	30 mins easy
Tuesday:	10 min warm-up 5 x 1 km tough with 2 mins easy, 10 mins cool-down
Wednesday:	Rest
Thursday:	Threshold run 45 mins (10 min warm-up, 25 mins challenging pace, 10 mins cool-down)
Friday:	Rest or cross-train
Saturday:	30 mins easy

12

Sunday:	Long run 20 miles
Monday:	30 mins easy
Tuesday:	10 min warm-up 5 x 1 km tough with 2 mins easy, 10 mins cool-down
Wednesday:	Rest
Thursday:	Threshold run 45 mins (10 min warm up, 25 mins challenging pace, 10 mins cool-down)
Friday:	Rest or cross-train
Saturday:	30 mins easy

13

Sunday:	Long run off-road easy 150–180 mins
Monday:	30 mins easy
Tuesday:	60 mins at marathon pace
Wednesday:	Rest
Thursday:	Threshold run 45 mins (10 min easy, 25 mins challenging pace, 10 mins easy)
Friday:	Rest or cross-train
Saturday:	30 mins at marathon pace

14

Sunday:	Half marathon or 10 mile race at predicted marathon pace*
Monday:	30 mins easy
Tuesday:	45 mins fartlek session including 8 efforts of 30–180 seconds at tough pace
Wednesday:	Rest
Thursday:	Threshold run 45 mins (10 min easy, 25 mins challenging pace, 10 mins easy)
Friday:	Rest
Saturday:	30 mins at marathon pace

*Use your half marathon (or 10 mile) race time to predict your marathon time using an online race pace prediction calculator

15

Sunday:	Long run 80–90 mins easy (last 30 mins at marathon pace)*
Monday:	30 mins easy (last 3 mins tough)
Tuesday:	30 mins fartlek session including 6 efforts of 30–60 seconds at tough pace
Wednesday:	Rest
Thursday:	35 mins: 10 mins easy, 15 mins challenging pace, 10 mins marathon pace
Friday:	Rest
Saturday:	30 mins easy

* Use this session as a dress rehearsal for kit and nutrition strategies

16

Sunday:	50 mins easy (last 15 mins at marathon pace)
Monday:	Rest
Tuesday:	Threshold run 20 mins (5 mins easy, 10 mins challenging, 5 mins easy)
Wednesday:	Rest
Thursday:	20 mins steady in race kit
Friday:	Rest
Saturday:	20 mins easy (last 5 mins at marathon pace)
RACE DAY!	

real world
marathon training programme
for first-timers

1

Sunday:	Long run 60 mins easy
Monday:	20 mins easy
Tuesday:	40 mins steady (ideally off-road) with 6 x 1 minute hill repeats
Wednesday:	Rest
Thursday:	Strength/circuit training 30–45 mins
Friday:	Rest
Saturday:	Rest or low-impact cross-training

2

Sunday:	Long run 70 mins easy
Monday:	20 mins easy
Tuesday:	45 mins steady (ideally off-road) with 6 x 1 minute hill repeats
Wednesday:	Rest
Thursday:	Strength/circuit training 30–45 mins
Friday:	Rest
Saturday:	Rest or low-impact cross-training

3

Sunday:	Long run 80 mins easy
Monday:	30 mins easy
Tuesday:	45 mins steady (ideally off-road) with 8 x 1 minute hill repeats
Wednesday:	Rest
Thursday:	Strength/circuit training 30–45 mins
Friday:	Rest
Saturday:	Rest or low-impact cross-training

4

Sunday:	Rest
Monday:	30 mins steady
Tuesday:	45 mins steady (ideally off-road) with 8 x 1 minute hill repeats
Wednesday:	Rest
Thursday:	Strength/circuit training 30–45 mins
Friday:	30 mins easy
Saturday:	Rest or low-impact cross-training

5

Sunday:	Long run 90 mins easy (last 20 mins steady)
Monday:	30 mins easy
Tuesday:	30 mins including 10 x 1 minute challenging/1 minute easy
Wednesday:	Rest
Thursday:	45 mins steady (ideally off-road) with 2 x 5 mins Kenyan hills
Friday:	Rest
Saturday:	Rest or low-impact cross-training

6

Sunday:	10 km race*
Monday:	30 mins easy
Tuesday:	30 mins including 10 x 1 minute challenging/1 minute easy
Wednesday:	Rest
Thursday:	45 mins steady (ideally off-road) with 2 x 5 mins Kenyan hills
Friday:	Rest or low-impact cross-training
Saturday:	Rest

*Use your 10 km time to predict your marathon time using an online race pace prediction calculator

7

Sunday:	Long run 100 mins easy
Monday:	30 mins easy
Tuesday:	40 mins including 6 x 2 mins challenging/2 mins easy
Wednesday:	Rest
Thursday:	45 mins steady (ideally off-road) with 10 mins Kenyan hills
Friday:	Rest or low-impact cross-training
Saturday:	Rest

8

Sunday:	Long run 120 mins easy off-road
Monday:	30 mins easy
Tuesday:	40 mins including 6 x 2 mins challenging/2 mins easy
Wednesday:	Rest
Thursday:	45 mins steady (ideally off-road) with 10 mins Kenyan hills
Friday:	Rest or low-impact cross-training
Saturday:	Rest

9

Sunday:	Long run 140 mins easy (last 30 mins steady)
Monday:	20 mins easy
Tuesday:	40 mins threshold run: 6 mins easy, 4 x 5 mins challenging/2 mins easy, 6 mins easy
Wednesday:	Rest
Thursday:	40 mins steady (ideally off-road)
Friday:	Rest or low-impact cross-training
Saturday:	20 mins at marathon pace

10

Sunday:	Rest
Monday:	30 mins steady (last 3 mins tough)
Tuesday:	40 mins threshold run: 6 mins easy, 4 x 5 mins challenging/2 mins easy, 6 mins easy
Wednesday:	Rest
Thursday:	50 mins steady (ideally off-road)
Friday:	Rest or low-impact cross-training
Saturday:	20 mins easy

11

Sunday:	Long run 160 mins easy (last 30 mins steady)
Monday:	20 mins easy
Tuesday:	45 mins threshold run: 5 mins easy, 5 x 5 mins challenging/2 mins easy, 5 mins easy
Wednesday:	Rest
Thursday:	50 mins steady (ideally off-road)
Friday:	Rest or low-impact cross-training
Saturday:	Rest

12

Sunday:	Long run 160–180 mins easy (last 20 mins of each hour steady)
Monday:	30 mins easy
Tuesday:	45 mins threshold run: 5 mins easy, 5 x 5 mins challenging/2 mins easy, 5 mins easy
Wednesday:	Rest
Thursday:	30 mins at marathon pace
Friday:	Rest or low-impact cross-training
Saturday:	30 mins easy

13

Sunday:	Half marathon or 10 mile race (or time trial)*
Monday:	30 mins easy
Tuesday:	35 mins threshold run: 5 mins easy, 3 x 6 mins challenging/2 mins easy, 5 mins easy
Wednesday:	Rest
Thursday:	40 mins at marathon pace
Friday:	Rest or low-impact cross-training
Saturday:	30 mins easy

*Use your half marathon (or 10 mile) race time to predict your marathon time using an online race pace prediction calculator

14

Sunday:	Long run 180 mins easy (last 20 mins of each hour at marathon pace)
Monday:	30 mins easy
Tuesday:	40 mins threshold run: 5 mins easy, 3 x 8 mins challenging/2 mins easy, 5 mins easy
Wednesday:	Rest
Thursday:	50 mins easy (last 15 mins at marathon pace)
Friday:	Rest or low-impact cross-training
Saturday:	Rest

15

Sunday:	Long run 70–90 mins easy (last 20 mins at marathon pace)*
Monday:	20 mins easy
Tuesday:	20 mins threshold run: 5 mins easy, 10 mins challenging, 5 mins easy
Wednesday:	Rest
Thursday:	20 mins steady including 5 x 1 min challenging, 1 min easy
Friday:	Rest
Saturday:	20 mins at marathon pace

* Use this session as a dress rehearsal for kit and nutrition strategies

16

Sunday:	45 mins easy
Monday:	Rest
Tuesday:	Threshold run 15 mins (5 mins easy, 5 mins challenging, 5 mins easy)
Wednesday:	Rest or 20 mins easy in race kit
Thursday:	Rest
Friday:	Rest
Saturday:	20 mins easy (last 5 mins at marathon pace)
RACE DAY!	

real world
marathon training programme
for experienced runners

1

Sunday:	Long run 8 miles easy
Monday:	30 mins easy
Tuesday:	40 mins steady (ideally off-road) with 8 x 1 minute hill repeats
Wednesday:	Rest
Thursday:	Threshold run 40 mins: 10 mins easy, 5 x 4 mins challenging, 90 secs easy, 5 mins easy
Friday:	Rest
Saturday:	Rest or low-impact cross-training

2

Sunday:	Long run 9 miles steady
Monday:	Rest
Tuesday:	40 mins steady (ideally off-road) with 8 x 1 minute hill repeats
Wednesday:	3 mins easy
Thursday:	Threshold run 40 mins: 10 mins easy, 5 x 4 mins challenging, 90 secs easy, 5 mins easy
Friday:	Rest
Saturday:	Rest or low-impact cross-training

3

Sunday:	Long run 90–100 mins off-road easy
Monday:	20 mins easy
Tuesday:	45 mins steady (ideally off-road) with 10 x 1 minute hill repeats
Wednesday:	Rest
Thursday:	Threshold run 45 mins: 10 mins easy, 6 x 4 mins challenging, 90 secs easy, 5 mins easy
Friday:	Rest
Saturday:	Rest or low-impact cross-training

4

Sunday:	10 km race*
Monday:	Rest
Tuesday:	45 mins steady (ideally off-road) with 10 x 1 minute hill repeats
Wednesday:	Rest
Thursday:	Threshold run 45 mins: 10 mins easy, 6 x 4 mins challenging, 90 secs easy, 5 mins easy
Friday:	20 mins easy
Saturday:	Rest or low-impact cross-training

*Use your 10 km time to predict your marathon time using an online race pace prediction calculator

5

Sunday:	Long run 12 miles easy (last 20 mins steady)
Monday:	30 mins easy
Tuesday:	30 mins including 10 x 1 minute tough/1 minute easy
Wednesday:	Rest
Thursday:	Threshold run 50 mins: 10 mins easy, 5 x 5 mins challenging, 2 mins easy, 5 mins easy
Friday:	Rest
Saturday:	Rest or low-impact cross-training

6

Sunday:	Long run 120–130 mins off-road easy
Monday:	30 mins easy
Tuesday:	30 mins including 10 x 1 minute tough/1 minute easy
Wednesday:	Rest
Thursday:	Threshold run 50 mins: 10 mins easy, 5 x 5 mins challenging, 2 mins easy, 5 mins easy
Friday:	Rest or low-impact cross-training
Saturday:	Rest

7

Sunday:	Rest
Monday:	30 mins easy
Tuesday:	40 mins including 6 x 2 mins tough/2 mins easy
Wednesday:	Rest
Thursday:	Threshold run 40 mins: 10 mins easy, 2 x 10 mins challenging, 2 mins easy, 5 mins easy
Friday:	Rest or low-impact cross-training
Saturday:	Rest

8

Sunday:	Long run 15 miles easy (last 20 mins steady)
Monday:	30 mins steady
Tuesday:	40 mins including 6 x 2 mins challenging/2 mins easy
Wednesday:	Rest
Thursday:	Threshold run 40 mins: 10 mins easy, 2 x 10 mins challenging, 2 mins easy, 5 mins easy
Friday:	Rest or low-impact cross-training
Saturday:	Rest

9

Sunday:	Half marathon or 10 mile race
Monday:	20 mins easy
Tuesday:	45 mins fartlek session including 6 efforts of 30–180 seconds at tough pace
Wednesday:	Rest
Thursday:	Threshold run 45 mins: 10 mins easy, 2 x 12 mins challenging, 2 mins easy, 5 mins easy
Friday:	Rest or low-impact cross-training
Saturday:	20 mins at marathon pace

10

Sunday:	Long run 18 miles easy (last 30 mins steady)
Monday:	20 mins steady (last 3 mins tough)
Tuesday:	45 mins fartlek session including 6 efforts of 30–180 seconds at tough pace
Wednesday:	Rest
Thursday:	Threshold run 45 mins: 10 mins easy, 2 x 12 mins challenging, 2 mins easy, 5 mins easy
Friday:	Rest or low-impact cross-training
Saturday:	20 mins easy

11

Sunday:	45 mins off-road easy
Monday:	30 mins easy
Tuesday:	45 mins fartlek session including 6 efforts of 30–180 seconds at tough pace
Wednesday:	Rest
Thursday:	6 miles at marathon pace
Friday:	Rest or low-impact cross-training
Saturday:	Rest

12

Sunday:	Long run 160–180 mins easy off-road
Monday:	30 mins easy
Tuesday:	45 mins fartlek session including 6 efforts of 60–180 seconds at tough pace
Wednesday:	Rest
Thursday:	4 miles at marathon pace
Friday:	Rest or low-impact cross-training
Saturday:	20 mins easy

13

Sunday:	Long run 20 miles easy
Monday:	Rest
Tuesday:	30 mins threshold run: 5 mins easy, 20 mins challenging, 5 mins easy
Wednesday:	Rest
Thursday:	50 mins marathon pace
Friday:	Rest or low-impact cross-training
Saturday:	30 mins easy

14

Sunday:	Half marathon or 13 miles at marathon pace
Monday:	Rest
Tuesday:	60 mins easy (last 15 mins at marathon pace)
Wednesday:	Rest
Thursday:	30 mins threshold run: 5 mins easy, 20 mins challenging, 5 mins easy
Friday:	Rest or low-impact cross-training
Saturday:	30 mins steady (last 3 mins tough)

15

Sunday:	Long run 80–90 mins easy (last 30 mins at marathon pace)*
Monday:	30 mins easy
Tuesday:	20 mins threshold run: 5 mins easy, 10 mins challenging, 5 mins easy
Wednesday:	Rest
Thursday:	40 mins at marathon pace
Friday:	Rest
Saturday:	Rest or low-impact cross-training

* Use this session as a dress rehearsal for kit and nutrition strategies

16

Sunday:	45 mins easy (last 10 mins at marathon pace)
Monday:	Rest
Tuesday:	20 mins (10 mins easy, 5 mins challenging, 5 mins easy)
Wednesday:	20 mins easy in race kit
Thursday:	Rest
Friday:	Rest
Saturday:	20 mins easy (last 5 mins at marathon pace)
RACE DAY!	

bare minimum
marathon training programme
for first-timers

1

Sunday:	Long run 60 mins easy
Monday:	Rest
Tuesday:	40 mins steady (ideally off-road) with 4 x 1 minute hill repeats
Wednesday:	Rest
Thursday:	30–45 mins strength/circuit training or rest
Friday:	30 mins steady
Saturday:	Rest

2

Sunday:	Long run 70 mins easy
Monday:	Rest
Tuesday:	40 mins steady (ideally off-road) with 4 x 1 minute hill repeats
Wednesday:	Rest
Thursday:	30–45 mins strength/circuit training or rest
Friday:	35 mins steady
Saturday:	Rest

3

Sunday:	Long run 80 mins easy
Monday:	Rest
Tuesday:	45 mins steady (ideally off-road) with 6 x 1 minute hill repeats
Wednesday:	Rest
Thursday:	30–45 mins strength/circuit training or rest
Friday:	35 mins steady
Saturday:	Rest

4

Sunday:	Rest
Monday:	45 mins steady
Tuesday:	45 mins steady (ideally off-road) with 6 x 1 minute hill repeats
Wednesday:	Rest
Thursday:	30–45 mins strength/circuit training or rest
Friday:	30 mins easy
Saturday:	Rest

5

Sunday:	Long run 100 mins easy off-road
Monday:	Rest
Tuesday:	40 mins including 10 x 1 minute challenging/1 minute easy
Wednesday:	Rest
Thursday:	45 mins steady
Friday:	Rest
Saturday:	Rest or low-impact cross-training

6

Sunday:	10 km race (or time trial)*
Monday:	Rest
Tuesday:	40 mins including 10 x 1 minute challenging/1 minute easy
Wednesday:	Rest
Thursday:	45 mins at marathon pace
Friday:	Rest
Saturday:	Rest or low impact cross-training

*Use your 10 km time to predict your marathon time using an online race pace prediction calculator

7

Sunday:	Long run 120 mins easy (last 15 mins of each hour steady)
Monday:	Rest
Tuesday:	40 mins including 5 x 2 mins challenging/2 mins easy
Wednesday:	Rest
Thursday:	35 mins steady
Friday:	Rest
Saturday:	Rest or low impact cross-training

8

Sunday:	60 mins steady
Monday:	20 mins easy
Tuesday:	40 mins including 5 x 2 mins challenging/2 mins easy
Wednesday:	Rest
Thursday:	45 mins steady (ideally off-road)
Friday:	Rest
Saturday:	Rest

9

Sunday:	Long run 140 mins easy off-road
Monday:	Rest
Tuesday:	45 mins including 5 x 3 mins challenging/2 mins easy
Wednesday:	Rest
Thursday:	35 mins steady
Friday:	Rest
Saturday:	Rest or low-impact cross-training

10

Sunday:	Long run 150 mins (last 20 mins steady)
Monday:	Rest
Tuesday:	45 mins including 5 x 3 mins challenging/2 mins easy
Wednesday:	Rest
Thursday:	40 mins steady (ideally off-road) with 2 x 5 mins Kenyan hills
Friday:	Rest
Saturday:	Rest or low-impact cross-training

11

Sunday:	60 mins at marathon pace
Monday:	20 mins easy
Tuesday:	45 mins threshold run: 10 mins easy, 5 x 4 mins challenging/2 mins easy, 5 mins easy
Wednesday:	Rest
Thursday:	30 mins steady (last 3 mins tough)
Friday:	Rest
Saturday:	Rest

12

Sunday:	Long run 165 mins easy off-road
Monday:	Rest
Tuesday:	45 mins threshold run: 10 mins easy, 5 x 4 mins challenging/2 mins easy, 5 mins easy
Wednesday:	Rest
Thursday:	30 mins steady (ideally off-road) with 2 x 5 mins Kenyan hills
Friday:	Rest or low-impact cross-training
Saturday:	Rest

13

Sunday:	Half marathon or 10 mile race (or time trial)*
Monday:	Rest
Tuesday:	50 mins threshold run: 10 mins easy, 4 x 6 mins challenging/2 mins easy, 5 mins easy
Wednesday:	Rest
Thursday:	30 mins steady (ideally off-road) with 2 x 5 mins Kenyan hills
Friday:	Rest
Saturday:	Rest or low-impact cross-training

*Use your half marathon (or 10 mile) race time to predict your marathon time using an online race pace prediction calculator

14

Sunday:	Long run 180 mins easy (last 15 mins of each hour at marathon pace)
Monday:	Rest
Tuesday:	50 mins threshold run: 10 mins easy, 4 x 6 mins challenging/2 mins easy, 5 mins easy
Wednesday:	Rest
Thursday:	40 mins easy (last 15 mins at marathon pace)
Friday:	Rest
Saturday:	Rest or low-impact cross-training

15

Sunday:	Long run 70–80 mins easy (last 15 mins at marathon pace)*
Monday:	Rest
Tuesday:	20 mins threshold run: 10 mins easy, 5 mins challenging, 5 mins easy
Wednesday:	Rest
Thursday:	30 mins easy (last 3 mins tough)
Friday:	Rest
Saturday:	Rest or low-impact cross-training

* Use this session as a dress rehearsal for kit and nutrition strategies

16

Sunday:	45 mins easy (last 10 mins at marathon pace)
Monday:	Rest
Tuesday:	Threshold run 15 mins (5 mins easy, 5 mins challenging, 5 mins easy)
Wednesday:	Rest
Thursday:	Rest or low-impact cross-training
Friday:	Rest
Saturday:	20 mins easy
RACE DAY!	

bare minimum
marathon training programme for experienced runners

1
Sunday:	Long run 8 miles easy
Monday:	Rest
Tuesday:	40 mins steady (ideally off-road) with 8 x 1 minute hill repeats
Wednesday:	Rest
Thursday:	30–45 mins strength/circuit training or rest
Friday:	30 mins steady
Saturday:	Rest

2
Sunday:	Long run 9 miles steady
Monday:	Rest
Tuesday:	40 mins steady (ideally off-road) with 8 x 1 minute hill repeats
Wednesday:	Rest
Thursday:	30–45 mins strength/circuit training or rest
Friday:	Threshold run 40 mins: 10 mins easy, 4 x 4 mins challenging, 90 secs easy, 5 mins easy
Saturday:	Rest

3
Sunday:	Long run 90–100 mins easy off-road
Monday:	Rest
Tuesday:	45 mins steady (ideally off-road) with 10 x 1 minute hill repeats
Wednesday:	Rest
Thursday:	30–45 mins strength/circuit training or rest
Friday:	40 mins steady
Saturday:	Rest

4
Sunday:	10 km race*
Monday:	Rest
Tuesday:	45 mins steady (ideally off-road) with 10 x 1 minute hill repeats
Wednesday:	Rest
Thursday:	30–45 mins strength/circuit training or rest
Friday:	Threshold run 40 mins: 10 mins easy, 4 x 4 mins challenging, 90 secs easy, 5 mins easy
Saturday:	Rest

*Use your 10 km time to predict your marathon time using an online race pace prediction calculator

5
Sunday:	Long run 12 miles easy (last 20 mins steady)
Monday:	Rest
Tuesday:	45 mins steady off-road including 2 x 5 mins Kenyan hills
Wednesday:	Rest
Thursday:	20 mins easy or rest
Friday:	30 mins marathon pace
Saturday:	Rest

6

Sunday:	Long run 120–130 mins easy off-road
Monday:	Rest
Tuesday:	45 mins steady off-road including 2 x 6 mins Kenyan hills
Wednesday:	Rest
Thursday:	Rest
Friday:	Threshold run 40 mins: 10 mins easy, 4 x 5 mins challenging, 90 secs easy, 5 mins easy
Saturday:	Rest

7

Sunday:	Long run 14–15 miles easy (last 2 miles at marathon pace)
Monday:	Rest
Tuesday:	45 mins steady off-road including 2 x 6 mins Kenyan hills
Wednesday:	Rest
Thursday:	35 mins marathon pace or 5 km time trial
Friday:	Rest
Saturday:	Rest or low-impact cross-training

8

Sunday:	60 mins steady
Monday:	Rest
Tuesday:	30 mins easy off-road
Wednesday:	Rest
Thursday:	30 mins steady
Friday:	Threshold run 40 mins: 10 mins easy, 4 x 5 mins challenging, 90 secs easy, 5 mins easy
Saturday:	Rest

9

Sunday:	Half marathon or 10 mile race (or time trial)*
Monday:	Rest
Tuesday:	Threshold run 45 mins: 10 mins easy, 4 x 6 mins challenging, 120 secs easy, 5 mins easy
Wednesday:	Rest
Thursday:	Rest
Friday:	45 mins steady off-road including 2 x 8 mins Kenyan hills
Saturday:	Rest or low-impact cross-training

*Use your half marathon (or 10 mile) race time to predict your marathon time using an online race pace prediction calculator

10

Sunday:	Long run 17–18 miles (last 30 mins steady)
Monday:	Rest
Tuesday:	45 mins fartlek session including 6 efforts of 30–180 seconds at tough pace
Wednesday:	Rest
Thursday:	Rest
Friday:	Threshold run 45 mins: 10 mins easy, 4 x 6 mins challenging, 120 secs easy, 5 mins easy
Saturday:	Rest or low-impact cross-training

11

Sunday:	140–160 mins off-road easy
Monday:	20 mins easy
Tuesday:	30 mins fartlek session including 6 efforts of 30–180 seconds at tough pace
Wednesday:	Rest
Thursday:	30 mins at marathon pace (last 3 mins tough)
Friday:	Rest
Saturday:	Rest

12

Sunday:	Long run 180 mins easy off-road
Monday:	Rest
Tuesday:	45 mins at marathon pace
Wednesday:	Rest
Thursday:	Rest
Friday:	Threshold run 45 mins: 10 mins easy, 3 x 8 mins challenging, 120 secs easy, 5 mins easy
Saturday:	Rest

13

Sunday:	60 mins at marathon pace
Monday:	Rest
Tuesday:	40 mins fartlek session including 6 efforts 60–180 seconds at tough pace
Wednesday:	Rest
Thursday:	45 mins steady (ideally off-road) with 2 x 5 mins Kenyan hills
Friday:	Rest
Saturday:	Rest or low-impact cross-training

14

Sunday:	Long run 20 miles easy
Monday:	Rest
Tuesday:	15 mins easy, 15 mins marathon pace
Wednesday:	Rest
Thursday:	Rest
Friday:	Threshold run 45 mins: 10 mins easy, 3 x 8 mins challenging, 120 secs easy, 5 mins easy
Saturday:	Rest or low-impact cross-training

15

Sunday:	Long run 70–90 mins easy (last 20 mins at marathon pace)*
Monday:	Rest
Tuesday:	30 mins marathon pace (last 3 mins tough)
Wednesday:	Rest
Thursday:	Threshold run 35 mins: 10 mins easy, 3 x 5 mins challenging, 120 secs easy, 5 mins easy
Friday:	Rest
Saturday:	Rest or low-impact cross-training

* Use this session as a dress rehearsal for kit and nutrition strategies

16

Sunday:	45 mins steady
Monday:	Rest
Tuesday:	Threshold run 15 mins (5 mins easy, 5 mins challenging, 5 mins easy)
Wednesday:	Rest
Thursday:	Rest or low-impact cross-training
Friday:	Rest
Saturday:	20 mins easy (last 5 mins at marathon pace)
RACE DAY!	

12 half marathon – from start to finish

:: How to make yours a swifter half

ADVICE ON TRAINING AND RACING

The half marathon could be described as the perfect running race distance. For new runners, it is far enough to pose a genuine challenge (with the all-important word 'marathon' in its title), but less daunting than the full distance event and easier to recover from. For more experienced runners, it's an opportunity to put both endurance and speed to the test in a single race. The half is also an ideal stepping stone towards a full marathon. No wonder it's the fastest-growing running event in the United States, and the UK's second most popular race distance.

Of course, most of the same principles apply when laying down plans for a successful half marathon race as they do for a full one (we'll recap on these

in a moment). But there *are* differences. For a start, the distance is significantly shorter, so your overall weekly mileage or 'time on your feet' need not be so high. Second, you may want to consider running the full distance of the event (13.1 miles) one or more times in training, which isn't normally advisable when training for 26.2 miles. (It's particularly advisable to run 'over-distance' if you are training for a half marathon as part of a longer-term build-up to a full one.)

A third factor is pace. While you still need to pace yourself wisely, the issue of 'hitting the wall' or running out of energy doesn't apply in a half marathon, because the body is able to store sufficient carbohydrate to fuel your efforts over this distance. This means you can run at a faster pace than you would if you were participating in a full marathon. A final difference is the 'taper' period, which, due to the lower weekly mileage, does not need to be as long as it would be for a full marathon (the taper period in the programmes on pages 196–207 is two weeks). Once the race is over, it should take you only a few days to recover, and less time before you can get back into full training.

Half measures

So where do you start? You should have at least three months of regular running (three to five days per week) behind you before you begin training for a half marathon – and, ideally, you will also have a few shorter races under your belt too (such as 5 km or 10 km races).

The training programmes in this chapter are ten-week schedules, including an easier fortnight as you taper towards race day. Like the full marathon programmes in Chapter 11, these schedules are based not on 'goal' finish times but on the amount of training you are willing and able to put in.

The *Perfect World* is for those with the time and motivation to train five days per week on average. The *Real World* programme is based on four days' training per week, and is well suited to those who need to balance other time and energy commitments with their training. Finally, there is the *Bare Minimum* programme (averaging three sessions per week). This schedule still includes some quality training – you'll just be performing fewer sessions overall.

Whichever programme you start with, it is perfectly possible to switch to a different one if you are finding you want or need to do more or less training. You can also switch from the 'first-timer' level to the 'experienced' version of the same programme, if you want to increase or decrease

your efforts without changing the number of days you are putting in.

You'll find more information about the half marathon programmes themselves over the page, but first let's recap on the general principles of training.

The golden rules of training (revisited)

∷ Make haste slowly. In other words, don't try to build up your speed or distance too soon. The body needs time to adapt to the unique demands of running, and pushing yourself too hard puts you at risk of injury and excessive fatigue.

∷ Only think about introducing quality sessions – like threshold running, hills and intervals – once you are able to run comfortably for 30–45 minutes and have been training consistently for two to three months. (You may want to precede your specific half marathon training with the 'Absolute beginner' programme on page 9.)

∷ Ensure you take enough rest days. These are just as important a part of your training programme as the running sessions. Read more about the vital role of rest on page 12.

∷ Remember, running is a repetitive, high-impact sport. It's well worth including some strength and core stability training to ensure your musculoskeletal system is up to the challenge, as well as regular stretching, to prevent muscles becoming short and tight. See pages 61–64 and 54–57 for running-specific strength and stretching workouts.

∷ Your half marathon training should include a variety of different types of training. You should be performing some runs slower than the pace you intend to run on the day (easy runs), some

The half as a stepping stone

A half marathon race is included in all the full marathon training programmes in this book. Running a half gives you the opportunity to get used to the racing environment, test out kit and hydration strategies, and practise running at different paces. It also gives you a good insight into your marathon potential – enabling you to estimate your marathon finish time from how well you do in the half.

But if your half marathon is part of a bigger plan, and not your end goal, approach with caution. If you push yourself too hard, you will waste valuable training days recovering. Any half marathon that you take part in during the final month of marathon training should be run at marathon pace, not half marathon pace.

faster (such as interval training) and some at 'race pace' (read more on this on pages 16–21).

∷ Vary the terrain that you run on. Softer surfaces are more forgiving on the joints than hard concrete and asphalt, so try to run a good proportion of your sessions off-road. See page 33 for more information on running surfaces.

∴ Half marathon training programmes

Ready to get started with your half marathon training? Great! Once you've decided which programme and level to begin with, get out your diary and schedule the runs in on the days that work for you. Not only does this help you determine what kind of realistic training commitment you are able to make, it also turns your runs into appointments that you are likely to keep, rather than something you just hope you'll fit in around your normal life. Here's some advice on how to follow the programmes successfully . . .

∴ Start each session with a warm-up (page 49) and finish with a cool-down (page 51).

∴ Follow the advice about how hard you should be working for each session – do not simply run as hard as you can every time. See the descriptions in the box below.

∴ Make sure you carry fluid with you on the longer runs (those that last 60 minutes or more). An isotonic sports drink is a better option than water on these longer sessions.

∴ Work back from the date of your race to determine the appropriate 'week commencing' dates for each session (weeks begin on a Sunday). You don't have to do the sessions on the days stipulated, however it is important to follow the 'hard/easy' format – in other words, spread out the tougher sessions.

∴ A 10 km race is scheduled along the way to give you a little racing experience and monitor your progress – if you can't find a race on the day suggested, it's fine to do it the week before or after the one suggested, or do a time trial with friends, alone or even on the treadmill.

∴ Some sessions that denote time are rounded up to the nearest 5 or 10 minutes.

∴ The runs on the beginners' programmes are given in time, rather than distance. The programmes for more experienced runners use a mix of time and distance to enable you to gauge your mileage and race pace more accurately.

∴ If you have to skip some training sessions for any reason, try at least to maintain the weekly long run and one of the quality sessions (such as intervals, hills or threshold training).

∴ Remember, you can always use a walk/run strategy on your long runs (*see* page 134). This is particularly useful for first-timers, as a way of increasing your 'time on your feet'.

∴ The final two weeks of training gradually reduce in volume. This is your race taper. Do not be tempted to keep training hard as you will not be optimally recovered.

∴ Finally, these and all other running training programmes are not set in stone. If the programme says 'long run, 100 mins' and your muscles are shrieking 'No!', then listen to your body and adapt, or skip, as necessary. I'm not suggesting you should cop out whenever things get tough, but to avoid injury and get the maximum enjoyment out of your training, it's important to keep it all in perspective.

Pace yourself

Easy
Use the lower end of this pace range (60–65 per cent) for recovery runs, the 'recovery' sections of your interval training, hills and fartlek. Your long runs, particularly if you are a beginner, should also fall into the 'easy' category, equating to 65–70 per cent of heart rate reserve (*see* page 14).
RPE rating 5–6 out of 10: 'I could do this for hours.'

Steady
This pace is for your steady runs, and some long runs (to ensure you don't only become accustomed to doing longer runs at a very slow pace). Equates to around 70–80 per cent of heart rate reserve.
RPE rating 7 out of 10: 'I'm working, but I feel comfortable.'

Challenging
Use this pace on your threshold runs and longer intervals and hill training. Equates to 80–85 per cent of heart rate reserve.
RPE rating 8.5 out of 10: 'Hmmm, I seem to have stepped outside my comfort zone.'

Tough
Use this pace, which is above your lactate threshold, for shorter intervals. Equates to 85–95 per cent per of heart rate reserve.
RPE rating 9–10 out of 10: 'When can I stop?!'

Predicting times

Wisdom has is that your predicted marathon time is twice your half marathon time plus 10–20 minutes, which will give you a broad idea of what you are capable of achieving.

Or, to predict your half marathon time from a 10 km run, multiply the time in minutes by 2.22.

perfect world
half marathon training programme for first-timers

1
Sunday:	Long run or run/walk 60 mins easy
Monday:	20 mins easy
Tuesday:	Strength/circuit training 30–45 mins
Wednesday:	Rest
Thursday:	30 mins steady (ideally off-road)
Friday:	Rest
Saturday:	20 mins easy

2
Sunday:	Long run or run/walk 70 mins easy
Monday:	20 mins easy
Tuesday:	Strength/circuit training 30–45 mins
Wednesday:	Rest
Thursday:	30 mins steady (ideally off-road)
Friday:	Rest
Saturday:	20 mins easy

3
Sunday:	30 mins steady
Monday:	20 mins easy
Tuesday:	Strength/circuit training 30–45 mins
Wednesday:	Rest
Thursday:	30 mins steady (ideally off-road) with 6 x 1 min hill repeats
Friday:	Rest
Saturday:	20 mins easy

4
Sunday:	Long run or run/walk 80 mins easy
Monday:	20 mins easy
Tuesday:	Strength/circuit training 30–45 mins
Wednesday:	Rest
Thursday:	30 mins steady (ideally off-road) with 6 x 1 min hill repeats
Friday:	Rest
Saturday:	20 mins easy

5
Sunday:	Long run or run/walk 90 mins easy
Monday:	20 mins easy
Tuesday:	Interval session 30 mins: 10 mins easy, 5 x 1 min challenging, 1 min easy, 10 mins easy
Wednesday:	Rest
Thursday:	35 mins steady (ideally off-road) with 8 x 1 min hill repeats
Friday:	Rest
Saturday:	20 mins easy

6

Sunday:	10 km race*
Monday:	20 mins easy
Tuesday:	30 mins: 10 mins easy, 10 mins at half marathon pace, 10 mins easy
Wednesday:	Rest
Thursday:	35 mins steady (ideally off-road) with 8 x 1 min hill repeats
Friday:	Rest
Saturday:	20 mins easy

*Use your 10 km race time to predict your half marathon finish time and determine your half marathon pace

7

Sunday:	Long run 100 mins easy
Monday:	20 mins easy (last 5 mins at half marathon pace)
Tuesday:	Interval session 30 mins: 10 mins easy, 6 x 1 min challenging, 1 min easy, 10 mins easy
Wednesday:	Rest
Thursday:	40 mins steady (ideally off-road) with 10 x 1 min hill repeats
Friday:	Rest
Saturday:	20 mins steady

8

Sunday:	50 mins easy
Monday:	20 mins easy
Tuesday:	Interval session 35 mins: 10 mins easy, 8 x 1 min challenging, 1 min easy, 10 mins easy
Wednesday:	Rest
Thursday:	40 mins steady (ideally off-road) with 10 x 1 min hill repeats
Friday:	Rest
Saturday:	20 mins steady

9

Sunday:	Long run 120 mins easy off-road
Monday:	20 mins easy
Tuesday:	Interval session 35 mins: 10 mins easy, 8 x 1 min challenging, 1 min easy, 10 mins easy
Wednesday:	Rest
Thursday:	40 mins steady (ideally off-road)
Friday:	Rest
Saturday:	20 mins at half marathon pace

10

Sunday:	45 mins easy
Monday:	Rest
Tuesday:	Interval session 30 mins: 10 mins easy, 5 x 1 min challenging, 1 min easy, 10 mins easy
Wednesday:	Rest
Thursday:	20 mins: 5 mins easy, 10 mins at half marathon pace, 5 mins easy (wear race kit)
Friday:	Rest
Saturday:	20 mins easy (last 5 mins at half marathon pace)
RACE DAY!	

perfect world
half marathon training programme for experienced runners

1

Sunday:	Long run 7 miles easy
Monday:	20 mins easy
Tuesday:	Threshold session 35 mins: 10 mins easy, 15 mins challenging, 10 mins easy
Wednesday:	Rest
Thursday:	30 mins steady (ideally off-road) with 8 x 1 minute hill repeats
Friday:	Rest
Saturday:	20 mins steady

2

Sunday:	Long run 8 miles steady
Monday:	20 mins easy
Tuesday:	Threshold session 35 mins: 10 mins easy, 15 mins challenging, 10 mins easy
Wednesday:	Rest
Thursday:	30 mins steady (ideally off-road) with 8 x 1 minute hill repeats
Friday:	Rest
Saturday:	20 mins steady

3

Sunday:	45 mins steady
Monday:	20 mins easy
Tuesday:	Threshold session 40 mins: 10 mins easy, 20 mins challenging, 10 mins easy
Wednesday:	Rest
Thursday:	35 mins steady (ideally off-road) with 10 x 1 minute hill repeats
Friday:	Rest
Saturday:	20 mins easy

4

Sunday:	Long run 10 miles easy
Monday:	20 mins easy
Tuesday:	Threshold session 40 mins: 10 mins easy, 20 mins challenging, 10 mins easy
Wednesday:	Rest
Thursday:	35 mins steady (ideally off-road) with 10 x 1 minute hill repeats
Friday:	Rest
Saturday:	20 mins steady

5

Sunday:	Long run 100 mins easy off-road
Monday:	20 mins easy
Tuesday:	Interval session 45 mins: 10 mins easy, 5 x 3 mins tough, 2 mins easy, 10 mins easy
Wednesday:	Rest
Thursday:	35 mins steady
Friday:	Rest
Saturday:	20 mins easy

6

Sunday: 10 km race*
Monday: 20 mins easy
Tuesday: 40 mins: 10 mins easy, 20 mins at half marathon pace, 10 mins easy
Wednesday: Rest
Thursday: 40 mins steady and undulating (ideally off-road)
Friday: Rest
Saturday: 20 mins steady

* Use your 10 km race time to predict your half marathon finish time and determine your half marathon pace

7

Sunday: Long run 8 miles: 4 miles easy, 4 miles at half marathon pace
Monday: 20 mins easy (last 5 mins at half marathon pace)
Tuesday: Interval session 45 mins: 10 mins easy, 5 x 3 mins tough, 2 mins easy, 10 mins easy
Wednesday: Rest
Thursday: 40 mins steady and undulating (ideally off-road)
Friday: Rest
Saturday: 20 mins at half marathon pace

8

Sunday: Long run 120 mins off-road easy
Monday: 20 mins easy
Tuesday: Interval session 50 mins: 10 mins easy, 5 x 4 mins tough, 2 mins easy, 10 mins easy
Wednesday: Rest
Thursday: 40 mins steady and undulating (ideally off-road)
Friday: Rest
Saturday: 20 mins at half marathon pace

9

Sunday: Long run 10 miles easy (last 20 mins at half marathon pace)
Monday: 20 mins easy
Tuesday: Interval session 50 mins: 10 mins easy, 5 x 4 mins tough, 2 mins easy, 10 mins easy
Wednesday: Rest
Thursday: 40 mins steady (ideally off-road)
Friday: Rest
Saturday: 20 mins at half marathon pace

10

Sunday: Long run 45 mins easy (last 3 mins tough)
Monday: Rest
Tuesday: Threshold session 25 mins: 10 mins easy, 5 mins challenging, 10 mins easy
Wednesday: 20 mins steady (wear race kit)
Thursday: Rest
Friday: Rest
Saturday: 20 mins easy
RACE DAY!

real world
half marathon training programme for first-timers

1
Sunday:	Long run 60 mins easy
Monday:	Rest
Tuesday:	Strength/circuit training 30–45 mins
Wednesday:	Rest
Thursday:	30 mins steady (ideally off-road)
Friday:	Rest
Saturday:	20 mins easy

2
Sunday:	Long run 70 mins easy
Monday:	Rest
Tuesday:	Strength/circuit training 30–45 mins
Wednesday:	Rest
Thursday:	30 mins steady (ideally off-road)
Friday:	Rest
Saturday:	20 mins steady

3
Sunday:	30 mins steady
Monday:	Rest
Tuesday:	Strength/circuit training 30–45 mins
Wednesday:	Rest
Thursday:	35 mins steady (ideally off-road) with 6 x 1 min hill repeats
Friday:	Rest
Saturday:	20 mins easy

4
Sunday:	Long run 80 mins easy
Monday:	20 mins easy
Tuesday:	Strength/circuit training 30–45 mins
Wednesday:	Rest
Thursday:	35 mins steady (ideally off-road) with 6 x 1 min hill repeats
Friday:	Rest
Saturday:	20 mins steady

5
Sunday:	Long run 90 mins easy
Monday:	Rest
Tuesday:	Interval session 30 mins: 10 mins easy, 5 x 1 min challenging, 1 min easy, 10 mins easy
Wednesday:	Rest or low-impact cross-training
Thursday:	40 mins steady (ideally off-road) with 8 x 1 min hill repeats
Friday:	Rest
Saturday:	20 mins easy

6

Sunday:	10 km race*
Monday:	20 mins at half marathon pace
Tuesday:	Interval session 30 mins: 10 mins easy, 5 x 1 min challenging, 1 min easy, 10 mins easy
Wednesday:	Rest or low-impact cross-training
Thursday:	40 mins steady (ideally off-road) with 8 x 1 min hill repeats
Friday:	Rest
Saturday:	20 mins steady

* Use your 10 km race time to predict your half marathon finish time and determine your half marathon pace

7

Sunday:	Long run 100 mins easy
Monday:	Rest
Tuesday:	Interval session 35 mins: 10 mins easy, 8 x 1 min challenging, 1 min easy, 10 mins easy
Wednesday:	Rest or low-impact cross-training
Thursday:	45 mins steady (ideally off-road) with 10 x 1 min hill repeats
Friday:	Rest
Saturday:	20 mins easy (last 2 mins tough)

8

Sunday:	Long run 50 mins easy
Monday:	Rest
Tuesday:	Interval session 35 mins: 10 mins easy, 8 x 1 min challenging, 1 min easy, 10 mins easy
Wednesday:	Rest or low-impact cross-training
Thursday:	45 mins steady (ideally off-road) with 10 x 1 min hill repeats
Friday:	Rest
Saturday:	20 mins steady

9

Sunday:	Long run 120 mins easy off-road
Monday:	Rest
Tuesday:	10 mins easy, 15 mins half marathon pace, 10 mins easy
Wednesday:	Rest or low-impact cross-training
Thursday:	45 mins steady (ideally off-road)
Friday:	Rest
Saturday:	20 mins easy

10

Sunday:	Long run 45 mins easy
Monday:	Rest
Tuesday:	Interval session 25 mins: 10 mins easy, 5 x 1 mins challenging 1 min easy, 5 mins easy
Wednesday:	Rest or low-impact cross-training
Thursday:	20 mins: 5 mins easy, 10 mins at half marathon pace, 5 mins easy (wear race kit)
Friday:	Rest
Saturday:	20 mins easy (last 2 mins tough)
RACE DAY!	

real world
half marathon training programme for experienced runners

1

Sunday:	Long run 7 miles easy
Monday:	Rest
Tuesday:	Threshold session 30 mins: 10 mins easy, 10 mins challenging, 10 mins easy
Wednesday:	Rest
Thursday:	30 mins fartlek (ideally off-road) with 6 x 30–180 second efforts
Friday:	Rest or low-impact cross-training
Saturday:	30 mins steady

2

Sunday:	Long run 8 miles steady
Monday:	Rest
Tuesday:	Threshold session 35 mins: 10 mins easy, 15 mins challenging, 10 mins easy
Wednesday:	Rest
Thursday:	30 mins fartlek (ideally off-road) with 6 x 30–180 second efforts
Friday:	Rest or low-impact cross-training
Saturday:	30 mins steady

3

Sunday:	50 mins steady
Monday:	Rest
Tuesday:	Threshold session 35 mins: 10 mins easy, 15 mins challenging, 10 mins easy
Wednesday:	Rest
Thursday:	30 mins fartlek (ideally off-road) with 6 x 30–180 second efforts
Friday:	Rest or low-impact cross-training
Saturday:	30 mins easy

4

Sunday:	Long run 10 miles easy
Monday:	Rest
Tuesday:	Threshold session 40 mins: 10 mins easy, 20 mins challenging, 10 mins easy
Wednesday:	Rest
Thursday:	30 mins fartlek (ideally off-road) with 6 x 30–180 second efforts
Friday:	Rest or low-impact cross-training
Saturday:	30 mins steady

5

Sunday:	Long run 100 mins easy off-road
Monday:	Rest
Tuesday:	Threshold session 40 mins: 10 mins easy, 20 mins challenging, 10 mins easy
Wednesday:	Rest
Thursday:	40 mins steady (ideally off-road) with 8 x 1 minute hill repeats
Friday:	Rest or low-impact cross-training
Saturday:	20 mins easy

6

Sunday:	10 km race*
Monday:	Rest
Tuesday:	55 mins: 10 mins easy, 2 x 15 mins at half marathon pace (2 mins recovery), 10 mins easy
Wednesday:	Rest
Thursday:	40 mins steady (ideally off-road) with 8 x 1 minute hill repeats
Friday:	Rest or low-impact cross-training
Saturday:	30 mins steady

* Use your 10 km race time to predict your half marathon finish time and determine your half marathon pace

7

Sunday:	Long run 8 miles: 5 miles easy, 3 miles at half marathon pace
Monday:	Rest
Tuesday:	Threshold session 45 mins: 10 mins easy, 25 mins challenging, 10 mins easy
Wednesday:	Rest
Thursday:	40 mins steady (ideally off-road) with 10 x 1 minute hill repeats
Friday:	Rest or low-impact cross-training
Saturday:	20 mins at half marathon pace

8

Sunday:	Long run 120 mins off-road easy
Monday:	Rest
Tuesday:	45 mins at half marathon pace
Wednesday:	Rest
Thursday:	40 mins steady (ideally off-road) with 10 x 1 minute hill repeats
Friday:	Rest or low-impact cross-training
Saturday:	20 mins at half marathon pace

9

Sunday:	Long run 10 miles easy (last 15 mins at half marathon pace)
Monday:	Rest
Tuesday:	Threshold session 35 mins: 10 mins easy, 15 mins challenging, 10 mins easy
Wednesday:	Rest
Thursday:	30 mins easy (ideally off-road)
Friday:	Rest or low-impact cross-training
Saturday:	20 mins at half marathon pace

10

Sunday:	Long run 45 mins steady
Monday:	Rest
Tuesday:	Threshold session 25 mins: 10 mins easy, 5 mins challenging, 10 mins easy
Wednesday:	20 mins steady (wear race kit)
Thursday:	Rest
Friday:	Rest
Saturday:	20 mins easy
RACE DAY!	

bare minimum
half marathon training
programme for first-timers

1
Sunday: Long run or run/walk 60 mins easy
Monday: Rest
Tuesday: 30–45 mins strength/circuit training or rest
Wednesday: 30 mins steady (ideally off-road)
Thursday: Rest
Friday: 10 mins easy, 10 x 1 min challenging/1 min easy, 10 mins easy
Saturday: Rest

2
Sunday: Long run or run/walk 70 mins easy
Monday: Rest
Tuesday: 30–45 mins strength/circuit training or rest
Wednesday: 30 mins steady (ideally off-road)
Thursday: Rest
Friday: 10 mins easy, 10 x 1 min challenging/1 min easy, 10 mins easy
Saturday: Rest

3
Sunday: 30 mins steady
Monday: Rest
Tuesday: 30–45 mins strength/circuit training or rest
Wednesday: 40 mins steady (ideally off-road) including 6 x 1 min hill repeats
Thursday: Rest
Friday: 10 mins easy, 5 x 2 mins challenging/2 mins easy, 10 mins easy
Saturday: Rest

4
Sunday: Long run or run/walk 80 mins easy
Monday: Rest
Tuesday: 30–45 mins strength/circuit training or rest
Wednesday: 40 mins steady (ideally off-road) including 6 x 1 min hill repeats
Thursday: Rest
Friday: 10 mins easy, 5 x 2 mins challenging/2 mins easy, 10 mins easy
Saturday: Rest

5
Sunday: Long run or run/walk 90 mins easy off-road
Monday: Rest
Tuesday: Rest
Wednesday: 45 mins steady (ideally off-road) including 8 x 1 min hill repeats
Thursday: Rest
Friday: 10 mins easy, 5 x 3 mins challenging/2 mins easy, 10 mins easy
Saturday: Rest

6

Sunday:	10 km race*
Monday:	20 mins at half marathon pace
Tuesday:	Rest
Wednesday:	45 mins steady (ideally off-road) including 8 x 1 min hill repeats
Thursday:	Rest
Friday:	10 mins easy, 5 x 3 mins challenging/2 mins easy, 10 mins easy
Saturday:	Rest

* Use your 10 km race time to predict your half marathon finish time and determine your half marathon pace

7

Sunday:	Long run 100 mins easy off-road
Monday:	Rest
Tuesday:	Rest
Wednesday:	50 mins steady
Thursday:	Rest
Friday:	10 mins easy, 5 x 4 mins challenging/2 mins easy, 10 mins easy
Saturday:	Rest

8

Sunday:	Long run 50 mins easy
Monday:	Rest
Tuesday:	Rest
Wednesday:	50 mins steady (ideally off-road) including 10 x 1 min hill repeats
Thursday:	Rest
Friday:	10 mins easy, 5 x 4 mins challenging/2 mins easy, 10 mins easy
Saturday:	Rest

9

Sunday:	Long run 110 mins (last 10 mins at half marathon pace)
Monday:	Rest
Tuesday:	10 mins easy, 10 mins half marathon pace, 10 mins easy.
Wednesday:	Rest
Thursday:	50 mins steady (ideally off-road)
Friday:	Rest
Saturday:	Rest

10

Sunday:	Long run 45 mins easy (last 3 mins tough)
Monday:	Rest
Tuesday:	25 mins: 10 mins easy, 5 x 1 min challenging/1 min easy, 5 mins easy
Wednesday:	20 mins easy in race kit
Thursday:	Rest
Friday:	Rest
Saturday:	20 mins easy (last 5 mins at half marathon pace)
RACE DAY!	

bare minimum
half marathon training programme for experienced runners

1

Sunday:	Long run 7 miles easy
Monday:	Rest
Tuesday:	30–45 mins strength/circuit training or rest
Wednesday:	40 mins steady (ideally off-road) including 8 x 1 min hill repeats
Thursday:	Rest
Friday:	10 mins easy, 6 x 2 mins challenging/1 min easy, 10 mins easy
Saturday:	Rest

2

Sunday:	Long run 70 mins: 35 mins easy, 35 mins steady
Monday:	Rest
Tuesday:	30–45 mins strength/circuit training or rest
Wednesday:	40 mins steady (ideally off-road) including 8 x 1 min hill repeats
Thursday:	Rest
Friday:	10 mins easy, 8 x 2 mins challenging/1 min easy, 10 mins easy
Saturday:	Rest

3

Sunday:	40 mins steady
Monday:	Rest
Tuesday:	30–45 mins strength/circuit training or rest
Wednesday:	45 mins steady (ideally off-road) including 10 x 1 min hill repeats
Thursday:	Rest
Friday:	10 mins easy, 5 x 3 mins challenging/2 mins easy, 10 mins easy
Saturday:	Rest

4

Sunday:	Long run 9–10 miles steady
Monday:	Rest
Tuesday:	30–45 mins strength/circuit training or rest
Wednesday:	45 mins steady (ideally off-road) including 10 x 1 min hill repeats
Thursday:	Rest
Friday:	10 mins easy, 5 x 3 mins challenging/2 mins easy, 10 mins easy
Saturday:	Rest

5

Sunday:	Long run 100 mins easy off-road
Monday:	Rest
Tuesday:	Rest
Wednesday:	45 mins fartlek (ideally off-road) with 6 x 30–120 second tough efforts
Thursday:	Rest
Friday:	10 mins easy, 3 x 5 mins challenging/90 secs easy, 10 mins easy
Saturday:	20 mins easy

6

Sunday:	10 km race*
Monday:	20 mins at half marathon pace
Tuesday:	Rest
Wednesday:	45 mins fartlek (ideally off-road) with 6 x 30–120 second tough efforts
Thursday:	Rest
Friday:	10 mins easy, 3 x 5 mins challenging/90 secs easy, 10 mins easy
Saturday:	Rest

* Use your 10 km race time to predict your half marathon finish time and determine your half marathon pace

7

Sunday:	Long run 12 miles easy (last 10 mins at half marathon pace)
Monday:	Rest
Tuesday:	Rest
Wednesday:	50 mins fartlek (ideally off-road) with 6 x 60–120 second tough efforts
Thursday:	Rest
Friday:	10 mins easy, 4 x 5 mins challenging/90 secs easy, 10 mins easy
Saturday:	Rest

8

Sunday:	Long run 60 mins easy (last 10 mins at half marathon pace)
Monday:	Rest
Tuesday:	Rest
Wednesday:	50 mins steady (last 3 mins tough)
Thursday:	Rest
Friday:	10 mins easy, 20 mins challenging, 10 mins easy
Saturday:	Rest

9

Sunday:	Long run 120 mins easy (last 20 mins at half marathon pace)
Monday:	Rest
Tuesday:	15 mins easy, 15 mins half marathon pace, 10 mins easy.
Wednesday:	Rest
Thursday:	50 mins steady (ideally off-road)
Friday:	Rest
Saturday:	Rest

10

Sunday:	Long run 45 mins steady (last 3 mins tough)
Monday:	Rest
Tuesday:	Interval session 25 mins: 10 mins easy, 5 x 1 min challenging/1 min easy, 5 mins easy
Wednesday:	20 mins easy in race kit
Thursday:	Rest
Friday:	Rest
Saturday:	20 mins easy (last 5 mins at half marathon pace)
RACE DAY!	

⠶ Find a race

FIVE OF THE BEST HALVES ON THE UK CALENDAR

Half marathon races are burgeoning in popularity – you should have no difficulty finding an event in your area. Here are some of the key half marathons to consider in the UK. Remember to read the advice on page 151 about choosing your perfect race and chapter 8 to ensure that you prepare successfully for the big day.

The Great North Run

When?
Late September

Where?
Newcastle

Who?
A phenomenal 52,000 runners

What?
The world's biggest half marathon race, renowned for its fantastic atmosphere. A popular race with first-timers (if you can manage to get in), though perhaps, given the crowds, not a good bet for a PB (though there is the incentive of spotting yourself on TV when the race is broadcast!). The event begins in Newcastle city centre and follows an undulating point-to-point route to the coast at South Shields.
www.greatrun.org

Run to the Beat

When?
Late September

Where?
The O$_2$, London

Who?
12,500 runners

What?
A road race with music. There are 17 live music stages on the 13.1-mile route, to spur you on. The playlist is concocted by sport psychologist and music expert Dr Costas Karageorghis to help runners maintain the right tempo and rhythm, and stay motivated. The undulating traffic-free route takes in the Thames waterside and Greenwich park.
www.runtothebeat.co.uk

The Royal Parks Foundation Half Marathon

When?
Early October (places go on sale in March)

Where?
Hyde Park, London

Who?
15,000 runners

What?
A central London race taking in some of the best of the capital's green spaces as it passes through Hyde Park, St James's Park, Green Park and Kensington Gardens. Runners also pass some of London's most iconic landmarks, including Buckingham Palace, the Houses of Parliament, Marble Arch and the Royal Albert Hall. The route is largely flat, encompassing park paths and road.
www.royalparkshalf.com

The Bath Half

When?
Mid-March

Where?
Bath, Avon

Who?
15,000 runners including lots of first-timers

What?
A fast, flat traffic-free two-lap race in the centre of one of the UK's most beautiful cities. It's one of the largest charity fundraising events in the south-west of England, and always fills up early.
www.runninghigh.co.uk

The Adidas Silverstone Half Marathon

When?
Mid-March

Where?
Silverstone motor racing circuit

Who?
8000 runners, many of them runners in training for the London Marathon, which is organised by the same team

What?
A traffic-free flat (though exposed to the elements) race, of which the first and final 3 miles take place on the famous Formula One circuit. Attracts a strong field, alongside many marathon virgins in training.
www.adidashalfmarathon.co.uk

further information

Useful websites

Keep up-to-date with the latest running research, read articles on running, fitness and health and get information on my books, coaching services and women's running club *www.sam-murphy.co.uk*

Organisations
UK Athletics
To find details of nationwide running clubs and coaches, along with athletics news and event information *www.uka.org.uk*

Fetch Everyone
Fetch Everyone is an online running community with more than 17,000 registered users. The free-to-use site enables you to keep a record of your training and racing, and communicate, compare and compete with other members *www.fetcheveryone.com*

Jog Scotland
Jog Scotland is a recreational walk/jog/run programme with over 13,500 members in 300 groups in local communities and workplaces, and a 'junior programme' currently taken up by more than 800 Scottish primary schools and youth groups *www.jogscotland.org.uk*

NikePlus
Users of the Nike+ sports kit (a speed and distance monitoring device used in conjunction with an iPod) can register at NikePlus and become part of the international online running community, chat to other runners, download music to train to, take part in challenges and store training data *www.nike.com/nikeplus*

Parkrun
Free, friendly 5 km runs around the country *www.parkrun.com*

Real Buzz
One of the most comprehensive running websites, with information and advice on kit, shoes, racing, training, staying motivated and more *www.realbuzz.com*

Runner's World
The leading running magazine's vast website has everything from race details to shoe reviews, training

advice, pace calculators and a very active forum *www.runnersworld.co.uk*

Running Track Directory

There are more than 600 athletics tracks in the UK. To find your nearest one, check out the Running Track Directory *www.runtrackdir.com*

Suzy Lamplugh Trust

Offers advice on safety for women in all situations, including being out at night and while exercising *www.suzylamplugh.org*

The Women's Running Network

A national organisation of 600+ female-only running clubs, providing a supportive, friendly environment in which women can get into running 01392 841148 *www.womensrunningnetwork.co.uk*

Running techniques

The Art of Running – Canadian coach Malcolm Balk's take on running, incorporating the Alexander Technique *www.theartofrunning.com*

Chi running – a method that marries some of the principles of tai chi with a specific running technique *www.Chirunning.com*

Pose running – Dr Nicholas Romanov's take on running technique, favouring a forefoot strike *www.posetech.com*

Running kit

Shoes

adidas 0161 419 2500 *www.adidas.com/uk*
ASICS 01925 243360 *www.asics.co.uk*
Avia *www.avia.com*
Brooks *www.brooksrunning.co.uk*
Inov-8 01388 744900 *www.inov-8.com*
Keen *www.keeneurope.eu*
Mizuno 0118 936 2100 *www.mizuno.co.uk*
New Balance 0800 3891055 *www.newbalance.co.uk*
Newton *www.newtonrunning.com*
Nike 0800 056 1640 *www.nike.com*
Puma 01372 360255 *www.puma.com*

Reebok 0808 1560156 *www.reebok.co.uk*
Salomon *www.salomonsports.com*
Saucony 023 9282 3664 *www.saucony.co.uk*

Clothing

adidas 0161 419 2500 *www.adidas.com/uk*
ASICS 01925 243360 *www.asics.co.uk*
Gore 0800 833357 *www.gorerunningwear.co.uk*
Helly Hansen *www.hellyhansen.com*
Hilly 0161 366 8207 *www.hillyclothing.co.uk*
New Balance 0800 3891055 *www.newbalance.co.uk*
Nike 0800 056 1640 *www.nike.com*
Peak Performance 0800 389 8655 *www.peakperformance.se*
Reebok 0808 1560156 *www.reebok.co.uk*
Ron Hill 0161 366 5020 *www.ronhill.com*
Salomon *www.salomonsports.com*
For sports bras, try *www.lessbounce.com*, for a comprehensive range from brands including Sportsjock, Shock Absorber, Enell and Nike
Another great female-specific store is **SheActive**, which sells running gear as well as sports bras and equipment *www.sheactive.co.uk*

Socks

As well as most of the above companies, try:
1000 Mile 01923 242233 *www.1000mile.co.uk*
2xU (compression socks) *www.2xu.com*
Falke *www.falke.com*

Most UK towns now have a local independent running shop. Asics, Nike and adidas have their own stores. Otherwise, **Sweatshop** has more than 25 branches across the UK *www.sweatshop.co.uk* and **Up and Running** has 24 branches nationwide *www.upandrunning.co.uk*

Gear and gadgets

Nathan Sports Bumbags, MP3 player holders, visibility products *www.nathansports.com*
The Physical Company Swiss balls, resistance bands, weights, aqua running belts and more 01494 769 222 *www.physicalcompany.co.uk*
Wiggle Online retailer with a range of drinking vessels,

hydration packs, sports eyewear, visibility products, sports nutrition, shoes and clothing www.wiggle.co.uk

Heart rate monitors, speed distance and GPS systems

Garmin 0808 238000 www.garmin.co.uk
Nike www.nike.com/nikeplus
Polar www.polarelectro.co.uk
Suunto www.suunto.com

Energy drinks and supplements

For Goodness Shakes www.forgoodnessshakes.com
Gatorade www.gatorade.co.uk
High 5 www.highfive.co.uk
Lucozade www.lucozade.com
Science in Sport www.scienceinsport.com

Ultra running, trail running and mountain marathon resources

Fell Runner's Association Information on fell running in the UK and worldwide www.fellrunner.org.uk
Mud and Mountain Information on cross-country, orienteering, fell running, mountain running and more www.mudandmountain.com
Run Further Information on the Vasque series of UK-based ultra events www.runfurther.com
Trail Running Association Membership organisation promoting trail running and events in the UK www.tra-uk.org
Ultra Marathon Running Information on ultra running worldwide www.ultramarathonrunning.com

Injury prevention and gait analysis

Chartered Society of Physiotherapy Find a qualified physiotherapist in your area 020 7306 6666 www.csp.org.uk
Gait analysis Find a qualified podiatrist through the Society of Chiropodists and Podiatrists 020 7234 8620 www.feetforlife.org
Gait analysis also available at:
South Bank University, London 0207 815 7594 www.lsbu.ac.uk
Bimal Medical and Sports Rehabilitation Clinic, London 0208 742 7423

Exeter University, Devon http://sshs.exeter.ac.uk/biomech_files/biomech_exbirt.htm
Sports Massage Association This is the UK professional body representing sports massage practitioners, with a national register of qualified therapists 0870 005 2678 www.sportsmassageassociation.org

Running workshops, camps, holidays and race packages

2.09 Events offers training camps in Europe, and race entry and packages for international and national events and races 01252 373797 www.209events.com
The Art of Running Malcolm Balk offers 'Art of Running' workshops in Canada, Europe and the UK www.theartofrunning.com
Full Potential Training workshops and weekends in the UK and France; also offers coaching www.fullpotential.co.uk
Purple Patch Training camps across the UK; also offers coaching www.purplepatchrunning.com
Running the Highlands Training weekends and bespoke training holidays in the Scottish Highlands www.runningthehighlands.com
Sports Tours International Race entry and accommodation packages abroad and in the UK, and training camps in Europe 0161 703 8161 www.sportstoursinternational.co.uk
TrailPlus Running and adventure racing weekends in the Forest of Dean www.trailplus.com
Wildoutdoors Running holidays and weekends in Scotland www.wildoutdoors.info

Useful publications

Master the Art of Running by Malcolm Balk and Andrew Shields (Collins & Brown)
Nancy Clark's Sports Nutrition Guidebook (4th edition) by Nancy Clark (Human Kinetics)
Run for Life: The Real Woman's Guide to Running by Sam Murphy (Kyle Cathie)
Running Well by Sam Murphy (Kyle Cathie)
Stretching for Running by Chris Norris (A&C Black)

index